# The Idea of History in Constructing Economics

The relationship between the disciplines of economics and history has often been fraught. Economics has tended to be perceived as being quantitative, mathematical, abstracted, and generalising, whilst history is factual, discursive, and detailed. Methodological linkages have frequently been sought and made between economics and other disciplines, but history has been an exception to this. In this new volume, Michael H. Turk explores the relationship between economics and history, making the case that economics does in fact require the proper grounding in history that has so often been ignored.

A key element of this book is its examination of the gaps and associations that exist in, or are seen through, linkages with thermodynamics, classical mechanics, biology, literature, mathematics, philosophy, and sociology. This exploration is frequently undertaken through study of the work of one or more major figures in the history of economic thought, ranging from Quesnay and Smith, through Walras and Marshall, to Robinson, Krugman, David, and Arthur.

Through the possibility of an alternative to the gaps noted in each such comparison, the underlying, necessary connection between economics and history can be brought out. The book concludes by exploring the basis for the positive construction of a historical economics.

**Michael H. Turk** is Professor of Economics at Fitchburg State University, USA.

# Routledge Studies in the History of Economics

*For a complete list of titles in this series, please visit www.routledge.com*

# The Idea of History in Constructing Economics

Michael H. Turk

Routledge
Taylor & Francis Group

LONDON AND NEW YORK

First published 2016 by Routledge

2 Park Square, Milton Park, Abingdon, Oxfordshire OX14 4RN
52 Vanderbilt Avenue, New York, NY 10017

*Routledge is an imprint of the Taylor & Francis Group, an informa business*

First issued in paperback 2019

*British Library Cataloguing in Publication Data*
A catalogue record for this book is available from the British Library

*Library of Congress Cataloging in Publication Data*
Turk, Michael H.
The idea of history in constructing economics / Michael H. Turk.
pages cm
1. Economics--History. 2. Economic history. I. Title.
HB75.T86 2015
330.09--dc23
2015010362

ISBN: 978-1-138-80889-8 (hbk)
ISBN: 978-0-367-87096-6 (pbk)

Typeset in Times New Roman
by Taylor & Francis Books

# Contents

# Acknowledgments

As this book builds upon a set of five previously published articles and papers of mine, I would like to express my appreciation to the following publishers for kindly granting permission so as to enable these pieces to be included in this work:

To the Taylor & Francis Group for the use of two articles from the *European Journal of the History of Economic Thought*: "The Fault Line of Axiomatization: Walras' Linkage of Physics with Economics," vol. 13, no. 2, June 2006, 195–212; and "The Arrow of Time in Economics: From Robinson's Critique to the New Historical Economics," vol. 17, no. 3, August 2010, 471–92.

To Springer Publishers for the use of chapter 22 of *Evolutionary Biology: Concept, Modeling, and Application*, edited by Pierre Pontarotti, 2009, and titled, "Economics Pursuing the Mold of Evolutionary Biology: 'Accident' and 'Necessity' in the Quest to make Economics Scientific," pp. 379–92.

To Duke University Press for the use of the article from the *History of Political Economy*: "Economics as Plausible Conjecture," vol. 42, no. 3, Fall 2010, pp. 521–46; and

To Cambridge University Press for the use of the article from the *Journal of the History of Economic Thought*: "The Mathematical Turn in Economics: Walras, the French Mathematicians, and the Road Not Taken," vol. 34, no. 2, June 2012, 149–67.

# Introduction

## Ahistorical economics and its weak linkages

As an intellectual discipline, economics is often set in relation to other disciplines, intended to show linkages or contrasts, so as to validate by analogy its claim to a kind of "scientificality." Among these various fields of inquiry, physics, especially classical mechanics, tends to be touted most often, although biology, especially evolutionary biology, is frequently invoked as well, each presenting different shades of scientific rigor, and providing different notions of the role of "scientific" laws.

History is more likely to be paired in opposition; this is sometimes elevated to the neo-Kantian distinction between the idiographic reliance upon the particular in history and the nomothetic or rule-making characteristic of economics. In the end, these linkages may offer up less than appears to be the case, and the distinction noted above rendered more illusion than reality. The flaws or gaps in the scientific linkages, and the necessity and means of establishing a firm grounding of economics in history, are the subject of the chapters in this volume.

These chapters are intended to draw attention to, and cast a positive light upon, the nexus between economics and history, suggesting in the process that the field of economics would benefit from the reconstitution of a historical economics updated to the twenty-first century, constructing it in ways that have otherwise proven elusive. Geoffrey Hodgson characterized the disconnection of history from the mainstream of economics in the twentieth century in the title of his study of now heterodox historically conscious schools of economic thought like the Institutionalists as *How Economics Forgot History* (Hodgson 2001).

Moreover, in its – generally – ideational approach, this collection of previously published papers and new chapters brings together matters of economics, history, and philosophy, and so as a concomitant recasts the scope and purview of economic methodology, rendering the field more consciously historical.

The effort, often strenuous, to align economics with other, more clearly or established "scientific" disciplines to shore up or clarify economics' own claims to being scientific has fallen short. This is so, for among other reasons, because such alignments falter at crucial junctures. In the case of classical mechanics there are at least two critical strands.

For one, Léon Walras' attempt to axiomatize economics by analogy with classical mechanics, drawing in part upon the work of Irving Fisher, failed to meet its mark because a construction by analogy presumes a similarity based upon content, while axiomatization, as Walras' contemporary David Hilbert saw it, was strictly formal. Hence, the axiomatization of economics could succeed on that basis only if a parallel formalism could be established between the two disciplines in which one did not serve in any way as the model the other. This is the subject of Chapter 1.

Second, the critiques of classical physics emerging at the turn of the twentieth century, by mathematical physicists like Henri Poincaré and Émile Picard, pointed to unresolved questions about the scope of the applicability of the model of classical physics for economics amidst the growing use of mathematics in economics, touching upon matters like uncertainty, linkages formed by memory, and the potential for hysteresis to occur, all the while casting doubt upon the relevance of the classical model itself. This topic was taken up in the paper entitled, "The Mathematical Turn in Economics" (see Chapter 2).

In fact, by the first decades of the twentieth century classical physics itself faced challenges about both content and structure that philosophizers about economics could ignore only at their peril, from the asymmetries of time to the disjuncture between the macroscopic universe, governed by the laws associated with relativity, and a microscopic world of quantum physics. Joan Robinson had come to challenge what she saw as the mistaken conflation of space and time in economic theorizing and construction. The notion that an asymmetrical direction to time, as would be the case in the related field of thermodynamics, would produce a different and potentially more historically based and conscious economics, or, at the least, one that followed time-dependent pathways, an approach pursued by Paul David and Brian Arthur, is treated in Chapter 3, exploring in part the road not taken by the main stream of economics in the twentieth century.

In addition, Kurt Godel's proof of the incompleteness of any free-standing, self-referencing arithmetic system led more generally to an understanding that scientific structures required "outside" or auxiliary elements to reconcile the need for proof with any possibility of validating the truth of any such system. Drawing upon insights from the later Wittgenstein, like the rejection of the possibility of any private language, might this open the way to incorporating community standards and social context into the comprehension of intellectual disciplines like economics? If so, it would call into question the full-scale transformation of economic experience into games, as games are fundamentally akin to puzzles, dependent upon an isolation or separation from worldly experience so that a given set of rules might be applied. The implications for economic theorizing of the tension between creating and solving puzzles, on the one hand, and addressing problems arising from societal activities and arrangements, as well as business affairs, on the other, is the subject of Chapter 4.

As for the notion that an alternate course might be pursued through an alignment with biology, as Alfred Marshall had suggested the "complexity" of "living things" entailed, or, more recently, with evolutionary biology, one finds evocations of such complexity as an organizing principle said to link the two disciplines. Yet there is a teleology in biology, that is, an intended purposefulness, most assuredly evident in evolutionary biology, missing from economics, namely the process of selective adaptation. Many an economist would tout the virtues of efficiency; nonetheless, they would be hard pressed to transform it into a mechanism that would serve as an economic version of "intended and inherent purposefulness" applicable to human affairs and activities.

The relation between economics and evolutionary biology has also been sought in the ostensible similarity between the models for economics proposed by Brian Arthur and Paul Krugman, in which the accidents of history serve as inciting events upon which the rules of economics are then imposed, and the model of biology where selective adaptation is associated with gene mutation and changing gene expression. This approach, though, does not give sufficient weight to the continuing impact of historical events and developments upon the time-based economic pathways followed, nor does it provide a teleology like that of selective adaptation. These matters are discussed in Chapter 5.

Thus is the place of history in economics brought center stage. Might it be possible to visit anew the relation between economics and history, comprehended as the possibilities afforded by a historical economics? Tony Lawson has suggested that the quest to establish the "scientificality" of economics, typically through claims asserting the nomothetic, or rule-making, character of the discipline, is fundamentally wrong-headed. He contends that the capacity of economics to provide what he calls "social explanation" is rooted in the "identification and illumination of those structures responsible for producing, or facilitating, social phenomena of interest" (Lawson 2003: 36).

Lawson's recasting of the "ontology" of economics has the virtue of transcending the neo-Kantian distinction between the nomothetic and the idiographical, whether explicitly stated or only implied. Yet his notion that the "social explanation" afforded by economics is to be found in "structures" could and should be readily "reoriented" and expanded to include historical structures and thereby set more firmly in historical terms.

In this vein one might note the emphasis the economic historian Paul Bairoch placed on such structures in affecting economic explanation: "different [historical] structures mean different evolutions and different [economic] laws" (Bairoch 1993: 174). Or, for that matter, one might take up the historian Eric Hobsbawm's view that economic and social history are both shaped about, and give primary attention to, matters of "structure," inspired, he felt, in the mid-twentieth century by the work of Marxist historians like himself, but even more so by the French *Annales* school, especially the historian Fernand Braudel (Hobsbawm 2002: 292–4), and where Hobsbawm saw economics without history, and hence the structures of economic history, as vacuous.

How such structures then may serve to ground economics in philosophical terms would make the "idea of history" central to the construction of economics, especially as historical structure would necessarily be comprehended in relation to historical context. This task begins in Chapter 6, which examines the intertwining of fact and fiction in economics, and its literary roots in the eighteenth century marked by the remarkably close association of the emergence of political economy with the rise of the novel as the pre-eminent literary work mixing fictionalized characters and experiences with acute observation of daily life within a larger social world cognizant of historical events and developments.

Then, the nexus between economics and history is taken up in four new essays, exploring how economics might have been grounded more in history – or potentially might be. In part this serves as a historical review of some of the tensions between economists and historians from a methodological stand-point over the nature of their work, as well as a consideration of both the limitations encountered and possibilities that might be realized in establishing a coherent historical economics.

The first of these chapters treats the effort by Max Weber a century ago to grapple with the methodological questions arising out of the historical economics shaped by the German Historical School. Here one may look to the ways that Weber anticipated some of the concerns raised in the late twentieth century about the narratology of economics and the nature of model-building, though with obvious differences in language and conceptual focus, and where the more recent inquiries are set much more in the realm of relativist, naturalistic, or postmodern thought. But it may also occasion con-sideration of the extent to which Weber's methodological concerns about the possibilities of a historical economics represent a "lost thread" in economic thought across the twentieth century. Accordingly, Chapter 7 is entitled, "Max Weber and the Lost Thread of Historical Economics."

Two of the chapters address the often problematic relation between economics and history, in which it often appears that a chasm of some sort divides the two disciplines, much as the economic historian Carlo Cipolla characterized the division as if "between two cultures." At the same time, there are elements within the two disciplines that point to the possibility of a bridge that might be established between them, rather than a breach that is impassable.

The first of these chapters, Chapter 8, entitled, "Historical Proof in Economics," takes up the notion of proof in economics, but is framed largely through the question of the scope of historical proof in economics. This entails both an exploration of the kinds of proof possible in economics, but also a recounting of the disputes and tensions between economists and economic historians about the nature of their respective fields, tracing such contentions back to the early days of the twentieth century, where the controversy between John Clapham and Arthur C. Pigou in the 1920s over Clapham's charge of "empty economic boxes" is taken as paradigmatic.

Chapter 9, entitled, "The Fraught Relation between Economics and Economic History," pursues similar themes. Here greater attention is given to some of the differences cited by economists and economic historians over both method and measurement, where the latter is sometimes reduced to a distinction between an economics that can be rendered scientific by dint of its amenability to quantification, while economic history remains at its core more impressionistic and hence qualitative. The pioneering work of Simon Kuznets in forging such quantitative measures, establishing their scope and limitations while distinguishing economics from economic history, serves as the point of departure. At the same time, the interpenetration of theory and fact, a notion at the center of Weber's efforts to construct an economic comprehension of historical events and phenomena, though, vitiates any such bifurcation of the quantitative and the qualitative.

Finally, a fourth chapter, "Toward a Positive Construction of Historical Economics" (Chapter 10), attempts to draw some of the various strands together from the relations between economics and history into a set of possibilities for a philosophically, or methodologically, coherent historical economics.

In part this requires outlining what is entailed by any historical context for economic inquiry to provide the requisite structure for such inquiry. Among the elements informing historical context are: the setting of a stage, the formative mold into which the pertinent economic experience must be fitted; the identification of the threads provided by colligation, the linkages between past and present that typically flow from the present to the past, a temporal inversion but an interpretive practice inhering within history; the introduction of relevant periodization, so as to avoid an infinite regress in assaying historical experiences drawn upon; and the recognition of applicable genres and modes of presentation, a more literary aspect in the shaping of historical context, but one that offers atmospheric elements and grapples more directly with the role of narrative in economics and the interplay of fact and fiction in framing hypotheses and models.

This traces a route back from contemporary postmodernism through the "linguistic" and literary turn in the 1970s advanced by the historian Hayden White, in conjunction with the contextualization of meaning brought to the fore by the anthropologist Clifford Geertz, to turn-of-the-twentieth century figures like Max Weber and Otto Neurath, both of whom were influenced by the German Historical School, broad differences between them – and with the school – notwithstanding.

The revisiting of the place of narrative in economics assumes even greater significance when cast in the context of economic methodology. Even in the realm of narratology in economics and model building, there has been an emphasis upon matters of "scientific context" (see Morgan 2012: 244). By and large, economic methodology has been conceived of, as Wade Hands put it in *Reflections without Rules* (Hands 2001), as an application of the philosophy of science, or at the least has drawn heavily from it to establish its philosophical benchmarks, treating and explicating what economics does as a discipline on the basis of many of the major trends advanced in the philosophy of science over the course of the twentieth century. Following Hands' treatment, one can follow a trajectory from the logical positivism of the Vienna Circle through Karl Popper's demarcation of science through falsification, Carl Hempel's criteria for nomological–deductive systems, Thomas Kuhn's paradigmatic shifts, Imre Lakatos' scientific research programs, to the pluralism of a more "naturalistic" methodology by the century's end.

While both Kuhn's and Lakatos' notions raised aspects of professional identification and communities of interest, hence, at least implicitly, introduced matters of historical context and periodization into the mix, history, and, in particular, the nexus between economics and history, is generally missing from the picture.

Yet it is certainly the case that economics, however one may seek to cast it, including through the prism of the – changing – philosophy of science, is concerned with worldly matters. In order to encompass the broader range of activities comprehended by economics one is necessarily drawn to a social world subject to the vicissitudes of politics and an array of intellectual and cultural currents.

Moreover, in the process of exploring the idea of history in constructing economics a raft of methodological questions emerges, some related directly to historical considerations, others only indirectly so.

These include:

1   The interpretation of economics as a form of intellectual inquiry through the prism of other disciplines or the use of literary means: are these all aspects of "drydock" construction at sea, to borrow Neurath's expression, such that they necessarily hold for all intellectual disciplines; or, do these obtain with special force in economics as a compensatory act intended to shore up the scientific claims of economics?

2   If it is the latter, to what extent is that the product of the tensions within the "nomothetic paradox," that is, the seemingly centrifugal pulls between generalizing rules and a grounding in daily and worldly affairs that characterize the structure and epistemology of economics?

3   How characteristic – and singular – is it for economics to proceed through fiction to fact? This is a thread that runs through economics from its formative twinning with the novel in the eighteenth century, through the continuing primacy of conjecture and plausibility over proof, through the Weberian emphasis upon a "heightening" or "accentuation" of reality to produce "ideal-types" intended to provide conceptual models, to the late twentieth-century, ostensibly postmodern philosophy of model construction.

4   How broad is the gap and disputed the terrain between concept and law? Would preserving the validity and legitimacy of concepts as nomothetic elements suffice to maintain the generalizing aspects of economics, even as laws and rules are excluded or, along lines suggested by the economic historian Paul Bairoch and not altogether inconsistent with Weber's formulations about the relation of theory and fact, treated as delimited by time and place, hence shaped by conditions and situation?

5   How might that then affect the ways that economic models are constructed?

How, then, is it possible to ignore history, even within the framework of economic methodology? To a significant degree economic methodology resembles the economics about which it philosophizes in its being fundamentally ahistorical in its analysis and perspective. What I am raising here is the notion that this should not be the case; rather that there ought to be a blending of economics, history, and philosophy in reflecting upon method, complementing the reinfusion of history into economics.

## References

Bairoch, Paul (1993) *Economics and World History: Myths and Paradoxes.*Chicago: University of Chicago Press.

Hands, D. Wade (2001) *Reflection without Rules.* Cambridge: Cambridge University Press.

Hobsbawm, Eric (2002) *Interesting Times: A Twentieth-Century Life.* New York: Pantheon.

Hodgson, Geoffrey M. (2001) *How Economics Forgot History.* London: Routledge.

Lawson, Tony (2003) *Reorienting Economics.* London: Routledge.

Morgan, Mary S. (2012) *The World in the Model: How Economists Work and Think.* Cambridge: Cambridge University Press.

# 1 The fault line of axiomatization
## Walras' linkage of physics with economics

## Introduction

When economists seek to invoke the power of economic law and demonstrate the scientific cachet of their field of inquiry, they are likely to do so by comparing those laws to the laws of physics. At the level of textbook writing or popular presentation this is often reckoned to be a force like gravity: it simply cannot be defied.[1]

Implicit in this is an alignment of some sort between economics and physics, from which the scientific character of economics is confirmed. In an offhand form it was also conveyed in the somewhat distanced remark of Robert Solow, as he endeavored to construct a bridge between economics and economic history, about the lure of treating economics as a hard science: "My impression is that the best and the brightest in the profession [of economics] proceed as if economics is the physics of society" (Solow 1985: 330).

In fact, the invocation of a scientific foundation for economics has frequently underpinned claims made about the value and solidity of the discipline itself, but not without some unease and substantial controversy, especially when matters of economic method are posed. How strong a science can economics strive to be, if its subject matter involves human behavior and societal interactions? Moreover, how broad is its capacity to predict outcomes? And how clearly can economic theorizing avoid conflating assumptions and conclusions?

Economists for whom methodological considerations loom large often find that the social character of economics establishes a fundamental divide between the methods of economics and those of the physical sciences; these range across a wide swath of intellectual and ideological perspectives in economics, from those who follow Friedrich von Hayek's epistemological disjuncture between the physical and the social sciences, to the American Institutionalists who see "cumulative causation" as the central mechanism of change in economics, or even to contemporary French economists such as Claude Mouchot, who emphasize the circularity of causation between the physical world of resources and goods and the human agents who shape their economic world through them (Mouchot 2003: 171–203).

However, the far larger number of economists drawn significantly from its mainstream concur in seeing economics as essentially scientific, even if there are not inconsiderable modulations in the case made for its being so. On the one hand, it is possible to position the field of economics as distinct from the physical or "hard" sciences because of the limitations created by the irreducible place of humans and society in it, but as a nomothetic discipline find it more rigorous than other social sciences; thus, in Daniel Hausman's words, economics is an "inexact and separate" science (Hausman 1992). On the other hand, the embrace of mathematics by economists over the course of the twentieth century gives economics the appearance of theoretical consistency and solidity that would place it on a scientific par with what is generally accepted as the hardest of sciences: physics.

If, then, an alignment between economics and physics exists, one may ask when it took place, and what, more particularly, is its nature?

As to the question of origins, this might be understood as a matter of historical fact-checking: one determines when the first recorded statement occurred, or the first recognition of such a statement as significant. But it will also prove to be a matter of conception or reconception, in which political economy becomes the science of economics and this entails a process as well as an act or event captured in a moment, requiring a historical stage to be set. Included on this stage are historical actors, who often speak a common language and enunciate themes that, especially from a distance, tend to cohere with one another, within a context.

The "science" of economics, as distinct from the political economy from which it emerged, can rightfully be dated to the efforts of the marginalists of the 1870s and 1880s to produce a counter-revolution in economic thought. The new emphasis upon utility, scarcity and marginal effects and the greater reliance upon mathematics were hallmarks of the work of the marginalists and led, in general, to a turn away from the linking of the economic and the historical that had marked the political economy of Turgot and Smith in the eighteenth century or Marx in the nineteenth century. These three figures assume greater importance here because, into the nineteenth century, history was seen as a source of laws that other fields of inquiry might use as a model; such a model, for example, was found in Lyell's new geology, itself an inspiration for Darwin's inquiry into evolution.[2]

Through the first half of the nineteenth century, even among those figures identified as the antecedent champions of a new and more scientific economics, the link between what was regarded as scientific and what was historical remained strong. For example, A. A. Cournot, often cited as the first economist of note to make mathematics central to his economic analyses, produced a number of works exploring the philosophical links between science and history, including a treatise entitled: *Traité de l'enchaînement des idées fondamentales dans les sciences et dans l'histoire* (Cournot 1861). Even Quesnay, whose *Tableau économique* served as a model for later system-builders among economists, framed his inquiry largely as a matter of statecraft and governance.

The identification of the foundations of political economy in the physical sciences advanced dramatically in the latter part of the nineteenth century, and among the triumvirate of marginalists across Europe in this period, Léon Walras stands out as the most ardent exponent of the model of the physical sciences for a revamped, or at least highly mathematized political economy. His writings are replete with references to the founding figures of classical physics and astronomy, from Galileo and Kepler to Newton and Laplace, highlighting in every such reference the precedent for political economy in the physical sciences, which they had established.

In the Preface to the fourth edition of *Éléments d'économie politique pure*, which appeared in 1900, Walras asserted: "In any case, the establishment sooner or later of economics as an exact science is no longer in our hands and need not concern us. It is already perfectly clear that economics, like astronomy and mechanics, is both an empirical and a rational science" (Walras 1984: 47). He also compared the work of the seminal figures in astronomy and mechanics to that of the leading figures in the transformation of economics, himself included, noting that, effectively, economics had progressed more rapidly than either astronomy or physics:

> It took from a hundred to a hundred and fifty or two hundred years for the astronomy of Kepler to become the astronomy of Newton and Laplace, and for the mechanics of Galileo to become the mechanics of d'Alembert and Lagrange. On the other hand, less than a century has elapsed between the publication of Adam Smith's work and the contributions of Cournot, Gossen, Jevons, and myself. We were, therefore, at our post, and have performed our duty.
>
> (Walras 1984: 47–8)

Beyond the claim that economics was a "rational science," Walras' writings may also contain the first explicit statement of a correspondence between the laws of economics and the universal law of gravity. In an article entitled, "Une branche nouvelle de la mathématique," written in 1885, but not published until decades later, Walras boldly linked the operation of economics to the framework of Newton's laws. He did so by first characterizing Jevons" mathematical constructions as the "keystone" of pure political economy, where the proportionality of the maximum satisfaction of wants to "rareté" is combined with the equality of supply and demand. This then served as: "the necessary and sufficient reason for the equilibrium of the economic world, just as the universal attraction based directly on the mass and inversely upon the square of the distance is the reason for the equilibrium of the astronomical world" (Walras 1987: 320).

Walras himself would give pride of place to his father, Auguste Walras, who exerted a powerful influence over his program of research in economics. The younger Walras suggested that his father had introduced the notion of an analogy between the primitive forms of physics and political economy in his lectures dating from the early 1830s:

[He] enunciated and developed the proposition that political economy is, within certain limits, a mathematical science, and went so far as to indicate the corresponding analogy that exists, on the one hand, between speed, space, and time, and, "rareté," utility, and quantity, on the other.

(Walras 1987: 321)

Thus, it would appear that Léon Walras saw the relationship between economics and classical physics as one of analogy, in which both shared, or at least could share, a kinship as "mathematical sciences," and for which the "system," that is, the laws governing the operation of the physical world, but especially mechanics, served as the model for those guiding the operation of political economy. In that same article Walras expounded the idea directly:

As it is found that the problem of the system of the astronomical world is a problem of mechanics, then it is necessary to resolve it in consequence; if it is something of the same problem for the system of the economic world, then it is necessary to resolve it in an analogous manner.

(Walras 1987: 328)

There is a certain murkiness to this argument, despite, or perhaps because of, Walras' assertiveness. What exactly are "mathematical sciences"? Do the correspondences suggested by an analogy differ from those established through a model? In part, the question becomes one of discerning the extent to which the "system" of economics, in Walras' case what will become the system of equations defining a general economic equilibrium, is a matter of mathematics alone; or if it hinges upon the metaphorical borrowing from physics of the notion of a physical equilibrium. Is this program championed by Walras the mathematizing of political economy, through which it becomes a science, or the grounding of the new science of economics upon the model of the physical sciences, but especially and decisively mechanics?

While Walras' ideas and claims are directly at issue, an assessment of them may also shed light upon more claims about the universality and scientific precision of economics achieved through the primacy of mathematics either as the language of economics or through its capacity for axiomatization; or upon the correspondence of economics with physics. Thus, through Walras' system of equilibrium one may ask of economics more generally: does it cohere as a science through the force of mathematics or is it moved by forces akin to those of nature?

## The parallel or the analogy

It is evident that the nature of the correspondence between economics and physics, as well as the relationship between economics and mathematics, may be complicated, but also a matter of decisive importance regarding the foundations of economics. Does the science of economics constitute a parallel development to classical physics, especially "rational" mechanics, as it assumes a suitably mathematical structure and language; or is it built upon a metaphorical borrowing, an analogy between its fundamental elements and those of classical mechanics, most significantly the organizing principle of equilibrium, or an equilibrium state?

These questions arise directly from Walras' work, in that his strenuous and lifelong efforts to mathematize economics were embodied in his attempt to define and depict a general economic equilibrium; hence, his undertaking could be viewed as potentially, if not necessarily in actuality, establishing a parallel with mechanics or an analogy based upon it, or both.

The first approach to consider places economics on a parallel track with mechanics and other hard sciences through its mathematization. In turn, the notion that the science of economics is political economy made precise and mathematical is drawn from two sources; these overlap but are not the same. In addition, they inform different developments in the subsequent transformation of economics.

The first of these involves a reliance upon axiomatization. The source, ultimately, for such a reliance is Euclid's *Elements of Geometry*. Walras alluded to the role played by the model of the construction of Euclidean geometry in shaping the method of his *Éléments d'économie politique pure*:

> This much is certain, however, that the physico-mathematical sciences, like the mathematical sciences, in the narrow sense, do go beyond experience as soon as they have drawn their type concepts from it. From real-type concepts, these sciences abstract ideal-type concepts which they define, and then on the basis of these definitions they construct a priori the whole framework of their theorems and proofs. After that they go back to experience not to confirm but to apply their conclusions.
>
> (Walras 1984: 7)

Walras then brings to bear in this discussion of method his understanding of geometry, as then commonly taught, that is, Euclidean geometry:

> Everyone who has studied any geometry at all knows perfectly well that only in an abstract, ideal circumference are the radii all equal to each other and that only in an abstract, ideal triangle is the sum of the angles equal to the sum of two right angles.
>
> (Walras 1984: 71)

He turns to the subject of economics:

> Following this same procedure, the pure theory of economics ought to take over from experience certain type of concepts, like those of exchange, supply, demand, market, capital, income, productive services and products. From these real-type concepts the pure science of economics should then

abstract and define ideal-type concepts in terms of which it carries on its reasoning.

(Walras 1984: 71)

In particular, it is clear that Walras assigns great weight to the idealization of primitive definitions and concepts and sees pure economics as a construct built out of "theorems and proofs." Others, including William Jaffe and Lionel McKenzie, have focused less on the foundational role of Euclidean geometry in Walras' axiomatizing and more on the mediating role played by Louis Poinsot, a French physicist whose text on statics Walras claimed had had a formative influence upon his understanding of the explanatory range of equilibrium. In his *Classical General Equilibrium Theory*, McKenzie, a major figure himself in the development of modern general equilibrium theory, wrote:

> It is interesting that the originator of [general equilibrium] theory, Léon Walras, was influenced by the theory of static equilibrium in classical mechanics. According to Jaffe (1954) he was familiar with the book by Poinsot (1803) in which the theory of statics in mechanics is derived from axioms.
>
> (McKenzie 2002: 4)

Jaffe remarked upon the curious remembrance of Walras, late in life, that he had been so profoundly captivated by Poinsot's work that he had read through the entire text in two evenings (Jaffe 1965: 148, 161–2). Yet if one examines the eighth edition of Poinsot's (1984) *Statics*, the edition that Walras had perused, it is also evident that Walras was drawn to one of the short "mémoires" attached to it, entitled, "Théorie générale de l'équilibre et du mouvement des systèmes" (Jaffe 1965: 149–50).

This "mémoire," which contains relatively little technical material, in the tradition of French popular scientific writing,[3] presents the notion of a fundamental breakthrough having been achieved in the axiomatizing of a scientific system, based upon one overarching principle. This, Poinsot saw, was the analytical achievement of Lagrange, in his *Mécanique analytique*.

> This was then a happy idea to take as the point of departure the principle of "virtual velocity" as one of an axiom, and … to think of drawing from it a uniform method of calculation to form the equations for equilibrium and for movement in all possible systems. That way one overcame all the difficulties found in mechanics: avoiding, one might say, making the science itself by transforming it into a question of calculation; and this transformation, the object and the result of *Mécanique Analytique*, appears as a striking example of the power of analysis.
>
> (Poinsot 1842: 422)

Crucially, Poinsot modified Lagrange's approach by placing fundamental importance upon the coupling of forces to resolve equilibria, and substituted "force" for "virtual velocity" as the essential term from whose definition everything else flowed. Overall, though, Walras' reliance upon Lagrange's conception of an axiomatized system of equations is inescapable, however much he may have accepted Poinsot's alterations.

From another vantage, that of Pierre Duhem, the French historian of science who was a contemporary of Walras, the link between Poinsot and Euclid was clear: "From Archimedes to Varignon, the mechanicians never ceased to pursue the same ideal. They continue this pursuit from Varignan to Poinsot and from Poinsot to our own time. They dream of constructing a statics on the model of Euclid's *Elements of Geometry*" (Duhem 1991: 434).

Duhem's description of the intentions and expectations of those he terms the "mechanicians" makes clear the goal of axiomatization:

> By means of a thorough and ingenious analysis they hope to reduce the most complicated cases of equilibrium in the most diverse systems until they can see clearly simple and elementary instances of equilibrium. Furthermore, in those simple and elementary instances they want equilibrium to be a self-evident and certain as those truths of common sense to which Euclid appealed. The goal of Archimedes in his treatise *On the Equilibrium of Planes* was to provide statics with principles which would be acknowledged as just as clear and certain as the axioms of geometry.
>
> (Duhem 1991: 434)

In this version one need only substitute "economics" for "statics" and the goal of the program is evident. Moreover, substituting to create a parallel between these two fields affords one possible interpretation of the remarkable table of equivalent terms (as shown in Table 1.1) found in Walras' notes for "Économie et Mécanique," his last published article, which appeared in 1909.

Each of the terms listed in the first column might be viewed as the mechanical equivalent of the terms drawn from economics appearing in the second column; hence, the two listings provide a parallelism of primitive terms.

Alternative interpretations are available. Philip Mirowski, for one, sees the dual columns as compelling evidence of the grounding of economics in a metaphorical borrowing from physics, rather than a set of mathematical equivalents (Mirowski and Cook 1990: 189ff.). Also open to question is the extent to which this dual listing encompasses the process of axiomatization. The one set of equations put forward appears insufficient to establish any system, mechanical or economic. The reference to a "parallelogram of forces" does have possibilities in that regard, since such a law might be invoked as the overarching principle underlying statics (Duhem 1991: 434–5). However, Walras does not present a parallel rule in the table for economics, nor does he indicate that he envisions economics to be governed by the same law, at least in this particular depiction.

*Table 1.1* Equivalent terms

| In mechanics | In economics |
|---|---|
| a molecule | an individual |
| space | goods and services |
| force | marginal utility or disutility |
| work | disutility |
| energy | utility |
| work or energy = force × space | disutility or utility = marginal utility × goods |
| force is a vector (directed in space) | marginal utility is a vector (directed in goods) |
| forces added through addition of vectors | marginal utility added through addition of vectors |
| (parallelogram of forces) | disutility and utility |
| work and energy scalar quantities | scalar quantities |

Source: Walras (1991: 627)

Yet another interpretation is possible. It is manifested along the route that leads from the Euclidean approach to what has been described as the Cartesian approach to the mathematization of economics. With the latter, the axiomatic gives way to the quantifiable and the language of mathematics itself takes center stage. In other words, one might regard the dual listings as a set of equivalent vocabularies, each term of which is capable of being translated into the other and where both may be subsumed under a universal language of science. This is what Jan van Daal and Albert Jolink, who in surveying "Une branche nouvelle" see the Cartesian approach as central to Walras' thinking, refer to as the "universal language of mathematics" (Van Daal and Jolink 1993: 3–7).

The Cartesian approach differs in certain crucial respects from the Euclidean version, largely because of a shift in emphasis from the structure that informs an axiomatized system to the means or technique used to express or demonstrate. In this latter case, it is the capacity to create a science through the use of mathematics that matters most. Mathematical language affords a precision, perhaps even a kind of objectivity devoid of any nuance, which allows the elements of the science in question to treat quantities that can be maneuvered algebraically and represented graphically.

The extension of scientific range derived from the introduction of the language of mathematics into a field of inquiry had been seen as affecting, even transforming, "hard" sciences, such as physics, in the course of the nineteenth century. As Walras' near-contemporary the German mathematician Bernhard Riemann, noted: "The progress of recent centuries in the knowledge of mechanics depends almost entirely on the exactness of the construction which has become possible through the invention of the infinitesimal calculus" (Riemann 1999: 660) and, he added, not without significance, "through the simple principles discovered by Archimedes, Galileo, and Newton, and used by modern physics" (Riemann 1999: 660).

For that matter, Walras ended his exposition on the efficacy of the Euclidean method of axiomatizing in economics by trumpeting the virtues of the language of mathematics. In the event, Walras' words in "Une branche nouvelle" echo those of Riemann:

> Just as mechanics treats of movement, space, time, speed, mass, force, etc., so political economy treats of exchange, demand, supply, price, utility, quantity, etc. Demand, supply, price, utility, quantity are magnitudes. It is possible to express these magnitudes by numbers, or to represent them graphically; thus it is possible to apply algebra or geometry to political economy; and perhaps this application will transform it as it has transformed mechanics and astronomy.
>
> (Walras 1987: 310–11)

In a general way, the Cartesian approach can also be found in Walras' notes for "Économie et Mécanique": "When one treats of facts quantitatively, there are advantages in reasoning about them mathematically" (Walras 1991: 627).

In "Une branche nouvelle" the original notion of extending the role of mathematics into science, as expressed by Descartes, was filtered through a contemporary source, Duhamel, who had advocated the broader reliance upon mathematics in science in ways that Walras found appealing and essentially made his own (Walras 1987: 307). Here Walras' reliance upon Descartes and the powers of the language of mathematics was explicit:

> In reality, Descartes considers as mathematical sciences all those which deal with quantitative facts, that is to say, magnitudes susceptible … of being either expressed in numbers of represented graphically, and which, for this reason, can and should be elaborated either in the language of the science of numbers, or of algebra, or in the language of the science of figures, or geometry.
>
> (Walras 1987: 308)

The Cartesian program offered up the possibility of applying mathematics to various disciplines that might, at the time, seem beyond the ken of mathematical treatment, technique and conceptualization. For Descartes, this meant applying algebra – and, more generally, the abstractions of mathematical thinking – to geometry; the bold step led to the creation of analytic geometry and a new understanding of the role of mathematics in analyzing the physical world. The great innovations in seventeenth-century physics followed from the extension of mathematics into the conceptualization of the laws of nature. Why not, then, reasoned Walras, extend mathematics to the rational comprehension of political economy? This followed the historical parallelism that had marked the triumph of scientific thought between the seventeenth and the nineteenth centuries: first geometry; then physics and astronomy, but especially mechanics; and now political economy.

To establish this parallelism, however, was no easy task, since it involved applying mathematics not to the physical world but to the social world. Here Walras was at his cantankerous best: the steps taken by Descartes and Newton were, in their own time, bold, even revolutionary, so why should misgivings about extending mathematics to political economy be viewed any differently? Naysayers simply impeded progress; later they are proven wrong. Also Walras could point to the recent explorations in the development of social statistics, such as those advanced by Quetelet, to bolster his case. In particular, Walras cited the compilation and use of figures regarding birth rates and mortality, which, while pertaining to society rather than nature and affected by human actions that cannot be fully predicted beforehand, nonetheless produced statistical regularities amenable to further scientific inquiry (Walras 1987: 327).

Moreover, in his time Walras was hardly alone in touting the capacity of science to comprehend the "mechanics" of society. In a "mémoire" from 1898, Walras' colleague in Lausanne, Vilfredo Pareto, proclaimed this extension of mechanics in the baldest of terms: "This science [of pure economics] does not merely resemble mechanics, it is, properly speaking, a type of mechanics" (Pareto 1966: 109). But if economics is a "type of mechanics," how is it possible to avoid the conclusion that scientific economics, and especially such central notions as equilibrium, are based upon a borrowing from physics, grafted onto economics by analogy?

This type of borrowing is certainly reinforced for Walras by some of the materials found in his notes to "Économie et Mécanique." What else is one to make of his sketch of a lever, with its resolution of forces described as an alignment of "virtual velocity" with quantity consumed and forces with "rareté," and the notation, "Voilà!"; an echo of Archimedes' "Eureka!" (Walras 1991: 634).

Philip Mirowski has produced an extended critique of what he sees as Walras' grafting of physics onto economics. In particular, Mirowski emphasizes the reliance of Walras and other mathematically inclined marginalist or neo-classical economists of the same era upon a conception of classical physics that was already in a state of dissolution when they embraced it. Mirowski identifies the essential borrowing as one from energetics, in which the economists substitute utility for energy and the conservatizing principles of thermo-dynamics are translated into the economic principles of equilibrium and maximization (Mirowski 1991: 241ff.).

The critique is multifaceted, in that Mirowski faults the trumpeters of the new "science" of economics, like Walras, for borrowing from a physics that had become outdated, but also because they were unable to make the borrowing work, even on its own terms. Could utility be integrated as one might energy, or was the economic concept subject to a path dependence that barred that possibility? Could the system of equations establishing equilibrium be solved without "rareté" being perfectly differentiable? As Mirowski described it, whenever Walras, Pareto, Irving Fisher or any of the other leaders in the movement to mathematize political economy were challenged, they fell silent or changed the subject.[4]

One might fault Mirowski as well for imputing to Walras a knowledge of physics that he clearly did not have. Jolink has rightly pointed to the lack of any significant references in Walras' work and writings to any developments in physics since the beginning of the nineteenth century (Jolink 1991: 164ff.). On that basis one might see the brunt of Mirowski's critique directed at those economists who were far more fluent in classical physics and more recent developments in thermodynamics; this might establish a pathway from the American chemist, J. Willard Gibbs, to his student, Irving Fisher, who originated the table of correspondences between mechanics and economics, which found its way into Walras' notes (Fisher 1892: 85), or to Paul Samuelson, whose *Foundations of Economic Analysis* does indeed translate the language of thermodynamics into the language of economics.[5] But while this may change the cast of characters, it does not vitiate the essential terms of the argument made by Mirowski of a flawed and faulty borrowing by economists.

Nonetheless, Walras may continue to be a pivotal figure in this matter of the foundational links between economics and physics. The pre-eminence of a physical analogy and the limitations to the Cartesian standard can be found in Walras' identification of Newton, as well as Descartes, as an antecedent. Descartes" algebraizing geometry greatly expanded the range of mathematical techniques and made possible the development of a more abstract form of reasoning, analysis, that transformed both mathematical thought and the idea of abstraction itself. Newton made explicit his goal of subjecting the phenomena of the physical world to a system of mathematical laws, drawing upon new mathematical techniques that again extended the range of mathematical thinking with the introduction of the differential and integral calculus.

But what Descartes did is not the same as what Newton undertook to establish. There are new mathematical techniques, new forms of abstract reasoning, and new scientific laws. Walras does appear to partake of all three: greater reliance upon mathematical techniques and the language of mathematics will make political economy more precise and its relations more evident; awareness of these relations will permit a greater abstracted comprehension of the nature of political economy to emerge; and this more abstracted understanding of political economy can be formulated in laws.

In essence, though, the inducement to extend abstracted reasoning to other disciplines or fields of scientific inquiry, the Cartesian program, as seen by Walras, is subsumed by the effort to devise scientific laws as Newton did. Political economy is not going to be modelled upon, or parallel to, analytic geometry. The laws of economics do not correspond with the laws of geometry; rather, economics will be able to make use – extensive use – of the techniques developed in and through analytic geometry. However, the laws of economics are intended to correspond with the laws of mechanics and the obvious extension of abstract analysis and mathematical techniques championed by Walras is that which allows mathematical laws to be established governing society as well as nature. There is a borrowing that is taking place and the source for that borrowing should be taken at face value: Newton's law. But whether this borrowing can actually be effected is another matter.

A second look at the nature of axiomatization in newly scientific economics may prove revealing. In Walras' time, and this is captured by the lengthy citation from Duhem, to be "axiomatic" was to systematize on the basis of first principles. Less evident then was the definitional or tautological boundaries inherent within axiomatization; as for that matter were the importance of validation and consistency, so that one might have a Euclidean geometry or a non-Euclidean one, each consistent with and within its own terms, and both amenable to interpretations that would determine their usefulness.

For Walras it was a rougher cut: first principles, as noted in the preface to his *Elements*, were idealized from circumstance and experience, then applied. Their subsequent use was carefully distinguished; empirical evidence was not gathered to support their validity, that is, as a testing or confirmation, rather it was the stuff to be sorted out on the basis of those first principles.

One can see this nineteenth-century view of axiomatizing laid out by the mathematician David Hilbert in his 1918 address, "Axiomatic Thought," where he presented as a challenge the more rigorous version of axiomatization that would occupy the attention of twentieth-century mathematicians, philosophers and ultimately theorizers in general:

> Thus in geometry the proposition of the linearity of the equation of the plane and of the orthogonal transformation of point-coordinates is completely adequate to produce the whole broad science of spatial Euclidean geometry purely by means of analysis. Moreover, the laws of calculation and the rules for integers suffice for the construction of number theory. In statics the same role is played by the proposition of the parallelogram of forces; in mechanics, say, by the Lagrangian differential equations of motion; and in electrodynamics by the Maxwell equations together with the requirement of the rigidity and charge of the electron. Thermodynamics can be completely built up from the concept of energy function and the definition of temperature and pressure as derivatives of its variables, entropy and volume.
>
> (Hilbert 1999: 1108)

Hilbert's delineation of the various formative propositions underlying various respective fields of knowledge serves as a template for nineteenth-century axiomatizing. If used as such in ascertaining how economics would have been axiomatized, in accordance with these nineteenth-century rules and understandings, one encounters something rather anomalous: one would expect an independent proposition or propositions to "produce" the science of economics, rather than a substitution of terms within the propositions underlying either statics or mechanics, or both. In other words, in Hilbert's delineation the template consists of specified propositions underlying a specific field of knowledge within mathematics and physics; not an abstracted structure in which different sets of corresponding terms would be introduced. Each field has foundational propositions of its own. The Lagrangian differential equations of motion should not serve as the foundational proposition for both mechanics and economics, only with different primitive terms inserted in each.

But this is what does appear to have occurred, in Walras' thinking as well as that of the other mathematically inclined economists, whether the propositions were drawn from statics, mechanics or thermodynamics. The first principle itself was transferred over from mechanics, say, to economics. This is a borrowing of substance and content; not merely the parallelism of the forms of axiomatization. This may be where the analogy or borrowing is fundamentally flawed.

In short, what appears to be a parallel in axiomatization actually depends upon a borrowing or analogy from physics, and hence the economics constructed thereby lacks the requisite independence in foundation to stand firmly as the science envisioned by Walras.

## Epilogue

One could certainly contend that, whatever Walras himself had thought, or by whatever assumptions, images or metaphorical borrowings, he was guided, he had put forward a set of economic ideas that others, more skilled in mathematics, might – and did – develop further. In that process they may not only have sought to address weaknesses in Walras' mathematics, but also to skirt, or even circumvent, difficulties that emerged from Walras' particular line of reasoning about the bases for an axiomatized system of equilibrium.

There is a narrative running across the first half of the twentieth century that traces the transformation of Walras' system into a far more sophisticated formulation of the theory of general economic equilibrium. Among the figures involved were Abraham Wald, who identified the limitations attendant upon resolving a system in equilibrium by solving "n" equations in "n" unknowns; Shizuo Kakutani and John von Neumann, whose work taken together led to the application of the fixed-point theorem to economic equilibrium; and Gerard Debreu and Kenneth Arrow, who used topological methods to construct a proof of the existence of a general economic equilibrium.

As if to dissociate the notion of general economic equilibrium from any reliance upon ideas, images or representations from physics, or any other natural science, Debreu in particular emphasized the free-standing nature of the mathematical structure that he developed. In and of itself Debreu's model bore no relation to nature, and, by extension, to any models drawn from nature or society, for that matter. In aligning himself with the formalist mathematical tradition of Bourbaki, Debreu asserted: "Allegiance to rigor dictates the axiomatic form of the analysis where the theory, in the strict sense, is logically entirely disconnected from its interpretations" (Debreu 1987: x). This "disconnection," though, is double edged, since it begs the question as to the sources of meaning for those interpretations and the choices made in accepting or rejecting one or another of them.

In the event, the resort by economists to an analogy with or metaphorical borrowing from physics, especially when conceptualizing about economic equilibrium, clearly continued over the course of the twentieth century. On one level it has been treated simply as routine, embodied in the definition of equilibrium found in contemporary texts. In *The MIT Dictionary of Modern Economics*, equilibrium is defined as: "[a] term borrowed from physics to describe as a situation in which economic agents or aggregates of economic agents such as markets have no incentive to change their economic behaviour" (Pearce 1992: 129). It can also be plainly implied. One may draw upon Gregory Mankiw's definition of equilibrium in his text on macro-economics, in which he posits a "state of balance between opposing forces" (Mankiw 1994: 487); this, of course, is the metaphorical lever that had captured Walras' imagination. It is with this image of the lever to which more elaborated and reflective depictions of the essential nature of economic equilibrium return. In the introduction to their extended analysis of general equilibria from the early 1970s, Kenneth Arrow and Frank Hahn attempted to set the formulation of general equilibrium in a broad intellectual context pre-dating Walras, yet they too ended up placing the analogy to the lever on center stage. They introduced the notion of equilibrium, which they took to be the central contribution of economics to the thought of the social sciences, as follows:

> There are two basic, incompletely separable, aspects of the notion of the notion of general equilibrium as it has been used in economics: the simple notion of determinateness, that the relations describing the economic system must be sufficiently complete to determine the value of its variables and the more specific notion that each relation represents a balance of forces.
>
> (Arrow and Hahn 1971: 1)

Arrow and Hahn initially traced this idea back to Adam Smith and strove to deny any conscious link in Smith's mind between economics and mechanics, specifically contending that "there is no obvious evidence" Smith had conceived of the "invisible hand" on the basis of "an analogy with mechanics" (Arrow and Hahn 1971: 1). Yet Arrow and Hahn went on to identify the ultimate historical source of the idea of equilibrium as an "equal weight," referring to the condition for balancing a lever pivoted at its center (Arrow and Hahn 1971: 1).

Finally, the allure of directly substituting economic concepts and terms for mechanical or physical ones, as Fisher and Walras did so dramatically, has not vanished either. The exemplar for this may be found in the following discourse of Paul Samuelson, who, perhaps as much as any major economic thinker in the twentieth century, has carried forward, consciously, a program of incorporating Willard Gibbs" insights about the physical sciences into economics. Addressing the subject of economic method and mathematics at the American Economic Association at mid-century, he declared:

> We may say of Walras what Lagrange ironically said in praise of Newton: "Newton was assuredly the man of genius par excellence, but we must agree that he was also the luckiest: one finds only once the system of the world to be established." And how lucky he was that "in his time the system of the world still remained to be discovered." Substitute "system of equilibrium" for "system of the world" and Walras for Newton and the equation remains valid.
>
> (Samuelson 1952: 61)

Later, in the 1961 edition of his immensely popular textbook, Samuelson would portray Walras as recognized by a scholarly consensus to be "the Newton of economics" (Samuelson 1961: 836). Samuelson's words of praise for Walras echo Walras' own words about the equivalence between a general economic equilibrium and Newton's universal laws. In turn, then, the fault line of axiomatization in Walras' conception of the economic system of the world remains the case as well for those, like Samuelson, who assert the foundational role of Walras' system for economics. In that vein, economic theory in the century after Walras, especially when seeking a grounding as science, has not fully dissolved the bond between economics and physics, in which core elements of the former derive their sense, are interpreted as metaphors, or are simply substituted, from the latter. This is striking, not because metaphors drawn from nature or human experience have been employed in an academic discipline or adapted from another; metaphors are embedded in thought as well as language and appear in and among formative ideas. Instead, it is the unusual reliance upon metaphor and analogy to establish, and then validate, the core or foundation of a scientifically based economics that makes the field of economics stand apart and forms the basis of a serious challenge to its claims of being scientific.

## Notes

1  See, for example, Paul Krugman's column depicting rent control as attempting to defy the law of gravity, that is, the laws of supply and demand (*New York Times*, June 7, 2000).
2  Charles Lyell's *Principles of Geology*, which first appeared in 1830, emphasized the great length of time over which the earth had changed, hence giving geology a history and making it subject to historical law. Darwin, for his part, relied upon Lyell's contention in advancing the notion of natural selection; see Darwin (1998: 127).
3  In the tradition of, say, P.-S. Laplace's (1824) highly popular recasting of his own work in astronomy, *Exposition du système du monde*, which then proved to be quite influential across a broad intellectual community. Walras' use of the term, "system of the world," to characterize the scope of general economic equilibrium may well have been drawn from Laplace, even if its ultimate source was Newton.

4  See Mirowski 1988; Mirowski and Cook 1990.
5  Paul Samuelson (1983) [1947] *Foundations of Economic Analysis.* The motto reads: "Mathematics is a Language." See also Samuelson's adaptation of LeChatelier's principle in physical chemistry to economics, which he validates in the following footnote: "This is a purely mathematical theorem" (p. 38).

## References

Arrow, K. J. and Hahn, F. H. (1971) *General Competitive Analysis.* San Francisco: Holden-Day.

Cournot, A. A. (1861) *Traité de l'enchaînement des idées fondamentales dans les science et dans l'histoire.* Paris: Hachette.

Darwin, C. (1998) [1859] *The Origin of Species.* New York: Modern Library.

Debreu, G. (1987) [1959] *Theory of Value: An Axiomatic Analysis of Economic Equilibrium.* New Haven: Yale University Press.

Duhem, P. (1991) [1905–1906] *The Origins of Statics.* Boston: Kluwer Academic.

Fisher, I. (1892) "Mathematical investigations in the theory of value and prices." Thesis, Yale University.

Hausman, D. (1992) *The Inexact and Separate Science of Economics.* Cambridge: Cambridge University Press.

Hilbert, D. (1999) [1918] "Axiomatic Thought." In William Ewald (ed.), *From Kant to Hilbert: A Source Book in the Foundations of Mathematics,* vol. II. Oxford: Clarendon Press.

Jaffe, W. (ed.) (1965) Letters 1483 and 1495, with notes. *Correspondence of Léon Walras and Related Papers,* vol. 3. Amsterdam: North Holland.

Jolink, A. (1991) "Procrustean Beds and All That: The Irrelevance of Walras for a Mirowski Thesis." In Neil de Marchi (ed.), *Non-Natural Social Science.* Durham, NC: Duke University Press.

Laplace, P. S. (1824) [1796]. *Exposition du système du monde,* 5th edn. Paris: Bachelier.

Lyell, C. (1830–3) *Principles of Geology.* London: Murray.

McKenzie, L. W. (2002) *Classical General Equilibrium Theory.* Cambridge, MA: MIT Press.

Mankiw, N. G. (1994) *Macroeconomics,* 2nd edn. New York: Worth.

Mirowski, P. (1988) "The Sciences Were Never at War?" In Philip Mirowski (ed.), *Against Mechanism.* Totowa, NJ: Rowman & Littlefield.

Mirowski, P. (1991) *More Heat than Light.* Cambridge: Cambridge University Press.

Mirowski, P. and Cook, P. (1990) "Walras' 'Economics and Mechanics': Translation, Commentary, Context." In W. Samuels (ed.), *Economics as Discourse.* Boston: Kluwer Academic.

Mouchot, C. (2003) *Méthodologie économique.* Paris: Éditions du Seuil.

Pareto, V. (1966) [1898]. "Comment se pose le problème de l'économie pure." *Œuvres complètes,* vol. 9. Geneva: Droz.

Pearce, D. W. (ed.) (1992) *The MIT Dictionary of Modern Economics,* 4th edn. Cambridge, MA: MIT Press.

Poinsot, L. (1842) *Éléments de statique.* 8th edn. Paris: Bachelier.

Riemann, G. F. B. (1999) [1868]. "On the Hypotheses Which Lie at the Foundation of Geometry." In W. Ewald (ed.), *From Kant to Hilbert: A Source Book in the Foundations of Mathematics,* vol. II. Oxford: Clarendon.

Samuelson, P. (1952) "Economic Theory and Mathematics: An Appraisal." *American Economic Review*, 42(2): 56–66.

Samuelson, P. (1961) *Economics: An Introductory Analysis*, 5th edn. New York: McGraw-Hill.

Samuelson, P. (1983) [1947] (ed.) *Foundations of Economic Analysis, Enlarged.* Cambridge, MA: Harvard University Press.

Solow, R. (1985) "Economic History and Economics." *American Economic Review*, 75(2): 328–331.

Van Daal, J. and Jolink, A. (1993) *The Equilibrium Economics of Léon Walras.* London: Routledge.

Walras, L. (1984) [1874]. *The Elements of Pure Economics*, 4th edn, translated by William Jaffe.Philadelphia: Orion Editions.

Walras, L. (1987) [1927]. "Une branche nouvelle de la mathématique." In Pierre Dockès et al. (eds), *Auguste et Léon Walras, œuvres économiques complètes*, vol. VII. Paris: Economica.

Walras, L. (1991) "Notes pour 'Économie et mécanique.'" In Pierre Dockès et al. (eds), *Auguste et Léon Walras, œuvres économiques complètes*, vol. XI. Paris: Economica.

# 2 The mathematical turn in economics

## Walras, the French mathematicians, and the road not taken[1]

The effort to make economics mathematical is set in different historical moments, each according a transformed place for mathematics in economics. Among them one may cite the first introduction of calculus in the 1860s, the increased use of statistics in the late nineteenth century, or the development of econometrics in the 1920s and 1930s.

The one, though, that served as a critical turn, where economics, conceived as a science akin to physics, but especially to mechanics, was to be comprehended as mathematical in its language, techniques, and formal relations or structures, occurred with the rise to prominence of neoclassical economics at the turn of the twentieth century. But as is the case for any historical moment, one ought to inquire as well about paths not pursued. What alternative ways of thinking about or constructing economics might have been available in that mathematical turn?

Two essential and noteworthy developments in the period of the ascendancy of neoclassical economics mark the mathematical turn within it. First of all, the marginalist rethinking of the field tended to encourage the greater use of and reliance upon geometric representation, culminating in Alfred Marshall's early synthesis of neoclassical economics, which, despite Marshall's own reluctance and ambiguity about the role of mathematics in economics, produced what still remains a recognizable microeconomics replete with graphical techniques.

Second, for all the broad differences on the subject among the marginalist schools, with Carl Menger the most notable exception, there were those like Stanley Jevons, Francis Edgeworth, Leon Walras, Vilfredo Pareto, and Irving Fisher who championed the mathematizing of economics. As distinct from those who sought to create statistical measures in economics (Porter 2001: 17–18), they envisioned linking the quantification of economic phenomena to establishing algebraic or other mathematical relationships across economics variables.

Among such economists Walras was perhaps the most ardent, as he saw his relentless and seemingly unyielding advocacy of a suitably mathematical economics met with disdain in France, resulting in his being regarded as an outsider by its established academic world of political economy. His main economic work, *Elements of Pure Political Economy*, through its revisions the cynosure of his writing over a lifetime, was intended to demonstrate the possibilities of an algebraic construction of and solution to the interplay of resources, output, and demand in any national economy. His extensive correspondence, organized and made available to a wider public audience by William Jaffe (Walras 1965), reveals Walras' dogged and sometimes beleaguered campaign to win support for his *idée fixe*.

Yet there is more than one irony in this period's turn towards mathematizing economics, especially as one looks more closely at Walras and his intellectual milieu. For one, as Philip Mirowski noted, the case for mathematizing economics was typically advanced as a way of making economics more scientific, through an alignment of economics with classical mechanics, at a time when its presumptive universality was already being delimited by contrasts with thermodynamics and when the core ideas of classical physics would shortly undergo the challenges of relativity and quantum theory (Mirowski 1989: 59–89). Moreover, both relativity and quantum theory drew upon and entailed a recasting of the nature and understanding of physical measurement, with the introduction of the idea of space–time through the former and the principle of uncertainty through the latter.

It was also a period in which mathematicians found themselves engaged in strenuous debate, lasting several decades, as efforts to achieve greater rigor – typically with greater formality – and to counter inconsistencies in mathematics led to a crisis about the nature of the foundations of mathematics. As E. Roy Weintraub has pointed out, there was a palpable shift over the course of the nineteenth century from an alignment of mathematical rigor with the capacity of mathematics to capture the truthfulness of the facts of the external world to an emphasis upon the need for internal consistency and the avoidance of contradiction (Weintraub 2001; also Weintraub 2002: 48–9). Yet the explicit grounding of all mathematics in the rules of logic or through a limited number of fundamental principles or axioms could not eliminate all such inconsistencies.

But perhaps most striking, if little noticed, in Walras' case was the fact that France's foremost mathematicians, including those whose views on the prospect of mathematizing economics he had sought out, raised questions and concerns that might easily have guided this project in another direction, away from the neoclassical tack it tended to take. Of the French mathematicians active and prominent in academic and professional circles around 1900 one might readily include, among others, Gaston Darboux, by then permanent secretary of the French Academy (Grattan-Guinness 1997: 487); Henri Poincaré, the most outstanding figure of the period who bridged the world of mathematics and physics; Émile Picard, who provided a similar bridge; Jacques Hadamard, Picard's foremost student; and Émile Borel.

If one considers carefully the specific exchanges between Walras, on the one hand, and Henri Poincaré and Émile Picard, on the other, one can discern within the writings of these mathematicians a raft of major elements for a modified economics program. Moreover, a similar set of such elements can be found as well in the writings of a third French mathematician with whom Walras corresponded, Émile Borel.

This modified economics program would include: the necessity of identifying with forthright clarity the assumptions underlying and limiting any economic hypothesis put forward; a recognition of the central role of uncertainty in assessing economic behavior; the complications posed by the discontinuities in economic measurement and the possibility of using qualitative measures that might require a different set of mathematical techniques; and an awareness of the place of memory and history in economic systems, or what has commonly become known as hysteresis, a term used by both Poincaré and Picard.

Yet for all intents and purposes, what these mathematicians proffered was a road not taken at that juncture. In part, one may read this as a desire on Walras' part to accept the apparent approbation of Poincaré and Picard, and cite the apparent approbation of Émile Borel, Gaston Darboux, Maurice d'Ocagne, and Jules Tannery (Walras 1965: 314, 352), rather than absorb broadly the points they raised, in either their responses to him or in their own writings.[2] To the end, in 1908 and 1909, Walras identified Poincaré, Picard, and Borel as supporters of his approach to economics, whom he hoped, without apparent success, might assist in promoting his last work, "Économique et mécanique," intended to make plain the alignment of a mathematical economics with mechanics, to the mathematical scientific community (Letters 1677, 1722, Walras 1965: 347, 388).

It was also the case that there were others, like the Italian mathematician Vito Volterra, who accepted the basic premise that economics ought to become more mathematical, along the lines of the physical sciences, though, as Pareto discovered, even Volterra could find difficulties in the details, notably in the integratibility of the utility function (Mirowski 1989: 248–9; Weintraub 2002: 32–5; 48–51).

The inclination not to modify the program of economics may reflect as well a seemingly common-sense understanding about the nature of science and the role of mathematics in it, where mathematics, whether in physics or economics, was intuitively grasped as serving as a medium, whereby number, and hence quantification, in words enshrined by Tobias Dantzig, became "the language of science" (Dantzig 1930). And, to the extent that a framework for mathematics might be applied to economics, Walras' own comprehension of the uses of mathematics in mechanics inclined him to view it as offering up an axiomatic structure, even though that structure and its primitives were actually dependent upon an analogy with classical mechanics (Turk 2006). This was quite distant and distinct from the conventionalism that characterized Poincaré's mathematical thought, where experience and imagination shaped mathematical concepts rather than being shaped by idealized principles and primitives, and influenced the choice of hypotheses that might be fitted to a given set of facts (Heinzmann and Nabonnand 2008).

## Language, technique, or formal relation?

To appreciate what matters hung in the balance in this century-old mathematical turn in economics it is necessary at the outset to step back and recognize the ambiguities and critical shadings entailed by the notion of "mathematizing." In part, the program of mathematization rested upon an understanding of mathematics as it was re-formed and shaped in the course of the nineteenth century into analysis, with a new emphasis upon rigor and a close bond with what came to be known as mathematical physics (Kneebone [1963] 2001: 139–40; Grattan-Guinness 1997: 312–17; 405–8).

This kind of mathematical thought was identified along a chronological and intellectual pathway through such figures as Joseph-Louis Lagrange, Augustin-Louis Cauchy, and Karl Weierstrass, where Lagrange sought to algebraize mechanics, while Cauchy replaced more loosely conceived notions about limits and the infinite with more formal and precise constructs of them, formalizing proofs in the process (Grattan-Guinness 1997: 373–6), and Weierstrass led the effort to set all mathematics as analysis, free of geometric representation and intuition (Grattan-Guinness 1997: 481–6). In this transformation it would prove difficult to distinguish the mathematics which economics would seek to appropriate, from the science, classical physics, that found mathematics essential to its expression. As Weintraub put it, by the late nineteenth century the effort to make economics as solid as a hard science required that it "emulate" mathematics itself (Weintraub 2002: 37).

The development of analysis represented a major trajectory in the broader advance of mathematical ideas, but, by the same token, this meant that other understandings of mathematics might exist and inform a mathematization of economics. In the case of the early twentieth-century turn in economics towards greater mathematization, one might think of topology, or, as it was then labelled, *analysis situs*, as one such alternative, a mathematical subfield pioneered by Poincaré and explored by Picard.

There are three different possible understandings of the nature of mathematics and the role it might play in economics that are routinely melded into each other, although they may be viewed as quite distinct in crucial ways.

The first of these is the notion that, as Paul Samuelson later put it in the motto for the *Foundations of Economic Analysis*: "mathematics is the language of science" (see Dantzig 1930). Walras himself had taken the position that mathematics would afford economists a clarifying and more precise language with which they might more readily engage in a scientific inquiry. In a letter to the Nobel Peace Prize Committee on January 22, 1906, Walras praised the work of the Vito Volterra, citing the latter's article entitled, "Les mathématiques dans les sciences biologiques et sociales," which had just been translated into French and published in *La revue du mois* twelve days before:

> The author, as he himself states, is more a mathematician than an economists; but, just the same, no one has better recognized in our "analytical

economics" the proceedings by the same means as which Maxwell and Helmholtz have transformed physics and physiology, and makes comprehensible how economic questions such as free exchange, for example, which are and remained so tangled and confused in everyday language, can be brought to a solution so clear and sure through the use of the mathematical method.

(Letter 1618, Walras 1965: 296)

It may be the case that Walras had not read – or read too closely – Volterra's article. In his notations to Walras' letter, Jaffe remarked that Volterra had made no reference to "free exchange" (Walras 1965: 296). It is also worthwhile to take note that in the article Volterra had approvingly cited Walras, along with Whewell, Cournot, and Gossen, for their "assimilation of mathematical methods" (Volterra 1901: 447). Of these four, three belonged to an earlier generation: Whewell died in 1866, Cournot in 1877, and Gossen in 1858. Thus, Walras stands out as the only listed living contemporary of Volterra, suggesting perhaps that Walras' overwhelming reaction served as more than a bit of an act of mutual admiration.

The identification of the mathematical method in economics with the resort to a language affording scientific precision can also be found a generation later in the writings of Charles Roos, an early American advocate of the mathematical method in economics. In *Dynamic Economics*, published in 1934, Roos stated: "In order to state hypotheses so clearly that they will not be misunderstood, it is necessary to choose language carefully" (Roos 1934: 10) He goes on to describe the need for and virtue of a "symbolic language" in any scientific inquiry:

> In fact, the more variables there are the more necessary it becomes to have a symbolic language to keep track of them. No one could advise an astronomer to develop a science of the stars without using mathematics.
>
> (Roos 1934: 11)

But mathematics could also be regarded as a toolbox, from which the best technique, or at the least the one most likely to succeed, would be chosen. In the process the mathematical economist became more of a professional craftsman, on the order of a jeweler whose skill in devising the best approach to cutting drew upon his/her experience and knowledge in sorting through the array of tools and techniques at his/her disposal. The range in technique has proven to be quite broad: as Walras made use of linear equations, so Roos made use of integral equations.

For his part, Edgeworth highlighted the possible gains to economic analysis through the use of the calculus of variations. He began by noting that "[i]t is the first principle of the calculus of variations that a varying quantity attains a maximum when the first *term of variation* vanishes, while the second term is negative (mutatis mutandis, for a minimum)" (Edgeworth [1881] 1932: 91).

He then applied this principle to economics: "In the simple cases which in the infancy of Mathematical Psychics are along presented in these pages, we know by observation not *what* the second term is, but *that* it is continually negative" (Edgeworth [1881] 1932: 91).

As Edgeworth's text suggests, mathematical methods and techniques might on occasion also be regarded as fundamentally formal and structural: as mathematical statements expressing universal relations that hold regardless of any specific content. This notion is akin to Ivor Grattan-Guinness' idea of "structure–similarity" in mathematical forms and patterns that precedes any attribution of meaning to them (Grattan-Guinness 1992: 93).

It may provide as well a mathematical resonance between economics and physics, like the one identified by Samuelson in his later reflections upon the genesis of the *Foundations of Economic Analysis* in the 1930s:

> I was vaccinated early on to understand that economics and physics could share the same formal theorems (Euler's theorem on homogeneous functions, Weierstrass's theorems on constrained maxima, Jacobi determinant identities underlying LeChatelier reactions, etc.), while still not resting on the same empirical foundations and certainties.
>
> (Samuelson 1998: 1376)

This, then, serves as the backdrop to the alternatives, whether expressed fully or only in inchoate ways, that economists early on in the twentieth century might divine as pertinent in mathematics to the nature and workings of economics. For Walras, whom Samuelson had praised as the Newton of economics (Samuelson 1965: 1756), both the power associated with the more scientific discourse of quantification through the use of algebra and the possibility of analogizing formal elements and structures from one discipline to another, had great appeal.

## On the importance of measure

The exchange of letters between Léon Walras and Henri Poincaré took place largely in 1901; the exchanges between Walras and Émile Picard in 1906.[3] Walras' letters to Émile Borel followed shortly thereafter. This was the last decade of Walras' life, and so his effort to confirm the legitimacy of his life's work and influence the future course of economics as a discipline was, if anything, reinforced in this period.

The exchange of letters between Walras and Poincaré has been largely overlooked, with the critical exception of an essay by William Jaffe dating from 1977 (Jaffe 1983: 213–20) and a discussion of the import of Poincaré's response for notions of attaining a general equilibrium by Bruna Ingrao and Giorgio Israel in *The Invisible Hand*, published in 1990 (Ingrao and Israel 1990: 154–61). Yet the discussion of the nature of scientific measurement and hence the role of mathematics in the construction of science is central to the question which prompted the exchange: what is the proper role and scope of mathematics in economics?

That is so at least in part because of the timing. For Walras the issue had been joined with greater urgency when Hermann Laurent, a mathematician with whom Walras had a longstanding relationship and had engaged in an especially extensive correspondence in December 1898 and again in May 1900, threw down the gauntlet at an annual conference of mathematical actuaries in 1900 and challenged the validity of applying mathematics to notions like satisfaction (Walras 1965: 113), a core element in Walras' "pure political economy," and, like Stanley Jevons' idea of utility, the essential concept in the reconstruction of economics in marginalism and ultimately in neoclassical economics.

Philip Mirowski has excoriated the feebleness of Walras' response to Laurent, emphasizing the weakness of Walras' mathematical intuition and skills and his tendency to cite the approbation of others, especially those with strong scientific credentials, as proof of the rightness of his theory. For Mirowski Walras' failing here to grasp the challenge and address it adequately – and a similar, contemporaneous such failing by Pareto in response to an otherwise highly supportive Vito Volterra – represented the hollowness of the mechanical analogy upon which they based their mathematization of economics (Mirowski 1989: 241–50).

As to Laurent's challenge to Walras, Mirowski paid particular attention to Laurent's "compression" of Walras' case into mathematical language, readily amenable to problem-solving through the technique of integration, and revealing thereby an unresolved factor of integration necessary for measuring rareté that called into question – and, in Mirowski's view – nullified the physical metaphor underlying Walras' economic model (Mirowski 1988: 32–44). Of course, the reference to metaphor also suggests that what was being sought by Walras, and contested by Mirowski, was a kinship of form or structure established through mathematics. As Mirowski saw it, the "program of mathematical economics" required both "a shared language and a shared metaphor" (Mirowski 1991: 147–8).

Mirowski, though, did not pursue the full extent of Walras' efforts to salvage and ultimately sustain his mission to mathematize economics.[4] Walras turned to Henri Poincaré, the pre-eminent French mathematician of his day, and asked if Laurent was right or not (Letter 1492). Initially, Poincaré responded by affirming the possibility that economics could be mathematized, within certain limits (Letter 1494). Walras pressed harder. Had he exceeded those limits? (Letter 1495). Poincaré then responded once more, again rather swiftly, within a week of receiving Walras' query (Letter 1496), in terms that Walras, not unreasonably, interpreted as positive, but which came with reservations and a difference in perspective that rendered the response quite ambiguous.

One may surmise, if only on textual grounds, that the rapidity of Poincaré's response was due in part to the attention he had been giving to the matter of measurement in science, most especially with regard to physics. That same year, 1901, saw the publication of the first of Poincaré's three popular works about the nature of science, *Science and Hypothesis*. One can identify phrases in Poincaré's letter to Walras that are drawn directly from *Science and Hypothesis*, specifically the subsection on "measurable magnitude," and his discussion of magnitudes that are not "measurable." In particular: "we can indeed say whether a given one of these magnitudes is greater than another, but not whether it is twice or thrice as great" (Poincaré 1905: 23).

One may compare this wording with Poincaré's response to Walras:

> Your definition of rareté impresses me as legitimate. And this is how I should justify it. Can satisfaction be measured? I can say that one satisfaction is greater than another, since I prefer one to the other, but I cannot say that the first satisfaction is two or three times greater than the other. That makes no sense by itself and only some arbitrary convention can give it meaning. Satisfaction is therefore a magnitude but not a measurable magnitude.
>
> (Letter 1496, translated by and in Jaffe 1983: 217).

Thus, from Poincaré's perspective the matter raised by Walras had little to do with any questioning of the status of economics as a field of intellectual inquiry – should it be regarded as suitably and sufficiently scientific, or not? – but instead turned on the efficacy and appropriateness of scientific measurement itself, thereby challenging established notions about how science itself was constituted.

Poincaré's reflections on the nature of measurement drew upon a half-century of examination and reimagination among leading mathematicians of the "problem of space" (Friedman 1996: 335–8), initiated by the recognition that the intuitive understanding of space thought to have been captured by Euclidean geometry represented only one of several different possible geometries calling forth different standards of measurements and different shapes to and curvatures of space, and conditions for the stability of objects in such spaces, including celestial bodies, needed to be re-examined.

For Poincaré this led to seeing many of the physical concepts through which measurements were made, whether cast in terms of Newtonian physics or from the vantage point of energetics, as merely conventions (Poincaré 1905: 67ff.). He tried as well to introduce the pertinence of a more qualitative form of measurement, paradox notwithstanding, found in unmeasurable magnitude (Poincaré 1905: 23–4).

In effect, in responding to Walras, Poincaré set Walras' query about the possibility of giving "satisfaction" a suitable mathematical measure in the context of his own work. Thus, while Walras was keen to establish the efficacy of mathematics in the discourse of economics so as to buttress the scientific claims of the discipline, Poincaré was concerned with the limitations of a mechanistic view of science in general and hence the scope and limits of mathematics in any science.

Consider the following juxtaposition: in his letter to Poincaré, Walras relies upon an understanding of the notion of "mass" and its capacity to be measured through an imagined counting that Poincaré would in no way accept. Walras cites the definition of the mass of any physical body in Poinsot's *Statics*, the work from which Walras built his analogy of economics to classical physics, as "the number of molecules that compose it" (Letter 1495). Such a number was not actually countable, yet formed the basis of physical construction and informed mathematical formulations of physical laws. Why should the satisfaction of an individual be regarded as any less suitable for a similar quantification and mathematical construction? (Letter 1495). By contrast, in the section on measurement in *Science and Hypothesis* Poincaré challenged the concept of "mass" as found in and derived from Newton's laws as fundamentally tautological (Poincaré 1905: 73–6).

Moreover, from Poincaré's perspective, setting foundations for any scientific inquiry was questionable, as it was only "relations between objects" that mattered in the construction of any science (Poincaré 1905: 18). Hence, if satisfaction – or presumably any other economic category or variable – could be comprehended as elucidating a set of pertinent relations, then it passed the threshold of science. In his letter to Walras, Poincaré finds that relation in "defin[ing] satisfaction by any arbitrary function providing the function always increases with an increase in the satisfaction it represents" (Letter 1496, Jaffe translation).

At first blush this may appear to meet the terms of the third way that economics could be rendered mathematical, by establishing a structural correspondence between a formal mathematical relation and an economic relation, but the strictures of Poincaré's conventionalism rapidly call that into doubt. First, there would have to be a basis in experience that "guides" the construction of that formal relation (Poincaré 1905: 53). Otherwise, a "formal relation" would remain an abstraction, a product merely of a choice of words. Second, the arbitrary functions used to construct the correspondence constitute a scaffolding that must in the end be removed for the relation exhibited to be meaningful. "If the arbitrary functions still appear in the conclusions, the conclusions are not false, but they are totally without interest, because they depend upon the arbitrary conventions made at the start" (Letter 1496, translation in Jaffe 1983: 217).

Intriguingly, Poincaré gave Walras a pass on this objective. Yet Jaffe correctly noted that that was not the case.

> In [Walras'] own proof of the fundamental theorem of proportionality of marginal utilities to parametric prices as a condition of equilibrium … the arbitrary assumption of diminishing utility remains embedded in the conclusion and entails the retention throughout of the further arbitrary assumption of cardinally measurable utility.
>
> (Jaffe 1983: 218)

Ingrao and Israel also found that Walras did not meet Poincaré's strictures, but from an altogether different vantage point. They take as suspect and arbitrary the assumption retained by Walras that different individuals respond uniformly in their satisfaction to various combinations of goods (Ingrao and Israel 1990: 158). One suspects that this challenge, rooted in the subjectivity of human response, was at the heart of Laurent's initial rebuke to Walras. If Ingrao and Israel are right, then Poincaré also completely missed the mark. Poincaré's focus was upon whether satisfaction itself was measurable, rather than how satisfaction that is experienced by different individuals would meet a standard of sufficient uniformity and consistency as to be measurable.

## Poincaré's reservations

Overall, Poincaré appeared supportive of Walras' efforts. Nonetheless, it may be fair to ask if Walrasian "satisfaction" did meet the further test laid out by Poincaré. Poincaré had offered up two reservations. First, he took the positing of unbridled self-interest as a plausible approximation of individual behavior. Second, and with greater hesitation, he questioned the reliance upon full clairvoyance, the notion that individuals have a complete and certain grasp of the future.

Walras did not explore the implications of either of these reservations. Instead he marginalized their gist, taking note of them essentially as subsumable deviations of an idealized treatment of consumer behavior, akin to the frictionless world of classical physics. What follows is his response to Poincaré:

> As to hypotheses, it is quite certain that one must be on guard when one passes from abstractions to reality. In reality there are frictions in the economic mechanism; and as to the other concerns [raised by Poincaré] men are not utterly self-interested nor perfectly clairvoyant. From this it follows that the applied theory of the production of wealth should indicate these frictions with care and bring about their suppression as completely as possible in view of approximating the maximum of utility as closely as possible.
>
> (Letter 1498, Walras 1965: 167)

Nevertheless, one could envision the potential impact of probabilities or asymmetries if such reservations were taken fully into account. More generally, Poincaré's reservations could be regarded as the basis for weighing and incorporating the consequences of a lack of sufficient information in the analysis and interpretation of consumer behavior. In Walras' schema, as it was for Irving Fisher and Vilfredo Pareto, the individual in economics was aligned with the molecule in mechanics. Yet nowhere in statistical mechanics did molecules have to contend with clairvoyance, or the lack thereof, as they collided with one another. Even if at only an initial stage Poincaré had opened the way to an appreciation of the problem of integrating intention and consciousness into economic matters.

In his paper examining the Walras-Poincaré correspondence, William Jaffé essentially cast the matters discussed into a narrative of realization whereby the recognition that utility ought to be understood as an ordinal rather than cardinal measure is seen as a "remarkable premonition [by Poincaré] of subsequent trends in microeconomic theory" (Jaffé 1983: 218) This, even on its face, seems unduly positive in its reach. There is no evidence that Walras took up Poincaré's insight or his conventionalist critique in his own work, or shared it with other economists. Nor is there any evidence that economists of the succeeding generation had knowledge of, or had somehow absorbed into their own thinking, his caution about the need to contemplate economic behavior beset by a lack of clairvoyance.

Moreover, that Poincaré's comments cannot simply be read as an endorsement of ordinal over cardinal measures of utility, as Jaffé envisioned them to be, is apparent from Poincaré's discussion of the physical continuum in *Science and Hypothesis*, where full transitivity, a critical element in the ranking system of ordinal measure, cannot be maintained. Relying upon Ludwig Fechner's standards for measurement, Poincaré saw contradictions in measurement emerge that led him to discern a disjuncture between the physical and the mathematical continuum (Poincaré 1905: 25–8). At the same time, it would be too facile to see Poincaré's critique of classical physics as effectively deconstructing the kind of scientific framework that Walras sought for economics, as Mirowski would have it, simply because Poincaré did give explicit support to the quest undertaken by Walras to mathematize economics, as long as it was done with suitably framed hypotheses. This means that the deconstruction one might reasonably see unfolding through Poincaré's insights and strictures must be somewhat more nuanced, establishing where the "relations between objects," built out of experience, would hold.

To what extent did Poincaré's introduction of the notion of "non-measurable" magnitudes into his exchange with Walras open up the possibility of making use of qualitative yet mathematical measurement in economics? Although Jaffé interpreted this as the case for ordinal as opposed to cardinal measurement, one might demur on a number of counts. For one, as Nicholas Georgescu-Roegen noted, it might be possible to devise instead a measure of weak cardinality, partaking of certain elements of quantitative measure (Georgescu-Roegen 1966: 51). For his part, Poincaré had identified a variability in the nature of measurement, using the example of temperature. He cited the introduction of the notion of absolute temperature as laying the groundwork for a new mathematical construct of temperature. While it had formerly been limited to unmeasurable magnitudes, based upon correspondences with changing intervals of columns of mercury, it could now be conceived as a mathematical function that was "constantly increasing" (Letter 1496, Walras 1965: 163).

One might extend Poincaré's critique of measurement further, to encompass qualitative changes for which a different kind of mathematics would be required, employing different sorts of techniques and drawing upon a different model for mathematical analysis, namely topology. It raises the possibility that mathematization, including that of economics, need not be viewed as synonymous with the quantification of economic phenomena into mathematical variables. As the French mathematician René Thom, one of the major developers of "chaos theory" and recipient of the 1958 Fields Medal, would later put it: "A topological analysis of a situation has a qualitative content which is not quantitative" (Thom 1991: 93). This stands as a refutation of Ernest Rutherford's apothegm that "Qualitative is nothing but poor quantitative" (Thom 1991: 93), a "formula" that recalls the contention by Walras, Roos, and Samuelson, among others, about the precision gained by mathematizing economics through a more scientifically established vocabulary.

In this context it is noteworthy that Poincaré is often viewed as having laid the groundwork for chaos theory in an 1890 paper in *Acta Mathematica* entitled, "Sur le problème des trois corps et les équations de la dynamique" (Grattan-Guinness 1997: 614–18). And, as Mirowski has noted, Poincaré's exploration of the implications of chaos theory led him to recognize the centrality of "stochastic processes" in classical mechanics itself (Mirowski 1989: 74–6).

## Of "frottements," irreversible phenomena, and hysteresis

In 1905 Émile Picard, one of France's leading mathematicians, published a popular work on the current state of science, entitled *La science moderne et son état actuel*. In the tradition of such popular writing in France, Picard's exploration of the subject was high-minded and intellectually engaging; not dissimilar, therefore, from Poincaré's popular writings about the nature of, and prospects for, science at the turn of the twentieth century.

Picard, while less well known than Poincaré, also had a distinguished career as a mathematician, making particularly noteworthy contributions in algebraic geometry and analysis, for the latter of which he produced a standard multi-volume treatise (copies of which he sent to Walras as a courtesy) (Letters 1634, 1636, and 1637). He first taught at the École normale supérieure in Paris, where his most famous student was Jacques Hadamard. From 1898 on he was ensconced at the University of Paris. Like Poincaré, Picard had an abiding intellectual interest in physics, especially mechanics, and in 1922 wrote one of the first textbooks on relativity. Picard's *Treatise*, first published in the mid 1890s, helped spread to a wider academic audience both Poincaré's and Lyapunov's theorizing about the conditions for establishing equilibrium in dynamical systems.

In *La science moderne et son état actuel* Picard produced a short treatment, no more than a couple of paragraphs, of the attempt made to apply mathematical analysis to economics, and attached it essentially as an addendum to a section entitled, "Analysis in its Relations with Chemistry and Biology." It was this passage to which Walras was drawn and responded so favorably, causing him to seek out Picard in October 1906 in further support of the effort to mathematize economics (Letter 1633). Walras' reaction appears somewhat outsized. The next month, as if offering blandishments, he inquired of Poincaré as to whether the rumors were true that Poincaré and Picard had made the case for a mathematized economics at an international conference at the 1904 World's Fair in St. Louis, Missouri (Letter 1638). The conference had been organized around the theme of the "unity of science" and had drawn, in addition to Poincaré and Picard, Gaston Darboux as head of the French delegation (Darboux 1912: 371–2). Poincaré, though, denied that the matter of a mathematized economics had ever been taken up at the conference (Letter 1639).

In this passage, presented below in its entirety in translation, one is struck by the cautionary notes sounded by Picard in his overview of the field.

Picard begins by stating: "[B]ut, despite legitimate hopes, it is clear that, overall, biology is still far from entering a truly mathematical period." He then goes on to say: "This is not the case, according to certain economists, for political economy" (Picard 1905: 45)

That case then follows:

> After Cournot, the Lausanne school made an extremely interesting effort to introduce mathematical analysis into political economy. Under certain hypotheses, which hold for at least limited cases, one finds in the scholarly treatises an equation between the quantities of goods and their prices, which corresponds to the equation for virtual velocities in mechanics: it is the equation of economic equilibrium. A function of quantities plays a role in this theory corresponding essentially to the potential function. Moreover, the most authoritative representatives of the school insist upon the analogy of economic phenomena with mechanical phenomena; "as rational mechanics, one of them says, considers material points, pure economics considers homo oeconomicus." Naturally, one also discovers the analogues of the equations of Lagrange, the obligatory model for all mechanics.
>
> (Picard 1905: 46)

However, Picard's assessment concludes in less than glowing terms. "All the while admiring these hardy efforts, one is led to fear that its authors have neglected certain *hidden masses*, as Helmholtz and Hertz might have put it. But, in the event, there are in these doctrines a keen application of mathematics, which, at least in cases that are well circumscribed, have already rendered service" (Picard 1905: 46).

What are those limits to which Picard refers? Or, more precisely, what are their implications for those seeking to mathematize economics? There were a host of masses or movements in the discourse of physics at the end of the nineteenth century that were regarded in the terminology of Helmholtz and Hertz as hidden. These included: the ether, vibrating materials, potential energy, and the dissipative motion association with entropy. Critically, the last of these involved actions or movements that were irreversible, though Picard's overall concern, like that of Poincaré, was with respect to all such actions or movements that could not be comprehended in a conservative force field.

Elsewhere in *La science moderne et son état actuel* Picard distinguishes between physical systems that acted upon the principle or postulate of *"non hérédité,"* in which "the future of the system depended solely upon its current state" (Picard 1905: 123), and those which were subject to the principle or postulate of heredity, in which the past or history did matter. The former were typically regarded as conservative, while the latter were taken not to be so. Picard saw these latter systems marked by certain "frottements," or frictions, which he felt were characteristic of systems where the past influenced the future. And it was to these "frottements" that Picard specifically drew Walras' attention, throwing out a clear-cut caution, in his response to him, restricting "the analogies of the problems of pure political economy" to "the problems of the rational mechanics of systems sans frottements" (Letter 1634, Walras 1965: 313).

In *La science moderne et son état actuel* Picard expatiated as well on the relation between "frottements" and the notion of irreversibility:

> The great majority of physicists are of the opinion that *irreversible* systems cannot be *conservative*; to discuss this assertion it is necessary to comprehend that the notion of irreversibility is not independent of the number and the nature of the variables envisaged in the system. A mathematical physicist of great penetration, M. Brillouin, thinks that rational mechanics is not essentially reversible, and irreversibility can introduce instability into mechanics.
>
> (Picard 1905: 124)

This carries with it the implication that when irreversible systems are involved, any reliance upon a natural movement toward an economic equilibrium may be mistaken. Attaining such an equilibrium would come to require the use of Lagrange's equations, through a direct borrowing from mechanics. But, as Poincaré had noted in *Science and Hypothesis*, the existence of "irreversible phenomena" called into question the scope of the applicability of Lagrange's equations: "It also has always been verified, at least in so far as concerns reversible phenomena which thus obey the equations of Lagrange, that is to say, the most general laws of mechanics" (Poincaré 1905: 125). The underlying principles here are those of the conservation of energy and least action. But Poincaré goes on to say: "Irreversible phenomena are much more rebellious" (Poincaré 1905: 125). These too can be comprehended by universal principles or laws, but of a somewhat different sort: Carnot's principle and that of entropy.

For his part, Picard links systems in which history or heredity matters to the phenomena of hysteresis:

> The word "heredity" ought not cause one to think necessarily of living beings; it signifies simply here the anterior history of the system under study. The type of these is found in the deformations said to be

permanent and in the phenomena called *hysteresis*. Here again one ought to remember the notice taken immediately of systems with "frottements."

(Picard 1905: 125)

As Émile Picard's extended discussion of the significance of irreversible phenomena in mechanics reveals, consideration of the scope, nature, and implications of such phenomena had clearly entered into the discourse of France's leading mathematical physicists at the turn of the twentieth century. Picard had specifically cited the insights of Marcel Brillouin. The latter was known for his contributions to the development of quantum mechanics, and was among the attendees at the first Solvay conference which would be held in 1911, an event that is widely regarded as the first international physics conference and brought together the most illustrious physicists of that generation.

Henri Poincaré, who also attended the first Solvay conference, had challenged the model of energetics, which had gained popularity among physicists in the second half of the nineteenth century, as failing to comprehend the import of irreversibility:

Another objections seems to me still more grave: the principle of least action is applicable to reversible phenomena; but it is not at all satisfactory in so far as irreversible phenomena are concerned; the attempt by Helmholtz to extend it to this kind of phenomena did not succeed and could not succeed.

(Poincaré 1905: 93)

## Economic hysteresis revisited

Hence, Rod Cross' version of the basis for the great dominance of reversibility in the conceptualizing of economic systems must be called into question. Writing in the *Journal of Economic Methodology* about "Metaphors and time reversibility and irreversibility in economic systems," Cross described a two-step process. First, he cited the "reluctance of physicists … to admit that time irreversible phenomena were other than aberrations" (Cross 1995: 127). Then he noted the "propensity of neoclassical economists to draw their metaphors from what they perceived to be the most prestigious scientific discipline" (Cross 1995: 128).

Yet it is clear that by the first decade of the twentieth century many leading physicists were not all that reluctant to take up the subject of irreversibility as a central matter in mechanics. That being the case, Cross' second proposition would also need to be modified: neoclassical economists tended to "draw their metaphors from what they perceived to be" physics, which they regarded as "the most prestigious scientific discipline." Or, in the alternative, it was a case of the tail wagging the dog, as nineteenth-century mathematical physics had produced an abstracted system and a set of mathematical techniques that appeared remarkably amenable to establishing analogous structures in other disciplines.

However, it cannot be denied that the existence and significance of irreversible phenomena had entered the domain of public discourse. Both Poincaré's and Picard's accounts of this matter were found in their popular writings, as was their use of the term "hysteresis." The introduction of it in their popular works is noteworthy on two counts: first, it meant that what had been a new technical coinage, as "magnetic hysteresis," in 1891 (Ewing 1891), had found its way into a more public discourse only a decade later; and, second, especially in Picard's hands, its use had been broadened to any system in which history or memory mattered. For his part, Borel also emphasized the likelihood of irreversibility in physical phenomena. While he did not use the term "hysteresis," his challenge to the scope of Ludwig Boltzmann's hypothesis on ergodicity introduced a way of thinking about physical phenomena that was closely allied to it. Jacques Hadamard was yet another contemporary French mathematician who had explored statistical mechanics (Hadamard 1906).

As for Walras, it is well known that he clung to Poinsot's *Statics* as his *vade mecum* to physics throughout his entire adult life (Turk 2006: 200–1). This is remarkable, as Poinsot first wrote his text on statics at the beginning of the nineteenth century, and even the edition which Walras used, Poinsot's eighth, was published in the early 1840s (Letter 1495), which pre-dated Clausius' work on the conservation of energy and Helmholtz's inquiry into the principle of least action. Thus, Walras' mental construction of physics also pre-dated the exploration of energetics, whose flourishing as a school of thought itself had come to an end by the time of Walras' exchanges with Poincaré.

Walras was aware of both Poincaré's and Picard's popular writing, and had in fact written to Picard precisely because of what he learned Picard had stated about the effort to mathematize economics in *La science moderne et son état actuel*. Moreover, in a letter to Georges Renard, Walras also claimed, shortly after his exchange of letters with Picard, that he was reading *La science moderne* along with Poincaré's *La valeur de la science* (Letter 1641). All courtesies aside, Picard had been explicit in his response to Walras that one might analogize from the rational mechanics of systems "*sans frottements.*" The text of *La science moderne et son état actuel* makes plain that such "frottements" or frictions are associated with memory, history, irreversibility, and thus hysteresis. While briefer in its depiction, Poincaré's *Science and Hypothesis* links the irreversible phenomenon of the friction of solids to hysteresis (Poincaré 1905: 125). Thus, even at the turn of the twentieth century, for anyone who wished to take into account current thinking in physics and attempt to address the role of hysteresis in analogized systems, the requisite materials and direction were fully in evidence. This appears to be especially so in the world of French mathematics and physics.

Moreover, Walras' exchanges with Poincaré and Picard were direct, and both pointed him to the problematic nature of friction for conservative mechanical systems. Picard in particular had judged it to be pertinent to any application of mechanics to economics. This was plainly a moment when the idea of hysteresis might have been taken up in the discourse and thinking of economics and thus might have come to occupy a formative role in economic thought, but it was not to be so.

Furthermore, the historical moment is all the more striking when one takes into account the fact that many of the same issues were taken up in Émile Borel's rethinking of the philosophical basis of economic measurement in his 1907 article, "Un paradoxe économique." Borel was a younger French mathematician with whom Walras had also corresponded, but, it appears, only in his capacity as editor of *La revue du mois*.[5]

In this article Borel turned his attention to the practical reality of the discontinuity of number inherent in economic matters like setting prices or applying taxes and other governmental rates. This extended his initial exposition about the general difficulty involved in quantifying sets of things ontologically, starting with what makes a "bundle" of wheat. (The article's subtitle was "The Sophism of a Bundle of Wheat.")

At the same time, Borel focused upon what he called "unstable equilibria" and the potential for seemingly minor and likely unnoticed events to introduce more profound destabilizing effects. As Borel put it, the "breach" of any equilibrium may be set in motion by a "very small action" that nonetheless leads to "important consequences." He saw the affinity of his notion of the instability of equilibrium with Poincaré's definition of chance ("hasard"), whereby "small causes produce large effects. The insignificant cause is not perceived, but the effect strikes us and appears to us as fortuitous" (Borel [1907] 1972: 2206f.).

These mathematicians thereby presaged, by nearly a century, the efforts by Brian Arthur and Paul David to incorporate similar ideas into economic thought (Turk 2010: 481–6). Arthur would champion a form of hysteresis propelled forward by the accident of "small events" (Arthur 1989: 122). Applying terminology that was first introduced by Boltzmann, both Arthur and David would seek to distinguish ergodic from non-ergodic pathways in economics, the latter of which linked past events to future developments, so that, in David's words, "history matters" (David 1997: 25).

Arthur has traced the scientific origins of his heterodox views in economics to, variously, Jacques Monod on the interplay of chance and necessity, and Ilya Prigogine on the irreversibility of physical systems, but also Henri Poincaré on a science of "complexity" drawn from an anti-Cartesian perspective on mechanics: "But there is another way to do science – a growing movement – and that is to look from the bottom up at how interactions form structures and patterns. Certainly there are many precedents for that, Poincaré's dynamics for example" (Delorme and Hodgson 2005: 20).

## Hysteresis, exact measurement, and discontinuity

What emerges from the critiques of classical mechanics by both Poincaré and Picard is an inclination to give greater weight to the role of history or memory in science, extending especially as Picard conceived of it, to all forms of scientific inquiry and including, therefore, economics among the disciplines so affected.

In their work there also appears to be a recognition of the discontinuities associated with the irreversible nature of many physical phenomena. This was also true for Borel, who saw a disjuncture between the continuity found in abstract mathematical measurement, with its assumption of unbounded enumeration or division, and the discontinuity and boundedness inherent in any physical measurement. To what extent, then, is hysteresis linked to the discontinuity inherent in such a lack of exactitude?

Those who have limned the history of hysteresis across disciplines have emphasized its roots in the notion of continuity. Writing in the 1970s, Jonathan Elster, who is often cited in this regard (Cross and Allan 1988: 26–7), traced a broadly conceived version of the idea of hysteresis back to Leibniz (Elster 1976). It was Leibniz who asserted that nature does not make leaps or jumps, that is, among natural phenomena changes assume an evolutionary form or follow an evolutionary path requiring a set of links between past events and experiences and the present state of affairs. The weight of the past then becomes the basis for the continuity implicit in historical experience. Though not cited by Elster, Alfred Marshall invoked the same expression as Leibniz in his support of continuity in economics: "the motto of my Principles ... is: – *Natura non facit saltum*: i.e., economic evolution is gradual and continuous on each of its numberless routes" (Marshall 1919: v).

But there is a countervailing theme among the critiques of the philosophical foundations of classical mechanics provided by the turn-of-the-century mathematicians.

Poincaré, Borel, and Volterra all appear to recognize that discontinuity must be reckoned with, however differently each pursued the matter. Poincaré pointed to the abstracted construct of the mathematical continuum, in contrast to the lack of smooth, continuous gradations evident in measures of the physical world.

In a similar vein, Borel saw a substantial and substantive gap or breach between the exactitude of abstract quantification as a mathematical operation and the blurred and less distinctive measurement of the physical world. Accordingly, he turned to measures of probability instead as the sole means whereby the reality of discontinuity in the external world could be addressed and reconciled: "[T]he calculus of probabilities alone permits us to exit from the logical impasse where the reasoning by continuity thrusts us" (Borel [1907] 1972: 2203).

By contrast, Volterra accepted the existence of discontinuity in the physical world, but allowed for the need of theorists of physics to create essentially a fiction of continuous change, extending this practice to economists as well:

Now, by analogy to that which the creators of the theory of elasticity have done, and Fourier with regard to heat, the economists suppose that the quantity of goods for which each may dispose, the nature of such would be known as discontinuous to them, vary by continuous degrees.

(Volterra 1901: 446–7)

The nomothetic view of economics, so essential to the neoclassical program of economics, appears to embrace continuity as a means of establishing universal patterns transcending time and place. Discontinuity, though, introduces additional nuances. On the one hand, one may envision the possibility that discontinuity alone is insufficient to bar identifying such universal patterns, as long as more disruptive patterns can be comprehended as recurring. On the other, discontinuity may help set in motion the irreversibility and hysteresis that mark many physical and economic processes.

Thus, the turn-of-the-century French mathematicians offered up the basis for embracing alternatives to the neoclassical program in both approach and conceptualization, by calling forth, instead, variously, a larger role for memory, hysteresis, and the inexact in concept and measure, as well as a recognition of the complexities accompanying discontinuity.

## Notes

1 Note: all translations in the text of the Walras correspondence with Poincaré and Picard are mine, with the exception of Letter 1496, which was translated by William Jaffe in Jaffe 1983: 213–20. The translation of portions of Picard's *La science moderne et l'état actuel* is mine, as well as portions of Borel's two cited articles and Volterra's 1901 article.

2 In writing to Georges Renard in December 1097 (Letter 1668), Walras listed "our principal approving mathematicians" as MM. Darboux, Tannery, Poincaré, and Picard. As to Borel, Walras expressed some concern that Borel had not yet written to him, but took him to be approving as well, on the basis of Renard's own opinion. In a subsequent letter from early 1908 (Letter 1681), Walras noted that among the attendees at the international congress of mathematics held that year in Rome, Poincaré, Picard, Borel, and d'Ocagne were "all adherents of my method" (Walras 1965: 352).

3 The correspondence between Walras and Poincaré, and later Walras and Picard, can be tracked through the numerical listings provided by Jaffe in his compilation of Walras' correspondence: (a) Letter 1448: Hermann Laurent's "denunciation" of Walras' effort to employ the principle of maximization of utility in deriving a theory of price determination at the Institut des Actuaires français in June 1900; (b) Letter 1492: Walras' appeal to Poincaré as arbiter (September 10, 1901); (c) Letter 1494: Poincaré's initial response (September 16, 1901); (d) Letter 1495: Follow-up letter to Poincaré (September 26, 1901); (e) Letter 1496: Poincaré's response (no later than October 1, 1901); (f) Letter 1498: Walras' response to Poincaré (3 October 1901); (g) Letter 1633: Walras' letter of appreciation to Picard for treating mathematical economics in *La science moderne et l'état actuel* (October 15, 1906); (h) Letter 1634: Picard's response to Walras (October 20, 1906); (i) Letters 1636/1637: Walras' anticipation of and then receipt of Picard's treatise on analysis; (j) Letter 1638: Walras' letter to Poincaré, inquiring as to Poincaré's and Picarad's supposed affirmation of the use of mathematics in economics at conferences held at the St. Louis World's Fair of 1904 (November 23, 1906); (k) Letter 1639: Poincaré's denial that such was the case (December 3, 1906); (l) Letter 1641: Walras' letter to

Georges Renard (January 3, 1907) in which he claimed to be reading Poincaré's *La valeur de la science* and Picard's *La science moderne et son état actuel* (January 3, 1907).

The correspondence between Walras and Poincaré, and later Walras and Picard, can be tracked through the numerical listings provided by Jaffe in his compilation of Walras' correspondence: (a) Letter 1448: Hermann Laurent's "denunciation" of Walras' effort to employ the principle of maximization of utility in deriving a theory of price determination at the Institut des Actuaires français in June 1900; (b) Letter 1492: Walras' appeal to Poincaré as arbiter (September 10, 1901); (c) Letter 1494: Poincaré's initial response (September 16, 1901); (d) Letter 1495: Follow-up letter to Poincaré (September 26, 1901); (e) Letter 1496: Poincaré's response (no later than October 1, 1901); (f) Letter 1498: Walras' response to Poincaré (October 3, 1901); (g) Letter 1633: Walras' letter of appreciation to Picard for treating mathematical economics in *La science moderne et l'état actuel* (October 15, 1906); (h) Letter 1634: Picard's response to Walras (October 20, 1906); (i) Letters 1636/1637: Walras' anticipation of and then receipt of Picard's treatise on analysis; (j) Letter 1638: Walras' letter to Poincaré, inquiring as to Poincaré's and Picarad's supposed affirmation of the use of mathematics in economics at conferences held at the St Louis World's Fair of 1904 (November 23,1906); (k) Letter 1639: Poincaré's denial that such was the case (December 3, 1906); (l) Letter 1641: Walras' letter to Georges Renard (January 3, 1907) in which he claimed to be reading Poincaré's *La valeur de la science* and Picard's *La science moderne et son état actuel* (January 3, 1907).

4 Mirowski cites eight letters, beginning with Letter 1374 and ending with Letter 1456. Save for letter 1448, these all precede the letters listed in note 3 above.

5 Vito Volterra's article on the virtues of applying mathematics to the social and biological sciences had been published in French translation in this journal in 1906. It was Borel's work in publishing this paper that prompted Walras' first letter to him. Coincidentally, Walras had written an article with virtually the same title as Borel's decades before. In his "Paradoxes économiques," which appeared in the *Journal des économistes* in 1860, Walras made the case that common sense was inadequate to the task of discovering the "vérités difficiles" that science alone could accomplish, and that this was especially so for political economy (Walras 1860: 381).

## References

Arthur, W. Brian (1989) "Competing Technologies, Increasing Returns and Lock-in by Historical Events." *Economic Journal*, 99: 116–131.

Borel, Émile [1907] (1972) "Un paradoxe économique." In *Œuvres de Émile Borel*, tome IV.
Paris: CNRS: 2197–2208.

Cross, Rod (1995) "Metaphors and Time Reversibility and Irreversibility in Economic Systems." *Journal of Economic Methodology*, 2(1): 123–134.

Cross, Rod and Andrew Allan (1988) "On the History of Hysteresis." In Rod Cross (ed.), *Unemployment, Hysteresis, and the Natural Rates Hypotheses.*Oxford: Blackwell.

Dantzig, Tobias (1930) *Number, the Language of Science.*New York: Macmillan.

Darboux, Gaston (1912) *Eloges académiques et discours.* Paris: Librairie Scientifique, A. Hermann et Fils.

David, Paul (1997) "Path Dependence and the Quest for Historical Economics." *Discussion Papers in Economic and Social History*, no. 20. Oxford: University of Oxford.

Delorme, R. and G. Hodgson (2005) "Complexity and the Economy: An Interview with W. Brian Arthur." In J. Finch and M. Orillard (eds), *Complexity and the Economy*. Cheltenham: Edward Elgar: 17–32.

Edgeworth, F. Y. [1881] (1932) *Mathematical Psychics*. London: Kegan Paul & Co. [reprint by London School of Economics]

Elster, Jonathan (1976) "A Note on Hysteresis in the Social Sciences." *Synthese*, 33: 371–391.

Ewing, James Alfred (1891) *Magnetic Induction in Iron and Other Metals*. New York: Van Nostrand.

Friedman, Michael (1996) "Poincaré's Conventionalism and the Logical Positivists." In Jean-Louis Greffe, Gerhard Heinzmann, and Kuno Lorenz (eds), *Henri Poincaré: Science et Philosophie, Congres International, Nancy, France 1994*. Berlin: Akademie: 333–344.

Georgescu-Roegen, Nicholas (1966) "Some Object Lessons from Physics" In *Analytical Economics: Issues and Problems*. Cambridge, MA: Harvard University Press: 47–82.

Grattan-Guinness, Ivor (1992) "Structure-similarity as a Cornerstone of the Philosophy of Mathematics." In Javier Echeverria*et al.* (eds), *The Space of Mathematics*. Berlin: Walter de Gruyter.

Grattan-Guinness, Ivor (1997) *The Rainbow of Mathematics: A History of the Mathematical Sciences*. New York: Norton.

Hadamard, Jacques (1906) "La mécanique statistique." *American Mathematical Society Bulletin*, 2: 12.

Heinzmann, Gerhard and Philippe Nabonnand (2008) "Poincaré: Intuitionism, Intuition, and Convention." In Mark van Atten*et al.* (eds.), *One Hundred Years of Intuitionism (1907–2007): The Cerisy Conference*. Basel: Birkhauser Verlag, pp. 163–177.

Ingrao, Bruna and Giorgio Israel (1990) *The Invisible Hand*, transl. IanMcGilvray. Cambridge, MA: MIT Press.

Jaffe, William (1983) "Poincaré and the Cardinal Measurability of Utility." In DonaldWalker (ed.), *Essays on Walras*. Cambridge: Cambridge University Press: 213–220.

Kneebone, G. T. [1963] (2001) *Mathematical Logic and the Foundations of Mathematics*. Mineola, NY: Dover.

Marshall, Alfred (1919) *Industry and Trade*. London: Macmillan.

Mirowski, Philip (1988) "The Sciences Were Never At War?" In *Against Mechanism*. Totowa, NJ: Rowman & Littlefield, pp. 31–44.

Mirowski, Philip (1989) *More Heat than Light*. Cambridge: Cambridge University Press.

Mirowski, Philip (1991) "The When, the How and the Why of Mathematical Expression in the History of Economic Analysis." *Journal of Economic Perspectives*, 5(1): 145–157.

Picard, Charles Émile (1905) *La science moderne et son état actuel*. Paris: Flammarion.

Poincaré, Henri (1905) *Science and Hypothesis*, authorized trans. George Bruce Halsted; special preface by Poincaré; introd. Josiah Royce. New York: Science Press.

Porter, Theodore M. (2001) "Economics and the History of Measurement." In Judy L. Klein and Mary S. Morgan (eds), *The Age of Economic Measurement*. Durham, NC: Duke University Press: 4–22.

Roos, Charles Frederick (1934) *Dynamic Economics*. Bloomington, IN: Principia.

Samuelson, Paul (1965) "Economic Theory and Mathematics – An Appraisal." In *Collected Scientific Papers: Volume 2*:1751–1761.

Samuelson, Paul (1998) "How Foundations Came to Be." *Journal of Economic Literature*, 36(3): 1375–1386.

Thom, René (1991) *Prédiren'est pas expliquer: entretiens avec Émile Noel*. Paris: Flammarion.

Turk, Michael (2006) "The Fault Line of Axiomatization: Walras' Linkage of Physics with Economics." *European Journal of the History of Economic Thought*, 13(2): 195–212.

Turk, Michael (2010) "The Arrow of Time in Economics: From Robinson's Critique to the New Historical Economics." *European Journal of the History of Economic Thought* 17(3): 471–492.

Volterra, Vito (1901) "Sui tentative di applicazione della mathematiche alle scienze biologiche e sociale." *Giornale degli economisi* 2a, 23: 436–458.

Walras, Léon (1860) "Paradoxes économiques." *Journal des économistes*: 373–391.

Walras, Léon (1965) *Correspondence of Leon Walras and Related Papers*: Volume III; ed. William Jaffe. Amsterdam: North-Holland.

Weintraub, E.Roy (2001) Measurement and Changing Images of Mathematical Knowledge." In Judy L. Klein and Mary S. Morgan (eds), *The Age of Economic Measurement*. Durham, NC: Duke University Press: 303–312.

Weintraub, E.Roy (2002) *How Economics Became a Mathematical Science* Durham, NC: Duke University Press.

# 3 The arrow of time in economics

From Robinson's critique to the new historical economics

## Introduction: time and history in economics

To what extent does the case for a historical economics rest upon an assessment of the nature and role of time in economics? In the long view of the history of economic thought one can discern a diminution in the role accorded a historically minded economics. While Adam Smith's seminal work *The Wealth of Nations*, published in 1776, advanced general principles, like the division of labor, that were intended to be universal in scope, large portions of his text might easily be read and regarded as economic history. Karl Marx, who brought a journalistic attentiveness to mid-nineteenth-century events, sought to construct a "law of motion of capitalism," but this was set in relation to a grand view of stages of history and societal transformation.

Yet by the late nineteenth century an immersion in the details of economic history tended to characterize schools of economic thought whose assertion of the priority of the inductive in economics landed them outside the mainstream of economics. This was the case for both the German Historical School and the American Institutionalists, who emphasized the primacy of amassing historical data and examining customary, cultural practices.

Over the course of the twentieth century, the relegation of history to the margins of economic theorizing did not dispel all doubts and concerns about the appropriate place of history in economics. At the century's end, Robert Solow commented that, since economics must draw upon the experience of the past, "[i]n one sense, economics is history ... [It] is about accounting for the past" (Solow 1997: 53). Yet, as Solow was all too aware, the widely accepted claim of universality for economic rules and models has led to a general alignment of economics with the hard science of physics and the construction of economics outside the bounds of history itself, notwithstanding the use of empirically drawn data (Solow 1985). The general economic equilibrium, associated with Walras, was taken as the archetype for this physical model of – or metaphor for – a scientifically grounded economics.

Meanwhile, critics of the Walrasian system such as Philip Mirowski and Roy Weintraub focused upon its inadequacies as either a wrongly conceived paradigm borrowed from nineteenth-century energetics (Mirowski 1988: 13–44;

Mirowski 1990) or as the product of a possible, but hardly definitive, construction of economic knowledge as a discourse about dynamics (Weintraub 1991). Both Mirowski and Weintraub sought to set economic theorizing in historical perspective, but neither directed much attention to the role of history itself in economics.

However, for other historically minded economists there has been a change in the bases upon which the rightful place of history in economics is seen as emerging; namely, the implications of the nature of time for the kind of economics created. Hence, the intertwining of economics and history no longer could be construed – solely – as a restatement of the case for an inductive, as opposed to deductive, economics, but – as the dissenters would contend – as a matter of comprehending the role of time to establish the essential underpinnings and structural coherence of economics.

In a historical economics there is a bedrock principle that time is unidirectional, advancing from past to present to future. The forward movement of time may be represented by an arrow in flight, drawing upon its depiction in the paradox of Zeno of Elea, dating from the sixth century BC of classical antiquity. How, according to Zeno, was it possible for the arrow, once released, to reach its target when, at any given moment in its flight, its position is fixed in location, and its movement forward can be captured in increasingly brief steps, each of which can be divided further, without any bound?

But asymmetry alone does not render time historical. The arrow of time is fraught with contradictions evident from the mathematical and physical twists and turns Zeno's paradox itself has produced, calling into question any easy acceptance of the notion of continuity of moment or motion, and hence the possibility of a linear progression of human activity in real time (Faris 1996).[1]

Moreover, the emergence of the theory of relativity in the first decades of the twentieth century raised new and unsettling questions about the nature of space and time, and led one of the theory's leading early proponents and popularizers, Arthur Eddington, to coin the expression "arrow of time" as a term of art in physics. This "arrow" has come to be regarded as the "thermodynamic arrow," "the direction of time in which disorder [or entropy] increases" (Eddington 1929: 74).

The problems posed by time in economics garnered the attention of economists across a broad ideological spectrum. For Friedrich von Hayek, an Austrian economist, and John Hicks, who straddled the realms of Keynesian and Austrian economics, the fixity of the past had to be contrasted with the uncertainty of the future. Hence, the linear motion from past to present and future was broken by a qualitative transformation in facing the future, where expectations and the concomitant limitations in information and knowledge prevailed.[2] Hicks took up as critical the distinction between "economics in time" and "economics of time" (Hicks 1976).

From the left Keynesians, Joan Robinson spoke of a distinction similar to the one made by Hicks, but characterized instead as distinguishing "historical time" from "logical time." Like Hayek and Hicks, Robinson saw the qualitative break between a set past and an uncertain future. For Robinson, however, it was much more historical experience itself – that is, events and developments – that had to be taken into account. Her call was most plainly for a historical economics.

## "Historical time" versus "logical time": Robinson's challenge

Of the historically minded critiques about the role of time in economics, the most thoroughgoing came from Joan Robinson, in a case constructed out of three elements, which were not necessarily fully integrated into each other. First, she challenged the applicability of the model of physics to economics, because it required a conflating of spatial measures with temporal ones; in effect allowing temporal changes to be reversible, comparable with physical displacements or oscillations. Here the distinction she draws echoes that of Eddington's "time's arrow."

Second, she also rejected the physical model because it placed economics outside human experience and historical time (Burstein 1991: 149). In spurning the mechanical analogy underlying the notion of a general equilibrium, Robinson noted: "Human life does not exist outside history and no one has correct foresight of his own future behavior, let alone of the behavior of all the other individuals which will impinge upon his" (1979: 49).

Third, while not elaborated upon in a formal sense, Robinson made the link between an economics set in historical time with an economic world characterized by monopolistic competition and increasing returns to scale, perhaps the central preoccupation of her career in economics.

Robinson's interest in the significance and implications of time in economic theory became evident in the early 1950s, when she took the bold step of rethinking publicly her most well-known contribution to economic thought, her analysis of "imperfect competition":

> In my opinion, the greatest weakness of the *Economics of Imperfect Competition* is one which it shares with the class of economic theory to which it belongs – the failure to deal with time.
>
> (Robinson 1964c: 222)

It is noteworthy that her description of the difficulties engendered by this "failure" also bears an uncanny resemblance, in philosophical and physical terms, to the puzzle posed by Zeno's paradoxes:

> Any movement must take place through time, and the position at any moment of time depends upon what it has been in the past. The point is not merely that any adjustment takes a certain time to complete and that (as has always been admitted) events may occur meanwhile which alter the position, so that the equilibrium towards which the system is said to be tending itself moves before it can be reached. The point is that the

very process of moving has an effect upon the destination of the movement, so that there is no such thing as a position of long-run equilibrium
which exists independently of the course which the economy is following
at a particular date.

(Robinson 1964c: 234)

It is also noteworthy that Robinson's rethinking of the economic implications
of time drew strongly upon her desire to resolve gaps in the ideas of Alfred
Marshall, who, along with Karl Marx and John Maynard Keynes, clearly
remained one of her most powerful influences (Robinson 1951: vii–ix).[3]
Among these gaps was the need to address "the *dimension of time* of equilibrium"
(Ingrao and Israel 1990: 224).

In 1953 Robinson had signaled her change in focus when she described her
premier work from the early 1930s as flawed by a "wrong turning" (Loasby
1991: 34). And so Robinson began to champion a more dynamic analysis of
economic processes, be they production, accumulation, or growth, where time
was regarded as irreversible and historical.

This oftentimes included a deriding of what she saw as the neoclassical
disregard of the implications of the nature of time for economic analysis,
where "movements through time [were treated] as though they occurred in
stationary equilibrium" (Robinson 1964a: 142).

She went on to identify as a fundamental flaw in the neoclassical approach
the presumed continuity of movement; in effect, a continuous path of change
and adjustment in the economy based upon the ability of all relevant economic agents to comprehend the implications of past events and to act
knowledgeably and effectively with regard to the future.

Robinson's use of the criterion of time to critique conventional economic
ideas extended to the nature of capital, a topic she took up in the early 1950s
when she challenged the notion of capital as a generic stock like putty measurable as such at any given moment (Robinson 1964b). In "A lecture delivered at
Oxford by a Cambridge economist," Robinson chose to demonstrate her
points through illustrations and diagrams using the "arrow of time." But her
embrace of the "arrow of time" also points to a more nuanced effort, as well,
to respond to, and distinguish from, the ideas and claims put forth by Piero
Sraffa about the nature of capital. Robinson links the problem of measuring
capital not only to its heterogeneity, but also to the illusion of an equilibrium
established outside of time:

> Let us apply the notion of equilibrium to capital. What governs the
> demand for capital goods? Their future prospective quasi-rents. What
> governs the supply price? Their past cost of production. For hard objects
> like blast furnaces and rolling stock demand is of its very nature ex ante,
> and cost is of its very nature ex post. The tutor cannot find any shelter
> here from the arrow of time.
>
> (Robinson 1973: 262)

In the same vein, Robinson later took up the relation between returns to scale and economic growth. By incorporating a dynamic view of time into the analytic framework, she felt it was possible to address difficulties unresolved in the stationary approach to equilibrium that Marshall had accepted (Marshall 1898 [1891]: 554–70). These included making sense of the irreversibility of investment, the trend toward falling costs in competitive markets, and the manifold effects of increasing returns and externalities upon the growth of economies (Robinson 1971: 61–2).

Finally, in two papers presented in the twilight of her career – "Equilibrium vs. History," which first appeared in 1974, and then "Time in Economic Theory," dating from 1980 – Robinson raised the conundrum of time in economic theorizing even more starkly. Robinson isolated the possibility of attaining equilibrium states from the actual workings of any economy in real – that is, historical – time (Robinson 1980a: 1ff.). It was here that she also contrasted "historical time," involving human experience and the vagaries of economic activities, with "logical time," the measure of duration which functions as a parameter in abstracted economic models (Robinson 1980b: 87–93).

This disjuncture of time and equilibrium presents a challenge to the alignment of the foundations of economics with those of classical mechanics, in which laws have universal efficacy and applicability, and equilibrium states provide the essential framework of analysis, without reference to specific historical moments. As such, the classical laws of physics – that is, the Newtonian model – conceive of time as symmetrical, a parameter applicable in the same way anywhere and everywhere. Time itself is undefined, serving solely as a mathematical marker, a metronome for the physical world; or better, perhaps, the laws guiding the physical world.

Yet what is equally noteworthy in these later writings is the overlay of the two different bases upon which, in Robinson's view, time undoes conventional economic theorizing. The first of these bases, concerned with the limitations of attaining equilibrium states, emphasizes the unidirectionality of time, set within a physical model. The motion, displacement, and continuity of the economy are all subject to reconsideration, as they constitute the spatial consequences – and concomitants – of temporal flows. How does the economy change over time, if one thinks correctly about the nature of time itself? Here, in line with her Marshallian legacy, emerges Robinson's keen interest in finding the right economic pathway that can exist in and through real time.

The second of these bases is grounded more in historical circumstance and context, tied implicitly to the longstanding division between the human sciences and the natural sciences that can be traced back at least to nineteenth-century German idealist philosophy. "Historical time" is not simply irreversible, in accord with the sense that time necessarily flows from past to future. Instead, it involves human activity and thus a stage, human history – especially economic history – on which economic activity and events transpire. As Robinson had concluded her discussion "Increasing and Decreasing Returns" in *Economic Heresies*:

> But once we bring historical time into the argument, it is not so easy to present the free play of the market as an ideal mechanism for maximizing welfare and securing social justice ... Economic history is notoriously a scene of conflicting interests, which is just what the neoclassical economists did not want to discuss.
>
> (Robinson 1971: 63)

Essentially, the first strand might be likened to determining the right pathway along which economies move, as well as the reasons for the breaks, shifts, and discontinuities that might occur en route; the second might be seen as establishing a historical context or set of conditions within which economic activity takes place. The first may retain elements of parametric time, only now limited as necessarily sequential or ratcheted. The second opens the way to historical description and depiction; what G. S. Shackle referred to as the "panorama" of history (Shackle 1967 [1958]: 33). In shorthand form, these two approaches evoke the different representations about how economic change takes place: via a pathway or in context.

It is apparent that Robinson intended to challenge, if not debunk, the standard, Walrasian treatment of equilibrium as fundamentally wrongheaded (Weintraub 1985: 146–9). What, though, might be constructed in its place?

Within the work of the post-Keynesians, where Robinson's ideas would have their most direct force and consequence, one can see an emphasis upon a dynamic approach, in which the economy evolves over time and there is a recognition of the importance of identifying pathways through which such an evolution might take place (Dasgupta 1985; Harcourt 2006). Certainly the pioneering inquiry of Robinson's colleague at Cambridge, Nicholas Kaldor, into plotting a "theory of the path," dating from 1934, with its concomitant understanding of the indeterminateness of equilibrium, also helped set the terms for this treatment of economic change or development over time (Kaldor 1934). This approach may have reached its culmination in Luigi Pasinetti's *Structural Change and Economic Growth*, published in 1981.

From the vantage point of Robinson's three-pronged critique of time in economics, however, the real successors to her in attempting to establish a new historical economics, or historically informed economics, can be found among a new generation of economists, who, since the mid 1970s, have remixed the elements of that critique in a markedly different fashion. For these economists, the economic rules themselves, especially as regards "scale effects" – from increasing returns to scale to spatial agglomeration effects – are viewed as establishing the essential place of history – and historical time – in economics. A possible marriage in theory of the historical approach with the physical model, this framework has been advanced in the new "historical economics" of Paul David and the "positive feedback loops" of Brian Arthur; as well as in the new spatial economics, with both regional and international applications, of Paul Krugman. How well do these efforts succeed in establishing a consistent notion of time and a clear sense of the historical in economics?

## The accident of initial conditions

If one treats the role and relative importance of history and economics in urban, regional, or international economics along the lines suggested by Paul Krugman, then it is an event, or series of events, that forms the initial or initiating conditions in historical time. Thereafter, however, the rules of economics are imposed upon the situation at hand, establishing subsequent outcomes in accordance with universal principles and therefore operating within the realm or terms of "logical" rather than "historical" time.

Over the past two decades or so Paul Krugman has endeavored to rethink both regional and international economics through a re-examination of spatiality in economics. In part, this has entailed integrating economic geography more fully into the theorizing about the workings of such economics (Krugman 1991a). But this greater interest in space called forth consideration of temporal change as well.

In *Geography and Trade*, a compilation of lectures given in 1991, Krugman emphasized further the role of initiating conditions in explaining the geography of industry; these conditions he regards as "accidents." Of the case of the US carpet-making industry and Dalton, Georgia, he writes:

> To a remarkable extent, manufacturing industries within the United States are highly localized; and when one tries to understand the reasons for that localization, one finds that it can be traced back to some seemingly trivial historical accident.
>
> (Krugman 1991b: 35)

He then links this formative historical moment with the operation of economic rules to explain what follows: "An accident led to the establishment of the industry in a particular location, and thereafter cumulative processes took over" (Krugman 1991b: 61). Couched in other terms, Krugman appears to be assigning to history the role of accident or contingency, while economic laws operate on the basis of necessity.

Krugman highlights the historical role of technological advance through spillover effects, a concentration of human capital, and the jump provided along a learning curve, among other factors. All of these, however, are intended to offer an economic rationale – that is, in accord with general, or at least generalizing, principles of economics – to a particular set of historical events or developments (Krugman 1991b: 36–54).

One might contend, with reason, that Krugman was primarily concerned about geography, rather than history. It is certainly true that Krugman has sought to reinvigorate the role of economic geography in economics; ranging from the ideas presented in *Geography and Trade* in 1991; through the Ohlin lectures, which became the volume *Development, Geography, and Economic Theory* in 1995; to his collaboration with M. Fujita and A. J. Venables in *The Spatial Economy* in 1999.

To do so, however, required adopting – and adapting – more complex theoretical models like the Dixit–Stiglitz model of monopolistic competition, which had entered economic discourse in the 1970s, and marking out common ground between theories of economic development and regional economics. It called for a reassessment of the nature of economic change over time, in essence a recasting of the role of history in economics. Krugman himself was explicit that the geographic concentration of economic activity resulting from increasing returns, with multiple equilibria possible, required a "story" set in time to explain which of these possible outcomes was actually pursued. These "natural stories" led to what Krugman regarded as a form of economic dynamics: "the cumulation of initial advantages that may be accidents of history" (Krugman 1995: 42).

This larger role for history is also evident in the central place accorded "linkages," a notion borrowed from A. O. Hirschman, in *The Spatial Economy*:

> [A large market and a good supply of inputs and consumer goods] correspond precisely to the backward linkages and forward linkages of development theory. Because of these linkages, a spatial concentration of production, once established, may tend to persist, and a small difference in the initial size of two otherwise equivalent locations may grow over time.
>
> (Fujita et al. 1999: 5)

In the end, while cast in terms of economic rules and analogies to physics, the "spatial" model ultimately describes an "evolution" (Fujita et al. 1999: 345), with its biological overtones.

Do these cumulative processes, to which Krugman refers as, effectively, the rules of economics set in motion, constitute evidence of an evolution or circular causation? There is a certain ambiguity on this point. Fujita et al. describe "forward" and "backward" linkages as an interaction of causal factors in line with circular causation.

On the other hand, Fujita et al. specifically characterize "the tension between ... centrifugal and centripetal forces" as "shap[ing] the evolution of the economy's spatial structure" (Fujita et al. 1999: 345). Cumulative processes could be viewed as compatible with evolution, advancing through a series of adaptations, where each change or modification builds upon – and, in crucial respects, is constrained by – previous changes or modifications.

Krugman's sequencing of historical event and accumulating consequences gives greater weight to an evolution based upon cumulative causation. But a closer examination of Krugman's model of the division between an economic core and periphery, developed most fully in *The Spatial Economy*, reveals the way that circular causation is melded with cumulative causation. In an adaptation of the Dixit–Stiglitz model establishing equilibrium conditions from the wage rate, price level, and relative initial size of the manufacturing and agricultural sectors, Krugman showed how the rate of change in the regional share of manufacturing depends upon its level, which may have been initially influenced by, but is then reinforced by the expansion of the potential consumer market. Krugman makes clear, however, that this introduces a cumulative effect, once a "critical mass" occurs in the concentration of manufacturing, resulting in a bifurcation of economic activity.

This, Krugman felt, was "strongly suggestive" of the division in the United States between North and South after the Civil War, and the gulf that emerged in Italy in the late nineteenth century between its industrial north and a depressed Mezzogiorno (Krugman 1997: 248).

In this approach it seems clear that Krugman tried to find, through economics, what he saw history as failing to do; namely, discovering the cause of historical change in economic life (Krugman 1995: 30). Yet, by the same token, one may ask how far does the pattern found by Krugman go in depicting how history, including economic history, unfolds?

One might well question the balance struck here between the historical and the economic. Could a different weighting be found for the role of historical events and developments, occurring over time, in its stead? In *Peddling Prosperity*, Krugman attempted to explain the "dominance" of the United States in the aircraft industry as a product of a "virtuous circle" that began with "the huge base of demand for aircraft that arose from the needs of the U.S. military during World War II and the early years of the Cold War" (Krugman 1994: 232).

By way of contrasting treatment of the same subject: over the course of a century, the earliest – and, to some extent, rival – centers of experimentation and innovation in aviation, located in the United States and France, remain the contemporary industrial centers of aviation, with Boeing and Airbus the two dominant manufacturers worldwide. While the early years of dabbling in aviation may reasonably be regarded as "initial" or "initiating" conditions, there were other, subsequent historical developments or events that cannot be excluded from consideration; these include the setting up of bases in both countries for mail routes in the interwar period, the expansion of production – and innovation – during World War II, the reconstitution of the industry after World War II, and the economic plans of the European Union, among others. All involved decisions by human agents that may have been influenced by economic considerations, but were not necessarily the product of, nor the inexorable operation of, economic laws.

As such, these circumstances can best be comprehended as "moments," signal events that redirect the course, or path, of economic development. They should not be thought of or seen as a continuum, or part of an economically determined cumulative process, but rather as episodic. Their episodic nature need not preclude them from being connected; the operable theory of history would be relevant to that determination.

Nonetheless, they would have to be understood as situated in historical time, set in the context of a web of interrelated events and developments.

## Along the pathway of time

As Dalton, Georgia serves as an exemplar for Krugman's approach and ideas, so the typewriter keyboard plays a similar role for Paul David. To borrow a cinematic term from Alfred Hitchcock, these are the "McGuffins" of their respective economic theories, serving as the specific moment or constellation of events that sets the theory in motion. Moreover, like Hitchcock's "McGuffin," the role of these exemplars is ultimately heuristic, less important in and of itself, but crucial in introducing the essential subject or theme under consideration. There are notable contrasts: David's McGuffin is a piece of technology, while Krugman's is a matter of geography. Nonetheless, each exemplar provides the means for launching a fundamentally abstracted treatment of the operation of economic laws or rules, with far broader, if not universal sweep.

From the outset, David's overriding interest has been in determining the appropriate bridge between economics and history, and in establishing an economic history sufficiently infused with analytical elements from economics as to be, in effect, a historical economics as well (David and Thomas 2003). His first major published work, *Technical Choice, Innovation and Economic Growth*, was, according to David, "inspired" by Alexander Gerschenkron (David 1975: ix). The issues it dealt with first became an abiding concern for David upon reading H. J. Habakkuk's comparison of US and British technology, a work of economic history (David 1975: 1–2).

In contrast to Krugman, David casts the matter of the role of history in economics as far more than a division between initial circumstances or conditions rooted in historical events and the economic rules applied thereupon. Instead, he distinguishes between the types of "allocative processes": one path independent, the other path dependent. The former are those "whose dynamics guarantee convergence to a unique, globally stable equilibrium configuration" or, as "stochastic systems ... have the ability eventually to shake free from the influence of their past state(s)" (David 1997: 13) The latter, then, are taken to be excluded from those categories, and hence are "unable to shake free of their history" (David 1997: 13). Rephrased positively, "[a] path dependent stochastic process is one whose asymptotic distribution evolves as a consequence (function of) the process' own history" (David 1997: 14). In such processes, time is irreversible, where a continuing formative role is accorded the past in establishing the range of future outcomes.

David's approach is also noteworthy for the distinction he draws between equilibrium states associated with path-independent processes and path-dependent ones. David in no way seeks to undermine or deny the validity of equilibria as economic outcomes; instead, he makes the case for different equilibrium outcomes resulting from different probabilistic possibilities (David 1997: 19ff.). Here David strikes a similar chord to Joan Robinson's in challenging the Walrasian treatment of equilibrium as momentary and static. He contends instead that path-dependent processes follow a "sequence of trades," at each stage "altering the distribution of possible outcomes" (David 1997:

21). Moreover, if such paths are dotted by positive externalities, they may lead to optimal outcomes not otherwise attainable (David 1997: 22).

Thus, the problematic connection between time and equilibrium, which Robinson saw as a central conundrum, if not outright illusion, in economic thought, is indeed addressed by David, essentially by separating "dynamic processes" into two categories, one operating in logical time, the other marked by the necessity of incorporating historical time into its workings. In so doing, David relies strongly upon a physical model, invoking the notion of "ergodicity," which characterizes systems in which "it is possible to transit directly or indirectly between any arbitrarily chosen pair of states, and hence, eventually to reach all the states from any one of them" (David 1997: 13). Economic equilibria would then be either ergodic, standing apart from historical time, or non-ergodic, existing "in time" or over time.

Does David in fact answer Robinson's question about the role of time in economics? The dynamic processes he characterizes as "path independent" raise immediate concerns in that regard. As the changing state of these processes is symmetrical with respect to time, it would appear that they might just as well move or "evolve" backward as forward, and hence be free of the "arrow of time." Such movements might be viewed as occurring spatially. This would make the resulting equilibria intelligible as a spatial phenomenon, thereby countering Robinson's contention that an economic equilibrium is based upon the mistaken conflation of space and time. Yet like production itself, these economic processes are ratcheted by sequence, if not historical time as such. Through what might be conceived of as an implied arrow of production, then, Robinson's criticism would still hold for these path-independent processes.

For David it is clear that non-ergodic equilibria, which establish a critical association of pathway with history, are his central interest. Whether the subject is the triumph of the QWERTY typewriter keyboard, the industrialization of Germany in the late nineteenth century, or the agrarian transformation of Victorian England, the changes that matter form a pathway (David 1985: 336).

David saw as crucial to such changes the importance of what may be deemed the external environment, finding, for example, QWERTY's "dominance" in a combination of "*technical interrelatedness, economies of scale*, and the *quasi-irreversibility* of investment" (David 1985: 334). These, it should be noted, are the same categories cited by Robinson to validate the "economic heresy" of an economics set in real time.

In the end, one may question whether this sort of pathway can be said to represent or otherwise capture "history," especially as distinguished from a process" "own history." Is David describing a pathway of development or a historical context – effectively, a broader framework or stage – within which economic changes can be comprehended? David speaks of a history that "mattered" in "economic theory" as one that:

> could begin openly to identify and formally analyze those processes where the influence of events in the past might be transmitted and

magnified in their power to significantly and enduringly affect the long-run patterns of resource allocation, for better or for worse.

(David 1997: 25)

History, however, may not so neatly conform to this model, even in the cases adduced by David. On the one hand, he sees the adoption of a particular technique or method of constructing typewriters and their keyboards as formative, creating a mold for subsequent events, developments, or technical changes. In this way it is akin to hysteresis. At the same time, he notes that the success of the QWERTY keyboard and the failure of seemingly more efficient alternatives, like the Dvorak construction, can be understood only as part of something larger: a "more complex system of production' (David 1985: 334). That larger "complex" of activity and possibility plays a determining role in establishing the pathway taken, and must be regarded as context, independent of the pathway itself.

This suggests the continuing tension in David's work between establishing a recognizable historical context for comprehending economic activity and making the notion of path dependence the key to when "history matters."

## "Small events" history

It was Brian Arthur who pioneered the case for path dependence and the linking of economic circumstances from past to present through a physical model. As intellectual antecedents for his own theorizing about economics Arthur identified Nicholas Kaldor, Joseph Schumpeter, Allyn Young, and Alfred Marshall (Delorme and Hodgson 2005: 27). From Kaldor, one can see the need to establish a theory of the path; from Schumpeter, the centrality of technology and technological change; from Young, the emphasis upon increasing returns; and from Marshall, an adumbration of the foundational role of complexity in economics.

In his work Arthur emphasized the role of increasing returns in producing a multiplicity of economic possibilities, rather than the single, atemporal equilibrium of "conventional" economics. Moreover, he characterized economic processes exhibiting increasing returns as "positive feedback loops," and saw the sequencing of economic events following certain probabilistic distributions and leading to a limited – and limiting – pathway, as an economic or technological "lock-in" (Arthur 1994a: 1–13).

Arthur's contributions dovetailed to a significant degree with David's analysis in comprehending the operation of increasing returns to scale in stochastic terms. For his part, Arthur had leaned heavily upon the notion of complex systems, especially as they pertained to biology, to establish a mathematical, but essentially probabilistic basis for translating the existence of increasing returns into a dynamic and non-ergodic economic process; that is, one that can only be understood as change occurring over time. Writing about "competing technologies, increasing returns, and lock-in," Arthur states:

Under increasing returns however, static analysis is no longer enough. Multiple outcomes are possible, and to understand how one outcome is selected we need to follow step by step the process by which small events cumulate to cause the system to gravitate toward that outcome rather than the others.

(Arthur 1994b: 28)

There is also a real resonance with Paul Krugman's emphasis upon the role of initiating conditions and the importance of spatial concentration. In "Industry Location Patterns and the Importance of History," Arthur makes this affinity clear, seeking "to provide a sound theoretical basis for the historical-accident-plus-agglomeration viewpoint," in which the sequence of historical events, "geographical attractiveness," and economic rules are blended into one analytical framework (Arthur 1994c: 51).

Arthur, like David, spatializes temporal changes by analogizing his version of history "essential" to economics to physical states through a reliance upon "the elementary theory of random walks" (Arthur 1989: 121). A random walk describes a Markov chain, where points are "joined by arrows that point in the possible directions of motion" (Dynkin and Uspenskii 2006 [1963]: 236), and an "irreducible" chain is one where "one can go from any position Ei to any other position Ej by means of a chain of possible transitions" (Dynkin and Uspenskii 2006 [1963]: 236).

Arthur's turn towards a physical model of this sort may be traced to the formative influence of Ilya Prigogine. Prigogine, the Nobel-Prize-winning chemist who took the heterodox tack of emphasizing the importance of disequilibria, would contend that the resort to probabilistic notions, in and of itself, introduces – indeed requires – a direction to time (Prigogine and Stengers 1997).

Arthur translated Prigogine's concern with time-directed hard science in thermodynamics into economics (Arthur 1994a: xiv). For Arthur it was the "urn model" proposed by the mathematician George Polya that proved decisive in forging his association of scale effects in economics with physical processes. With the urn model, both economic and physical outcomes depended upon the arrow of time.

And while Arthur and Prigogine may differ on the overall importance of equilibrium states, both appear to agree that dynamic processes – whether physical, in Prigogine's case, or economic, in Arthur's case – are time dependent and follow from complex states of affairs.

In actuality, however, what status does Arthur accord what he calls "small event history" (1989: 122)? It appears that he means, in the main, choices among technologies, for which past events limit future possibilities, and cloud clear prediction. History matters then in economics as alternatives among technologies present themselves, while the reasons why those different choices emerge remain somewhat obscure.

As Arthur appears to invoke the notion of a chain of transitions, one may question whether it is altogether consistent with the primacy of initiating conditions, placing Arthur somewhere between Krugman, for whom the initial state is decisive, and David, who gives great weight to the formation of the subsequent pathway.

Attracted as well to the model of science provided by the "complex" natural science of biology, Arthur distinguished between the "accidental" as historical, the specific choices among technologies, and the "necessary" as economic, the general rules underlying agglomeration. In this he drew upon the pairing in evolutionary biology made by the Nobel-Prize-winning biologist Jacques Monod in *Chance and Necessity*, another major and early source of inspiration (Delorme and Hodgson 2005: 17).

Yet the correspondence Arthur sought to establish appears somewhat flawed. There is a purposefulness or teleology to Monod's comprehension of evolutionary change in biology whose counterpart in economics is difficult to discern. In evolutionary biology, accidents are sorted out on a progressive basis, in that they "enter into" necessity when they advance the species (Monod 1971: 118). By contrast, economic rules do not proceed in a similar way; no inherent, progressive principle establishes which historical events will necessarily advance the economy. The evocation of a general tendency towards greater efficiency in economic affairs is challenged, even belied, by Arthur's own insight into the rigidifying tendencies of "lock-in." Elias Khalil, while identifying some measure of "purposeful activity" in economics at the level of the firm (Khalil 1990: 164), notes that the same cannot be said of the business cycle, or of economic structures in general (Khalil 1994: 191). Moreover, economic rules, even if taken to be universal, tend to be applied on an ad hoc basis. In fact, the economists most likely to be seen espousing some version of a progressive inner logic to economics would be those, like Anne Robert Jacques Turgot or Karl Marx, who melded economics into a historical framework where historical stages rather than economic laws prevailed.

Paradoxically, Arthur's grafting of Monod's dichotomy into economics, however flawed, grounded Arthur's insight into the importance of highlighting the tension between the nomological and the idiographic in economics.

## Economics "in time" versus in historical time

Of the three elements comprising Robinson's critique of time in economic theory, two are addressed with substantial success by Arthur, David, and Krugman. Arthur's "positive feedback loops," David's "historical economics," and Krugman's "economic geography" all advance the requirement that, in economic theory, time be comprehended as irreversible, moving from the past through the present to the future; all, in short, require the arrow of time. They also cite as crucial elements in their construction of economic theory the existence of scale effects and/or increasing returns.

Taken together these approaches all adhere to a physical model of economics that corresponds most decisively with the principles of thermodynamics; that is, the irreversibility of time in physics is seen as holding as well for economics, where both are founded upon the second law of thermodynamics or the existence of entropy (see, for example, Georgescu-Roegen 1973). This is evident in Arthur's and David's references to ergodicity, a notion originally introduced by Ludwig Boltzmann into the field of statistical mechanics in the 1880s. And Krugman, while emphasizing the role of critical mass and tipping points, gave great weight to broken symmetries and bifurcations in *The Spatial Economy*. Both play a central role in the thermodynamically based model of complexity advanced by Gregoire Nicolis and Ilya Prigogine, whose *Exploring Complexity* (Nicolis and Prigogine 1989) is cited by Fujita et al. (1999: 355).

Might this mean that, in economic terms, increasing returns are somehow associated with increases in entropy? Kenneth Boulding offered up the intriguing possibility of such a link. He cast entropy in positive terms – the "negentropy" of information theory – and saw it as the realization of "potential" from past events (Boulding 1976: 5). This certainly evokes a sense of, variously, evolution, cumulative processes, and path dependence. Would it be possible to extrapolate further, and to envision in this a necessary correspondence between changes in and over time and the concentration of economic activity?

Krugman clearly saw that connection: "An economic analysis that takes increasing returns seriously will normally involve dynamic models in which the choice of equilibrium also reflects history" (Krugman 1995: 42). As did David, who wrote:

> The pervasiveness of economies of scale opens up the prospect that past market configurations ... were in reality unstable positions away from which the system moved when disturbed.
>
> (David 1975: 15)

He then concluded: "To understand the process of modern economic growth and technological development in such an untidy world necessarily calls for the study of history" (David 1975: 16).

If so, economics "in time" would be the economics of concentrating effects, whether as scale or agglomeration effects. This would still leave intact a complementary universe of economics where the static resolution of equilibria is sufficient, and neither the past nor the future is relevant to the present.

Robinson herself saw the link between increasing returns and economic change occurring in historical time, tracing it back in *Economic Heresies*, which appeared in 1971, to the implications of Adam Smith's division of labor and specialization, and interpreting in particular Allyn Young's address entitled "Increasing Returns and Economic Progress," delivered in 1928, as laying the groundwork for such a link (Robinson 1971: 62). Writing only a few years later, David echoed Robinson's words, citing the foundational "vision" of both Smith and Young along similar lines (David 1975: 15–16).

This linkage can be extended to longstanding concerns that inform questions about economic growth, perhaps the nature of economics itself. Whether the subject is industrialization, the "life and death" of cities and regions, or the beginning of civilization itself, economics "in time" would be in accord with increasing returns to scale, thereby diminishing significantly the place of economic models of pure or perfect competition when accounting for changes over time.

However, it is in the comprehension of human experience and history that the approaches of Arthur, David, and Krugman fall short, even as all three see the capturing of historical change as essential to their own efforts, and can rightly claim to have carved out a place for time in economics that incorporates historical elements within a theoretical structure. Arthur, David, and Krugman all contend that history ought to be comprehended as events, accidental, even trivial; Arthur and David would add that those events, taken together in a sequence of some sort, can be matched to a pathway in time. Historians, across a wide range of methodological approaches, emphases, and ideologies, are likely to object, as this limits history at most to a largely sequential narrative when it is not reduced even further to singular, inciting – or formative – events, set in isolation. There is no clear place for institutions, historical (as opposed to economic) forces, intellectual currents, cycles of change, or upheavals of transformation.

What is missing, or appears only weakly, is the historical context. David comes closest, by providing pieces of an accompanying, more descriptive narrative, and using a series of external events as a surrogate for a changing historical backdrop. He characterized his own work as "genealogical," built from an initial set of conditions and a "sequence of connecting events" (David 1994: 206), with different outcomes possible, not all necessarily optimal and efficient. In this way, economic life would be subject to an evolution not bounded by a preconceived result, a criticism of neoclassical thinking akin to that levelled by Thorstein Veblen, a leading Institutionalist in its formative era.

Nonetheless, a genealogy is a history in only a limited sense. As a family history, and perhaps even a barebones version of one, a genealogy exists fundamentally in isolation from the surroundings in which it is set, without necessarily being integrated or merged into the larger world those surroundings constitute.

Not without reason is history seen as a seamless web, with a multiplicity of interpenetrating circumstances and factors to be comprehended. When a stage is set within which initial conditions may be discerned and scrutinized, historians invariably find themselves moving backwards, to provide an explanation or context for the stage that first appeared as the initiating scene. In a mathematical sense, historical contexts might be thought of as recursive, and their boundaries are always blurred. An evolutionary process may show the means by which one moved in time from A to B, but does not indicate how and why A emerged in the first place.

Crucially, the set nature of the past, to which Robinson referred, must be tempered by its retrospective reconstruction as history, affected in turn by the variation in the comprehension, consciousness, and memory of it – the "web of meaning," as Clifford Geertz has described it, that flows from human experience.

Hence, one must acknowledge Robinson's own difficulty in grasping historical time and human experience, despite her invoking of the term "historical time." A dynamic, evolutionary model may capture the network of steps that, taken altogether, give rise to a historical process, but may still fail to embrace or engage fully historical time and historical change.

It appears, then, that the effort by Arthur, David, and Krugman to establish an essential historical economics is ultimately grounded in making a bright-line distinction between history as a subject of particulars, and economics as a field of generality, rule-making, and model-building, revealing in a new way the methodological division between history as idiographic and economics as nomothetic. Their achievement has been to grasp the arrow of time in their remaking of a historically based economics, but the full measure of historical time has proved to be elusive.

Consequently, Joan Robinson's three-pronged critique of time in economics continues to raise fundamental questions about the scope of economics: can activities conducted by humans, the subject matter of economics, be understood in relation to changes in real time, and yet be analyzed through abstracted models that follow from a discrete set of general rules?

Finally, in assessing Joan Robinson's place in the history of economic thought, it is worth noting the disjuncture between the vision and challenge entailed by her critique of time in economics and the implications of other strands in her own thinking, especially the effort to pursue Marx's notion of the "law of motion of capitalism." In the latter instance it may be argued that colleagues and successors like Michael Kalecki and Richard Goodwin achieved considerable progress in devising cyclical models of growth by marrying Marxian ideas about the distribution of income as a primary determinant to a Keynesian emphasis upon effective demand (Kalecki 1962) and, ultimately, to Schumpeter's focus upon technological innovation, in Goodwin's case within the framework of the half-century Kondratiev cycle (Goodwin 1991: 30ff.). Both Kalecki and Goodwin saw the emergence of macroeconomic instability, structural change, and cyclical movement following from an accelerating pattern of investment linked to a new "stream" (in Kalecki's term) or "swarm" of innovations (Goodwin's term).

Yet this approach relies strongly upon parametric, or what Goodwin himself referred to as "endogenous" elements to the exclusion of historical events (Goodwin 1991: 30) and hence is set effectively in logical rather than historical time. Moreover, the effort to create a model for the law of motion of capitalism presents an obvious contradiction with Robinson's critique of time, in that any such law resonates with the Newtonian frame of reference she had rejected.

Thus, overall, this approach limits the contribution of these models to a new historical economics grounded in Robinson's insights about the problematic nature of time in economics.

## Notes

1 Zeno's paradoxes have informed controversies about the nature of time, the place of
   continuity and the infinite, and the possibility of change; figuring significantly, say,
   in Georg Cantor's work on the existence of transfinite numbers (Cantor 1955 [1895,
   1897]: 15), or in Kurt Godel's critique of classical and relativistic physics (Yourgrau
   1991: 31–41).
2 See, for example, John Hicks' scepticism about the use of the natural sciences as a
   model for economics and the need to accord history a larger role instead: "It is
   usually possible, in the natural sciences, for the reliability of a fact to be tested by
   repeated experiment ... But the facts of economics are not in that way fortified. An
   economic time-series is a sequence of observations of a historical process, each item
   having its own distinct individuality. Each of them is a historical fact; like other
   historical facts, it depends on someone's testimony" (Hicks 1983: 372).
3 It is telling that the first two essays appearing in the second volume of Robinson's
   *Collected Papers*, published in 1964, deal explicitly with her assessment of
   Marshall's work and legacy. One is entitled, "Marshall, Marx and Keynes"; the
   other, "Notes on Marx and Marshall."

## References

Arthur, W. B. (1989) "Competing Technologies, Increasing Returns and Lock-in by
   Historical Events." *Economic Journal*, 99: 116–131.
Arthur, W. B. (1994a) *Increasing Returns and Path Dependence in the Economy.* Ann
   Arbor: University of Michigan Press.
Arthur, W. B. (1994b) "Competing Technologies, Increasing Returns and Lock-in by
   Historical Events." In W. B. Arthur,*Increasing Returns and Path Dependence in the
   Economy.* Ann Arbor: University of Michigan Press, pp. 13–32.
Arthur, W. B. (1994c) "Industry Location Patterns and the Importance of History." In
   W. B. Arthur,*Increasing Returns and Path Dependence in the Economy.* Ann Arbor:
   University of Michigan Press, pp. 49–67.
Boulding, K. (1976) "The Great Laws of Change." In A. M. Tang,F. M. Westfield,
   and J. S. Worley (eds), *Evolution, Welfare, and Time in Economics.* Lexington, MA:
   Lexington Books, pp. 3–14.
Burstein, M. (1991) "History versus Equilibrium: Joan Robinson and Time in
   Economics." In Ingrid Rima (ed.), *The Joan Robinson Legacy.* Armonk, NY: M.E.
   Sharpe, pp. 49–61.
Cantor, G. (1955 [1895, 1897]) *Contributions to the Founding of the Theory of Transfinite
   Numbers.* trans. and intro. P. E. B. Jourdain.New York: Dover Publications.
Dasgupta, A. K. (1985) *Epochs of Economic Theory.* Oxford: Basil Blackwell.
David, P. (1975) *Technical Choice, Innovation and Growth.* London: Cambridge
   University Press.
David, P. (1985) "Clio and the Economics of QWERTY." *American Economic Review*,
   75(2): 332–337.
David, P. (1994) "Why Are Institutions the 'Carriers of History'?" *Structural Change
   and Economic Dynamics*, 5(2): 205–220.
David, P. (1997) "Path Dependence and the Quest for Historical Economics." *Discussion
   Papers in Economic and Social History*, no. 20. University of Oxford.
David, P. and M. Thomas (2003) "Introduction: Thinking Historically about
   Challenging Economic Issues."In P. A. David and M. Thomas (eds), *The Economic
   Future in Historical Perspective.* Oxford: Oxford University Press, pp. 1–27.

Delorme, R. and G. Hodgson (2005) "Complexity and the Economy: An Interview with W. Brian Arthur." In J. Finch and M. Orillard (eds), *Complexity and the Economy*. Cheltenham, UK: Edward Elgar, pp. 17–32.

Dynkin, E. B. and V. A. Uspenskii (2006 [1963]) "Random Walks." In *Mathematical Conversations*, trans. N. D. Whaland, Jr and O. Titelbaum. Mineola, NY: Dover, pp. 189–270.

Eddington, A. (1929) *The Nature of the Physical World*. New York: Macmillan.

Faris, J. A. (1996) *The Paradoxes of Zeno*. Aldershot, UK: Avebury.

Fujita, M., P.Krugman, and A. J. Venables (1999) *The Spatial Economy*. Cambridge, MA: MIT Press.

Georgescu-Roegen, N. (1973) "The Entropy Law and the Economic Problem." In H. E. Daly (ed.), *Toward a Steady-State Economy*, San Francisco: Freeman, pp. 37–49.

Goodwin, R. M. (1991) "Schumpeter, Keynes and the Theory of Economic Evolution." *Journal of Evolutionary Economics*, 1(1): 19–47.

Harcourt, G. C. (2006) *The Structure of Post-Keynesian Economics*. Cambridge: Cambridge University Press.

Hicks, Sir J. R. (1976) "Some Questions of Time in Economics." In A. M. Tang, F. M. Westfield and J. S. Worley (eds), *Evolution, Welfare, and Time in Economics*. Lexington, MA: Lexington Books, pp. 135–151.

Hicks, Sir J. R. (1983) "A Discipline Not a Science." *Classics and Moderns: Collected Essays on Economic Theory*, Vol. III. Oxford: Basil Blackwell, pp. 365–375.

Ingrao, B. and G. Israel (1990) *The Invisible Hand: Economic Equilibrium in the History of Science*, trans. I. McGilvary. Cambridge, MA: MIT Press.

Kaldor, N. (1934) "A Classificatory Note on the Determinateness of Equilibrium." *Review of Economic Studies*, 1(2): 122–136.

Kalecki, M. (1962) "Observations on the Theory of Growth." *Economic Journal*, 72(285): 134–153.

Khalil, E. (1990) "Entropy Law and Exhaustion of Natural Resources: Is Nicholas Georgescu-Roegen's Paradigm Defensible?" *Ecological Economics*, 2(2): 163–178.

Khalil, E. (1994) "Entropy and Economics." In *The Elgar Companion to Institutional and Evolutionary Economics A–K*. Aldershot, UK: Edward Elgar, pp. 186–193.

Krugman, P. (1991a) "Increasing Returns and Economic Geography." *Journal of Political Economy*, 99(3): 483–499.

Krugman, P. (1991b) *Geography and Trade*. Cambridge, MA: MIT Press.

Krugman, P. (1994) *Peddling Prosperity*. New York: Norton.

Krugman, P. (1995) "Incidents from My Career." In A. Heertje (ed.), *The Makers of Modern Economics*, Vol. II. Aldershot, UK: Edward Elgar, pp. 29–46.

Krugman, P. (1997) "How the Economy Organizes Itself in Space: A Survey of the New Economic Geography." In W. B. Arthur,S. N. Durlauf, and D. A. Lane (eds), *The Economy As an Evolving Complex System II*. Reading, MA: Addison-Wesley, pp. 239–262.

Loasby, B. (1991) "Joan Robinson's 'Wrong Turning.'" In I. Rima (ed.), *The Joan Robinson Legacy*. Armonk, NY: M.E. Sharpe, pp. 34–48.

Marshall, A. (1898 [1891]) *Principles of Economics*, 4th edn. London: Macmillan.

Mirowski, P. (1988) *Against Mechanism*. Totowa, NJ: Rowman & Littlefield.

Mirowski, P. (1990) *More Heat than Light*. Cambridge: Cambridge University Press.

Monod, J. (1971) *Chance and Necessity*, trans. A. Wainhouse,1st American edn. New York: Knopf.

Nicolis, G. and I. Prigogine (1989) *Exploring Complexity: An Introduction.* New York: Freeman.

Prigogine, I. and I. Stengers (1997) *The End of Certainty: Time, Chaos, and the New Laws of Nature.* New York: Free Press.

Robinson, J. (1951) *Collected Economic Papers,* Vol. 1. Oxford: Basil Blackwell.

Robinson, J. (1964a) "Accumulation and the Production Function." In *Collected Economic Papers,* Vol. 2. Oxford: Basil Blackwell, pp. 132–144.

Robinson, J. (1964b) "Some Problems of Definition and Measurement of Capital." In *Collected Economic Papers,* Vol. 2. Oxford: Basil Blackwell, pp. 197–208.

Robinson, J. (1964c) "'Imperfect Competition' Revisited." In *Collected Economic Papers,* Vol. 2. Oxford: Basil Blackwell, pp. 222–238.

Robinson, J. (1971) *Economic Heresies.* London: Macmillan.

Robinson, J. (1973 [1953]) "Re-reading Marx." In *Collected Economic Papers,* Vol. 4. Oxford: Basil Blackwell, pp. 247–268.

Robinson, J. (1979) "History versus Equilibrium." In *Collected Economic Papers,* Vol. 5. Oxford: Basil Blackwell, pp. 48–58.

Robinson, J. (1980a) "What Are the Questions?" In Joan Robinson, *What Are the Questions? And Other Essays.* Armonk, NY: M.E. Sharpe, pp. 1–32.

Robinson, J. (1980b) "Time in Economic Theory." In Joan Robinson, *What Are the Questions? And Other Essays.* Armonk, NY: M.E. Sharpe, pp. 86–95.

Shackle, G. L. S. (1967 [1958]) *Time in Economics.* Amsterdam: North-Holland.

Solow, R. (1985) "Economic History and Economics." *American Economic Review,* 75(2): 328–331.

Solow, R. (1997) "How Did Economics Get that Way and What Way Did It Get?" *Daedalus,* 126(1): 39–58.

Weintraub, E. R. (1985) "Joan Robinson's Critique of Equilibrium: An Appraisal." *American Economic Review,* 75(2): 146–149.

Weintraub, E. R. (1991) *Stabilizing Dynamics.* Cambridge: Cambridge University Press.

Yourgrau, P. (1991) *The Disappearance of Time.* Cambridge: Cambridge University Press.

# 4 Of puzzles and problems

## A methodological challenge in economics from a philosophical dispute

As a narrative about philosophical disputation, David Edmonds and John Eidinow's *Wittgenstein's Poker*, published in 2001, brings to light the alternatives posed to advancing intellectual inquiry in and across disciplines as a matter of either puzzle-solving or problem-addressing (Edmonds and Eidinow 2001). While cast as a philosophical wrangle, this division between puzzle and problem can serve to shine a spotlight on an essential feature of the methodology of economics, the often-resorted-to adoption of a metanarrative of puzzle-solving in order to secure a claim to scientific rigor, a feature manifested most plainly in economic game theory.

From the dramatic narrative about which *Wittgenstein's Poker* is constructed, describing the sole encounter – and confrontation – between Karl Popper and Ludwig Wittgenstein in 1946, one may first consider the terms of Popper's critique of Wittgenstein. For Popper the central issue was simple and direct: puzzles lacked the moral heft and seriousness of real-life problems in need of addressing, which he therefore identified as the worthy goal of philosophy, in contrast to the artifice of solving puzzles, which he saw in Wittgenstein's "language" or "word games" (Edmonds and Eidinow 2001: 185–6).

Yet Popper's neat dichotomy is but one of the problems with puzzles. As a matter of construction, their formation may influence strongly, even shape their solution. In effect, the rules that allow the puzzle to be constructed are sufficiently limiting as to assure a certain outcome. Astute selection of rules may yield ingenious results, but such creativity may also be viewed as trickery or artifice. Moreover, the construction of the puzzle requires an abstracting from the reality associated with the puzzle in such a way as to insulate and isolate it largely from any broader context.

Wittgenstein's critique of language introduces additional complexities to the place accorded puzzles and problems. Edmonds and Eidinow characterized Wittgenstein's outlook on "philosophical questions … as puzzles rather than problems" (Edmonds and Eidinow 2001: 183) by dint of the necessity of illuminating and avoiding the traps of language present in all such questions. Nonetheless, puzzles set in isolation and conjured up out of artifice were subject to stern criticism by Wittgenstein himself, especially when he adopted what is widely regarded as an "essentially social" conception of language associated with *The Philosophical Investigations* (Baker and Hacker 1985: 170). Here the Wittgensteinian critique, sometimes referred to as the necessity of interpreting all language through "community standards" (Putnam [2001] 2012a: 358–64), provides an entry into an examination of the role, meaning, and implications of context in shaping and defining either puzzles or problems.

Moreover, there is also an overarching narrative often invoked in mathematics that appears to transcend Popper's dichotomy. One may posit that it is possible to "graduate" from puzzles to problems, as one might contend is the case for topology, graph theory, among other parts of mathematics, and produce thereby a metanarrative for mathematics that might serve as a paradigm for other fields of inquiry, including economics. To entertain this possibility requires entering into an exploration of the range of formal correspondences and structures across philosophy, mathematics, and economics – and their limits.

## The economic case in a nutshell

A quick sketch of the tensions within the practice of economic theorizing reveals, on a continuing basis, the embedding of conclusions to be reached in the initiating assumptions. Where economic theorizing is thought of in terms of competing narratives, this might also be viewed as the "problem" associated with the selection of narrative, for the basis for selection may effectively "embed" conclusions in the assumptions underlying the economic model under construction.

In general, any grand model might well be comprehended as the result of a construction, with a limited number of limiting assumptions providing the foundation, and often many acknowledged omissions or deviations from experience or empirical reality. One of the most common – and favored – statements by economists engaged in such constructions is the ready acknowledgement that certain foundational assumptions do not comport at all with the reality that we routinely experience, but this seeming unreality will not stand in the way of effectuating the significant explanatory power of the model. Nancy Cartwright has given economists some leeway in this regard, likening it to the frictionless models of classical physics, only to call into question the abstracting assumptions typically made by economists. She characterizes these latter assumptions as "non-Galilean," that is, as ones undermining the rigor of the model by influencing, even guiding in crucial ways the conclusion sought (Cartwright, 2005: 143).

While model-building or, in a simpler form, the conducting of thought experiments, stands at the center of an economics mode of inquiry, the choices made in constructing thought experiments and models are of a fundamentally ad hoc nature, often suiting the moment rather than conforming to an established system, and increasing the likelihood that the choice of narrative will be influenced by an unreflected predisposition to find an agreeable outcome.

In concert with these methodological challenges is the disjuncture between the high, abstract language and tone of economic modeling and the more conventional and offhand form of the discussion of daily economic affairs and events by economists. One can see this in the recent critique of the scientific aspirations of economics by Bertrand Collomb, commenting upon the work of Maurice Allais:

> I then went to the Ecole des Mines, where I followed the teaching of Maurice Allais, the sole Nobel prize winner in economics of French nationality. His courses made a strong impression on me through the rigor of his concepts and methodological apparatus and through the force of his personality.
>
> (Collomb 2011: 15)

Later, though:

> I rediscovered the same Maurice Allais later, in reading his articles in *Le Figaro* ... His positions on the great economic problems of the world paradoxically made no reference to the methodological apparatus and mathematics that he had previously taught. Was this the sign of certain difficulties?
>
> (Collomb 2011: 16)

These difficulties might be regarded as a manifestation of the gap between an abstracted, mathematically based puzzle and an everyday problem encountered amidst the serious affairs of the world, the distinction, in short, that appears to underlie Popper's dichotomy.

But when one turns to the economic theorizing associated with "game theory," a further blurring of that dichotomy has occurred. For, while games follow from the rules set for them, and hence appear to have an artificial, or at least constructed quality to them, game theory is envisioned, not as an artifice or trick, but rather as foundational, encompassing the broadest range of economic analysis and providing, at least in potential, a more systematized set of ideas to be followed in constructing diverse models.

Yet there is a further twist here as well. If one turns to Robert Leonard's depiction of John von Neumann, perhaps the central figure in the early development of the mathematics for and the economic applications of the theory of games, it is play, with its reliance upon artifice and creative, even ingenious techniques, embodied in the Central European fascination with chess and other "parlor games," that drives the critical, initial phases of its development. Leonard entitled the section of his 1995 article on the history of game theory about von Neumann's background and initial forays into game theory as "Homo Ludens" (Leonard 1995: 732–5).

It is also evident in Harold Kuhn and A. W. Tucker's appreciation of John von Neumann's pathbreaking work on game theory, written shortly after his death. In it they highlighted the role of "play" and "chance" in the method he followed (Kuhn and Tucker 1958: 104).

However, one might also take note of John Maynard Keynes' caution at the conclusion of his *Treatise on Probability*, citing Quetelet, which expresses the conundrum of constructing reality from rule-driven games, but couched in terms of the laws (or rules) of probability itself. Does the urn with its black and white balls reflect nature, and, by extension, human activity, or has nature been made to conform to the urn, so as to validate the laws of probability which in fact depend upon the disposition of the urn? (Keynes [1921] 1963: 428). Written prior to Keynes' major economic writings, having begun as a dissertation in 1907, the concluding conundrum exposes a central methodological weakness in constructing economic life as if it conformed to the rules of a puzzle or game.

## The puzzle elevated

While Keynes' characterization of the rule-making underlying the determination of probabilities might be taken as a cautionary insight into the "puzzle problem" in economics, there is a countervailing sense that a metanarrative of mathematics holds sway, and that therefore puzzles present the gateway to broader knowledge and greater comprehension in economics. Clearly it is assumed that what begins as puzzle will become something deeper and more substantive, and that, accordingly, the method underlying the construction of the puzzle does not ensnare, by embedding limiting assumptions, those who might use it for other purposes.

Yet a raft of methodological concerns remains. How does one establish with any consistency the proper context or social epistemology in which the rules guiding the puzzle-making and solution need to be set? Here the difficulties associated with ad hoc choices surface quite plainly. Do these choices merely reinforce the bases for the conclusion sought? Does their ad hoc selection preclude the formulation and use of standard criteria for rule-making or rule-following?

The aggrandizing of the place of the puzzle, as in the case of game theory, makes these concerns all the more pressing. For example, the primacy of the puzzle is on display in the depictions of the situation or set of circumstances addressed by John Nash in his first major paper, "The Bargaining Problem," dating from 1950 (Nash 1950), as well as his seminal paper in 1951 on the formation of a strategic equilibrium, "Non-cooperative Games" (Nash 1951). Both papers are essentially mathematical constructions, open to possible applications in other disciplines. They capture formally the "situation" to be resolved. There is, clearly, the appearance of context, as the best possible decision by any one player depends upon knowing what other players' decisions would be. Moreover, this context has subsequently been refined, to make use of probabilities in decision-making and to account for other nuances, like non-credible actions or threats. Yet any broader context or social epistemology is cast aside. Hence, for all its subsequent economic applications the Nash equilibrium is, at its core, a solution to a puzzle.

To elaborate further: in game theory, the context is not comprehended as a social setting or social world as much as it is embodied or stated in the rules themselves. As David Krebs has described the "Nash Equilibrium," "how to play the game" would generally be based upon "explicit negotiation among the players" or conceivably results from an implicit understanding "*in some contexts, for some particular games*" (Krebs 1989: 169). In other words, even in the implicit case, for a particular set of conditions a related set of rules is associated or, more narrowly, a rulebook itself forms the context, rather than springing from a broader range of outside criteria. One might imagine, for example, a group of players entering into a game of poker, with its known and well-defined rulebook, as in the one specific application, "A Three-Man Poker Game," cited in Nash's 1951 article "Non-cooperative Games" (Nash 1951: 293–4). To establish a broader context, though, entails laying out the circumstances from which the rulebook itself came and the understanding by the players of what the rules are.

Cast in terms of Wittgenstein's later understanding of language, social context, in P. M. S. Hacker's view, calls for recognizing the distinction, even disjuncture, between rule and game:

> The rules of chess could not determine a game of chess in a society in which the chess moves were a religious ritual culminating in the sacrifice of the loser (or winner) to the gods, or a form of warfare engaged in by the use of human beings as pieces on a chessboard, who were killed when taken.
> (Hacker 2010: 37)

David Bloor, drawing upon Wittgenstein's identification of rule with institution, goes even further, seeing in it the necessarily "social character of rule-following" (Bloor 1997: 142).

In economics it is possible to posit that the broader context or its social epistemology is derived from one source: history; as the subject matter of economics is ultimately the worldly affairs of humans. Nonetheless, the draw of mathematics is quite strong, suggesting a tension between the pull of mathematics and history on economics. On the one hand, one may reasonably ask if there is any other discipline among the social sciences that proceeds from the puzzle-solving ways of mathematics in so close a manner. In the same vein, economics is replete with paradoxes, which hinge, explicitly or implicitly, upon a mathematical understanding or intuition of contradiction. On the other, how contexts are drawn is clearly a matter of choice: selecting narratives from human experience. Whatever the science that may be invoked in the narrative chosen, there remains a literary residual that cannot be altogether discarded. If the narrative takes place in and over time, the presence of history is unavoidable.

## Extending the narrative of mathematics

In the parlance and discourse of narratives in and about mathematics, "problem" and "puzzle" often appear to be essentially interchangeable, as the history of the origins and development of topology, for example, makes clear (Szpiro 2007).

This narrative form in mathematics consisted of an initiating event, like the challenge posed to Leonhard Euler in the eighteenth century of determining the possibility of traversing all of Konigsberg's bridges without crossing paths, that becomes first a solution to a specific problem or puzzle, then expands over time into a new subject area. Despite its appeal, this approach, even within the philosophical discourse of mathematics, has proved contentious.

Stephan Korner's *The Philosophy of Mathematics* reflected the impact of the crisis that loomed over the foundations of mathematics in the first decades of the twentieth century. Thus, Korner categorized the philosophy of mathematics into three parts: the logical, the formal, and the intuitionist approaches. Further, he concluded that philosophical or metaphysical assumptions, effectively constituting different and diverse *Weltanschauungen*, invariably found their way into reflections about mathematics (Korner [1960] 2009).

Now it is also the case, as Robert Leonard, among others, has pointed out, that an axiomatic, or formal, approach was favored over the course of the first half of the twentieth century by those who sought to use mathematical structures as a paradigm for scientific inquiry in other disciplines, including economics (Leonard 1995: 733). For all that, the resort to such axiomatization in economics faces serious limitations. For example, Leon Walras' signal work in "pure economics" of borrowing the elements of an "axiomatic structure" from mechanics suffers from a major flaw: axiomatization precludes any reference to content. As a result, rather than producing a "parallel" process of axiomatization across different intellectual disciplines, Walras instead treated classical mechanics as the defining field of inquiry analogized to economics (Turk 2006).

A generation after Walras the structuralist approach of the Bourbaki to the use of axiomatics renewed the claims for axiomatizing intellectual disciplines beyond mathematics. The case made by the Bourbaki to extend the use of the "abstract forms," essentially axiomatic structures, of mathematics to various aspects of "empirical reality," depended upon the notion of "preadaptation" (Bourbaki 1950: 230). That is, that mathematical structures, regarded as pure forms, or so emptied of content to be the case (an acknowledgment that content was likely associated with the mathematical intuition underlying the initial exploration of new mathematical fields), somehow comport with, or "fit", certain kinds of empirical reality.

But exactly how does that occur? In fact, is this not the essential question to be addressed in any effort to establish a correspondence between mathematics and other intellectual disciplines? According to this thesis, abstract structures, forms – or perhaps better – patterns, bring forth resemblances in fields with some measure of empirical content. But does the shoe – metaphorically – fit because it conforms to the foot, or is the foot simply shoehorned to conform to the shoe? This is another version of the conundrum posed by Keynes at the end of his *Treatise on Probability*. What criteria might be established to ascertain the validity or legitimacy of any such adaptation?

The problem of "preadaptation" seems most pertinent in relation to economics, for all that what it has meant to "mathematize" economics is itself a work in progress, and has undergone a considerable evolution from the latter part of the nineteenth century through the middle of the twentieth century (see, for example, Weintraub 2002). One highly influential version, drawing, consciously or not, from the Bourbaki paradigm, can be found in Paul Samuelson's retrospective look at the origins of his *Foundations of Economic Analysis*, published in 1947, where he noted that, "economics and physics could share the same formal theorems ... while still not resting on the same empirical foundations and certainties" (Samuelson 1998: 1376; see also Turk 2012: 152–4).

## The mathematics narrative and game theory

There is a second strand to the Bourbaki case that is also relevant in this instance. The Bourbaki saw as one of the virtues of this axiomatic or structuralist approach the capacity to generalize, beyond the elevation of the puzzle noted above, so that axioms first identified as underlying one particular subfield can be found, if suitably translated, to underlie other subfields as well (Bourbaki 1950: 230). In certain respects this tracks the grand mathematical narrative in which a puzzle presented and solved leads to the recognition of broader patterns or resonances that will inform a larger subject. Can or should the same case be made for economics?

The paradigmatic quality of the mathematics metanarrative is most likely to obtain in economics where mathematics is viewed as an essential, if not indispensable, framework, tool, or technique. This extends to the construction of economic models, especially when it is assumed that economic constructs or structures correspond with mathematical forms supposedly not laden with content or meaning.

Such construction, though, entails a critical translation from formal mathematical relation to economic rule, and such rules do require the infusion of meaning. This may be achieved by attributing a certain causality to an economic rule that might otherwise be viewed as a description, association, or correlation.

Robert Aumann's description of the "game solution concept" appears to capture critical elements of the challenge posed in this way:

> Born more than a century ago in connection with Cournot's (1838) study of duopoly, it is now extremely common in many different applications ... The Nash equilibrium is the embodiment of the idea that economic agents are rational; that they simultaneously act to maximize their utility. If there is any idea that can be considered the driving force of economic theory, that is it. Thus in a sense, Nash equilibrium embodies the most important and fundamental idea of economics.
>
> (Aumann 1989: 43–4)

It should be noted that Cournot was primarily a mathematician and philo-sopher, and his study of duopoly can best be understood as a mathematical puzzle, based upon a set of largely unrealistic assumptions so as to facilitate the solution. But then Aumann expands the scope of the "game solution concept" further, raising the explanatory power of the Nash equilibrium to the highest possible level.

In a similar vein, in overviewing the theoretical treatment of oligopoly, Aumann is explicit as well about the expanded explanatory reach of an "axiom system" attainable through game theory:

> In a sense, of course the doctrine[al or institutional assumptions are] built into the solution concept [for oligopoly]; as we have seen, the core implies competition, the stable set cartelization. It is not that game theory makes no assumptions, but that the assumptions are of a more general, funda-mental nature. The difference is like that between deriving the motion of the planets from Kepler's laws or from Newton's laws. Like Kepler's laws, which apply to the planets only, oligopoly theory applies to oligopolistic markets only. Newton's laws apply to the planets and also to apples falling from trees; stable sets apply to markets and also to voting.
>
> (Aumann 1989: 17–18)

Aumann thereby joins Walras in validating the scientific aspirations of economics through a comparison with the breakthroughs of the iconic figures of classical physics. There is this difference, though: while relying upon an analogy between economics and pure mechanics, Walras emphasized the importance of incorporating mathematical techniques into economics. For his part, Aumann gave central weight to the extension of mathematical structures to other fields, including economics, along the lines laid out by the Bourbaki.

Aumann's depiction of the explanatory power of game theory in economics can be, and has been, subject to criticism from a variety of perspectives, though each, in the end, touches upon matters of context. Ariel Rubinstein, who has played a significant role in exploring the use of game theory in economics, has also posed serious questions about the problems attendant upon the requisite infusion of meaning into any abstracted construction of economic relations, separating the pure formalism of mathematics from the need for interpretation in economics (Rubinstein 2000: 72–3).

For Leonard, assaying the history of economic thought, Aumann's outlook was shaped by his desire to create an ideational narrative of the "game solution concept," in which the past – in the instant matter the ideas and work of Cournot – was reconjured to establish the linear antecedents of the new scientific world of game theory (Leonard 1994).

John Sutton has sought to extract meaningful explanations of oligopolistic behavior through greater specificity rather than generality, for the latter, in his view, suffers from the potential liability of "explaining nothing" in consequence of "explaining everything." He finds the strongest case for game-theoretic models where "the context pins down the form of the game, and where the analysis of the game yields some sharp qualitative [and distinct] predictions" (Sutton 1990: 509).

Moreover, the generality about which Aumann speaks and upon which he grounds economics rests solely upon generic economic agents, presumed to be pursuing the greatest "utility" possible. From a societal or social perspective one may ask how valid is this reduction of economic agents, rather than categorizing them, for example, in groupings, like classes? Furthermore, how does this focus upon economic agents comport with the notion that economics is concerned with the matter of production itself, that is, the translation of resources into outcomes? Finally, how applicable is the notion of strategy, so central to game-playing and game theory, to matters of production?

On such matters there seems little place for the "play" associated with the formation and operation of strategies. Might one think of choices made among farming techniques as a "strategic" decision? While this is certainly possible, if not very likely, the imposition of the notion of strategy seems as anachronistic and culturally biased as Aleutian Islanders using the calculus of the "hedonistic" microeconomics of John Bates Clark in Thorstein Veblen's caustic critique written a century ago (Veblen [1919], 1990: 193). More likely the farmers' actions are a mix of customary practice and assessment of available resources.

Nor, set in a contemporary context, do matters of ecological resources come directly into play. One might reframe the economic game in question so as to address the problematic aspects of obtaining and maintaining resources, but this would require, as Pierre Duhem or Otto Neurath might have put it, the introduction of additionally determining or auxiliary hypotheses.

## Prisoner's dilemma and double-edged metaphor

Context may also be borne of metaphor, which by its nature extends the explanatory range but also calls forth certain limitations. It must be recognized that context cannot be reduced – entirely – to a set of objective facts, as it too is framed by interpretation. In the main, the context for the "prisoner's dilemma" game has been sought in the machinations of the Cold War, with fear and distrust extracted as the guiding motive principles, affecting the choice of strategies thereby. Mary S. Morgan has explored the contradictory implications of this model for economic theorizing, but crucially sees this game as arising out of the context of the Cold War (Morgan 2012: 345). It is also the case, though, that the model of the "prisoner's dilemma," one of the most potent game theoretic structures in its range of applications, evokes the atmospherics of "film noir," including its early development and exploration at the RAND Corporation based in southern California in the first years of the Cold War.

Albert Tucker, who first devised the model and then formalized it, brought the prisoner's dilemma forward as a classroom example to a group of psychologists at Stanford University in 1950. Tucker's – apparent – reference to prisoners being given the "third degree" by the police is suggestive (*Philadelphia Inquirer*, February 2, 1995), as it was a term widely in use during this period, routinely raised in the crime movies and films noirs of the 1930s and 1940s, and identified as a common practice of the police throughout the United States in the Wickersham Commission report, released in 1931.

What is commonly referred to as the "paradoxical" nature of the "prisoner's dilemma" would make perfect sense in the world of film noir, with beleaguered detainees, however tough, savvy, or villainous, bowing to the pressure of police interrogators, whose world-weariness or corruption, or both, provides a match of sorts to the street-smarts of the detainees, and in the end accepting an outcome less favorable than might have been secured. This is hardly a tale of the triumph of law and order; rather, it forms a narrative that emphasizes the seamy and constricted world of post-World War I German Expressionism translated to post-World War II America.

How could this dilemma, then, be generalized so greatly? Anatol Rapoport suggests that the "prisoner's dilemma" represents the conflict between individual and collective rationality, and so might be understood as a version of the "tragedy of the commons" (Rapoport 1989: 199–200). While this has come to be accepted as the standard interpretation of the dilemma, it seems to be misplaced. In economics the latter might better be captured by Keynes' paradox of thrift, in which, during sharp economic declines, the prudence of individuals to save contributes to the overall weakening of the economy and jeopardizes further the viability of individual households, including their saving.

Missing from Rapoport's interpretation of the prisoner's dilemma is its metaphorical context, which is one of physical coercion. The common distinction in law seems apt here: civil matters regard property; criminal matters life and physical liberty. While it may be both fruitful and enlightening to introduce or, better, account for the role of power and the prospects for risking physical liberty, it is worth recognizing that economic affairs typically concern the use, exchange, control, and disposition of property, and thus are commonly addressed as civil matters. Of course, one must also recognize that, ranging across diverse ideological perspectives, there are those who would emphasize the role of force by the state or through legal structures in economic affairs. It was Pierre-Joseph Proudhon who famously stated that the origin of "all property is theft." But to generalize the prisoner's dilemma to include a broad array of economic situations is to blur or even ignore the basic, underlying context for it.

Fundamentally, this inquiry into metaphor and cultural milieu is intended to grapple with the question of where ideas originate. What may seem so obvious at the moment may in turn seem "stuck in time" at a future date, limited in just those ways that had made it so compelling at an earlier time. In the case of the "prisoner's dilemma" the "shoehorning" of reality is effected not only by an enumeration of conditions or assumptions, but also by the power of the metaphorical conceit. Hence, Philip Mirowski's characterization of the "prisoner's-dilemma game" as algorithmic, one of the "natural rules" of game theory, rather than evolutionary or historical misses the temporal limitations of analogizing by metaphor (Mirowski 1986: 257–8), whereby the mixing of the "natural" with the social, which Mirowski categorizes as a "third tier" of rules, may be all-encompassing.

## On rules, strategies, and economic uncertainty

No matter the use or application, games (of any sort) have two characteristics: rules and strategies. The appearance of games in twentieth-century philosophy owes much to Wittgenstein's insights into the relation among language, thought, and the "states" or "facts" of the world, where the "rules of the game" are paramount. By contrast, game theorists give special weight to strategies, as these reflect the interests, concerns, and knowledge of the agents involved. For economic game theorists, the focus upon strategies facilitates the construction of an economic world moved and motivated by utilities.

There is, though, another piece to this puzzle. If economic forms, or formal relations, follow from mathematical ones, and these in turn result from the solution of puzzles, then the economic rules of the game are fundamentally set. This is the rulebook taken as a given, as was evident in the initial formulation of the Nash equilibrium, formally built upon the fixed point theorem. For good measure, as historians of game theory most certainly would do, one ought to incorporate the St Petersburg Paradox, a second mathematical puzzle, into the rules regarding risk as well. In Till Grune-Yanoff and Paul Schweinzer's treatment of the means by which game theory actually functions, these theorems would constitute core elements of the "theory proper" (Grune-Yanoff and Schweinzer 2008: 134).

The St. Petersburg paradox was initially "discovered" by the eighteenth-century mathematician Daniel Bernoulli. Karl Menger, the Austrian-American mathematician and economic thinker, described this paradox as the entry for "subjective probability" into economic theory. This is so because the paradox introduces an individualized assessment of risk-taking altering an outcome determined solely by the calculation of probability. Menger goes on to claim that his paper on this subject, presented to the Viennese Economic Society in 1927, spurred John von Neumann to "undertake a formal treatment of utility," hence initiating what would eventually become the "theory of games" (Menger [1934] 1979: 259)

The St. Petersburg paradox thus falls within the purview of the mathematics narrative in which problems are synonymous or at least congruent with puzzles, and these puzzle/problems, once solved, lend themselves to far broader application than the question that prompted the formulation of the puzzle. But it will also bring to the fore the contextual boundaries of uncertainty.

Menger appeared to be of two minds about the application of the St. Petersburg paradox to the world of economics. On the one hand, he states that it "may be useful in dealing with many as yet unsolved problems or confusedly treated questions of social science" (Menger [1934], 1979: 270).

However, he also appears to go on to delimit its scope, pointing to the need for set rules, as one might find "only in the case of games of chance" to establish a modicum of "quantitative precision" (Menger [1934], 1979: 273).

He elaborates further with regard to economic matters:

> In other domains of economic actions, uncertainty also plays a very important role indeed but can rarely be made numerically precise. This is most obvious in the case of general economic and political uncertainty, however important their influence on economic actions may be. If some piece of real estate lends itself only to a special use, say, the development of a luxury hotel or an armament factory, then its evaluation will largely depend upon the evaluator's views on the economic development of the country or the prospect of war – thus on his views about uncertain circumstances.
>
> (Menger [1934], 1979: 273)

Keynes' contemporaneous remarks about the nature of uncertainty in economics, found in a 1937 article "The General Theory of Employment," are striking in their resonance with Menger's cautionary comments, but highlight even more vividly the distinction between "games" played out as puzzles, and the problems associated with worldly affairs.

> By "uncertain" knowledge, let me explain, I do not mean merely to distinguish what is known for certain from what is known is only probable. The game of roulette is not subject, in this sense, to uncertainty; nor is the prospect of a Victory bond being drawn. Or, again, the expectation of life is only slightly uncertain. Even the weather is only moderately uncertain. The sense in which I am using the form is that in which the prospect of a European war is uncertain, or the price of copper and the rate of interest twenty years hence, or the obsolescence of a new invention, or the position of private wealth-owners in the social system in 1970. About these matters there is no scientific basis on which to form any calculable probability whatever. We simply do not know.
>
> (Keynes 1937: 213–14)

Keynes balked at the notion that "following the rules," as one might do in a game of chess, the prototype envisioned by Ernest Zermelo in his original 1912 inquiry into the possibility of a theory of games, was adequate and sufficient to encompass the method of economics. Instead, he envisioned such rules as a "guide" alone, from which and along which the variability of human choices and decisions, as well as larger events, would produce the totality of economic experience. (See Hoover 2006: 93.)

## Foundational tensions between rule-following and strategies

In the end, one may fairly question whether the pursuit of the puzzle in economics comes at the price of diminishing the scope of the field, essentially along the line of demarcation suggested by Popper. At the same time, the complexities of establishing meaning and context, evident in the extended ruminations about Wittgenstein's later epistemology of language, pose serious foundational challenges to economic theorizing, in the case of game theory exposing a substantial and substantive gap between the requirements of rule-making and the economic "problems" of the world.

This also brings to the fore a crucial distinction between philosophy and economics as to the nature of games. As noted above, within the realm of philosophy the most problematic aspects of games involve the rules that obtain. Within the world of economics it is instead the matter of strategies. In the construction of game theory the rules of the game are set by the formal relations taken from mathematics, making strategic considerations, and hence the behavior of economic agents, paramount.

As Marvin Shubik noted in his overview of the economic applications of game theory, one of the keys to its use was the notion that "dynamic phenomena" might be captured in "a static theory" through the use of "strategies" (Shubik 1982: 8–10). Or, as Ken Binmore has described the nature of a "Nash Equilibrium": "[It] is a strategy profile (one, possibly mixed, strategy for each player) that has the property that each player's strategy choice is an optimal response to the strategy choices of other players" (Binmore 1987: 189).

By contrast, there is greater flexibility and fluidity with regard to rule-making in philosophical circles, set against the challenges and controversies of comprehending context, meaning, and framework. For example, Saul Kripke grappled with Wittgenstein's claims about the nature of "language games" by writing a skeptical philosophical tract inquiring into what it means to "follow a rule," or even whether it is possible to do so, taking up the paradox presented in *The Philosophical Investigations* that "no course of action could be determined by a rule, because every course of action can be made to accord with the rule" (Kripke 1982: 7ff.). Setting himself apart from Kripke, Hilary Putnam has offered up a less stringent interpretation, seeing "attunement" as a less conscious or formal means of proceeding to act and comprehend in the world without necessarily following a rule. But a grappling with context remains: "[I]f anything is central to Wittgenstein's vision of language, it is that the meaning of our words does not determine the precise truth-evaluable content they have in particular contexts" (Putnam [2001] 2012b: 417)

Are there similar texts in economics, tackling the problematic aspects of rule formation in plumbing the philosophical foundations of economics?

Philip Mirowski's essay, cited above, delineated a broad typology of rules, applying it critically to any claims that game theory incorporated an institutionalist framework into a formal mathematical model. Mirowski, though, did not tackle the epistemological questions regarding the formation of rules or the means by which they might be followed. Otto Neurath's 1944 monograph entitled *Foundations of the Social Sciences* may have come closer to addressing such questions, with his emphasis upon the practice of the "systematized transfer of certain traditional institutions" in economic concept formation (Neurath 1944: 38). Neurath's characterization bears a close resemblance to the later Wittgenstein's "positive thesis," as depicted by Colin McGinn, as "grasp of a rule is mastery of a practice, the capacity to engage in a custom" (McGinn 1987: 122). However, Neurath's work appears to have gone virtually unnoticed among economists.

To the extent that concept formation is seen as a matter of words, it gives greater weight to the role of language, rooted in the inexorability of such concepts arising out of "language games," along the lines advanced by Wittgenstein. As E. Roy Weintraub has suggested for the central concept of equilibrium:

> Equilibrium is associated with a Wittgensteinian language game, and the meaning of the word is dependent on the players of the game and the rules they decide to play by at a particular moment in the history of economic thought.
>
> (Weintraub 1988: 154)

Weintraub's incorporation of the history of ideas into how the game is played provides a context for it, but it remains unclear if rule formation should be regarded as a matter of historical accident or the product of period-defining intellectual or ideological emphases? In either case such rule formation may fall prey to an "unreflected predisposition," as noted above.

In the 1990s Viktor Vanberg explored the relation between economic rules and choices, yet the methodological individualism he embraced may suffer from the fundamental failing ascribed by sceptics of rule-following to any private language isolated from outside experience, the crux of Wittgenstein's private language argument. Vanberg also drew strongly upon the work of Popper and Friedrich von Hayek in exploring the nature of "rule following," which he linked to a form of "evolutionary epistemology." Hayek in fact had referred to "man [as] a rule-following animal" (Vanberg 1998: 432). Here "the process of learning or knowledge acquisition and rule-following behavior" are viewed as "two sides of one coin" (Vanberg 1998: 433). The upshot of this approach is a form of adaptive psychology in which "all behavior concerns problem solving" (Vanberg 1998: 433). While rule-following is accorded a central role, the contextual difficulties raised by the private language argument, that is, what it means to follow a rule, or even Putnam's "attunements," are not directly addressed. Instead, such rules are assumed to follow an essentially internal process of rational adaptation.

Over the last two decades more has been done to tackle the matter of context, largely through a recognition of the need for narratives of some sort to supply meaning to the formal structure of the game-theoretic model, though there is the danger that narrative will somehow be conflated with context.

The necessity of incorporating stories or narratives into game theory has been taken up recently by Till Grune-Yanoff and Paul Schweinzer:

> To function as economic models, game theory has to represent real or hypothetical economic situations. A game structure is characterized only by formal properties. By itself, it does not connect in any way to an economic situation either real or imagined. To account for the use of games in economics, a game structure has to somehow acquire an interpretation. It has been proposed that formal models include a narrative that provides such an interpretation.
>
> (Grune-Yanoff and Schweinzer 2008: 133)

At the same time, Grune-Yanoff and Schweinzer emphasize the importance of what they call "theory proper" in game theory, in part to distinguish their understanding of the role of narrative in game theory from that of Mary Morgan:

> Game theory, even though it clearly operates with models, is also comprised of a sophisticated body of theoretical work, which cannot be accurately characterized as a set of models. Instead, this work betrays game theory's roots as a mathematical discipline.
>
> (Grune-Yanoff and Schweinzer 2008: 134)

Echoing Samuelson and the Bourbaki, they note: "The theory proper is empirically empty, because its forms do not have an interpretation" (Grune-Yanoff and Schweinzer 2008: 134). The construct they create establishes dual interactions across three foundational elements: theory proper, model, and world. One of these interactions links the "model narrative" with the "economic situation." This depiction thus advances significantly the notion that the narrative fits within, or is framed by, a broader context. A critical piece, nonetheless, is still missing. On what basis, or upon what criteria, does the narrative arise out of this broader context? In literary terms, what subtext informs the narrative and underlies the "construction" of the economic situation, as the latter cannot be construed as a compilation or amalgam of "economic facts," devoid of meaning?

Finally, it was Mary Morgan's extensive examination of the role of narrative in economic game theory, including her dissection of the prisoner's dilemma as an economic game, which has brought the subject of the relation between narrative and economic model to the fore.

In her recent *The World in the Model* (2012), Morgan's aim appears to be twofold: on the one hand, she wants to establish a larger place for interpretation in the construction and especially the use of game theory in economics, in particular, that games as presented mark out situations, and that these situations represent narratives, though generally unstated; on the other, she seeks to demonstrate the inconvenient conclusion of the prisoner's dilemma game for neoclassical economics, namely the inconsistency between individual self-interest and a less-than-optimal collective equilibrium outcome (Morgan 2012: 344–76).

Morgan's reference to the necessity of identifying the economic narrative in various economic situations seems right in seeking to meld the puzzle of the game with the economic problem – or situation – of the world (Morgan 2012: 361–3), but it remains insufficient. For one, what constitutes a narrative? Is it specific to specific and varying situations, so that different narratives apply to what have traditionally been described as "market structures"? In this regard Morgan invokes the work of Franklin Fisher to convey the possibility of the variability and hence variety of economic situations (Morgan 2012: 370–2). Or, are there overarching narratives that inform a whole array of situations, such as one might see in an evocation of the "invisible hand" as the lodestar of economic activity, which she extracts as one – challenged– strand of the prisoner's dilemma game? Here one might think in terms of subtexts that arise out of different historical contexts. Morgan does not appear to pursue this line of questioning; rather, she deems the "story" as the base against which "typical" situations conform, if not perfectly, and the model is constructed thereby. But there is a story to be told of such stories, suggesting a further set of steps to be taken: from whence do narratives come, and what may be discerned from their structure and historical roots, as well as the method by which they are selected? Moreover, there is the potential for the translation of narratives into puzzles to be an act of serious deformation beyond the imperfections noted by Morgan. Accordingly, the gap between puzzle and problem has yet to be bridged fully.

## References

Aumann, Robert (1989) "Game Theory." In John Eatwell, Murray Milgate, and Peter Newman (eds), *The New Palgrave: Game Theory*. Basingstoke: Macmillan.

Baker, G. P. and Hacker, P. M. S. (1985) *Wittgenstein: Rules, Grammar and Necessity*. Oxford: Basil Blackwell.

Binmore, Ken (1987) "Modeling Rational Players: Part I." *Economics and Philosophy*, 3(2): 179–214.

Bloor, David (1997) *Wittgenstein, Rules and Institutions*. London: Routledge.

Bourbaki, Nicolas (1950) "The Architecture of Mathematics." *American Mathematical Monthly*, 57(4): 221–232.

Cartwright, Nancy (2005) "The Vanity of Rigour in Economics: Theoretical Models and Galilean Experiments." In Philippe Fontaine and Robert Leonard (eds), *The Experiment in the History of Economics*. London: Routledge, pp. 135–153.

Collomb, Bertrand (2011) "La nécessaire ambition scientifique de l'économie." In *L'Economie, une science qui nous gouverne?* Actes Sud/IHEST, pp. 15–27.

Edmonds, David and Eidinow, John (2001) *Wittgenstein's Poker*. London: Faber & Faber.

Grune-Yanoff, Till and Schweinzer, Paul (2008) "The Role of Stories in Applying Game Theory." *Journal of Economic Methodology*, 15(2): 131–146.

Hacker, P. M. S. (2010) "Meaning and Use." In Daniel Whiting (ed.), *The Later Wittgenstein on Language*. Basingstoke: Palgrave Macmillan, pp. 26–44.

Hoover, Kevin D. (2006) "Doctor Keynes: Economic Theory in a Diagnostic Science." In Roger E. Backhouse and Bradley W. Bateman (eds), *The Cambridge Companion to Keynes*. Cambridge: Cambridge University Press, pp. 78–97.

Keynes, John Maynard [1921] (1963) *A Treatise on Probability*. London: Macmillan.

Keynes, John Maynard (1937) "The General Theory of Employment." *Quarterly Journal of Economics*, 51(February): 209–223.

Korner, Stephan [1960] (2009) *The Philosophy of Mathematics*. Mineola, NY: Dover.

Krebs, David (1989) "Nash Equilibrium." In John Eatwell, Murray Milgate, and Peter Newman (eds), *The New Palgrave: Game Theory*. Basingstoke: Palgrave Macmillan.

Kripke, Saul (1982) *Wittgenstein on Rules and Private Language*. Cambridge, MA: Harvard University Press.

Kuhn, Harold and Tucker, A. W. (1958) "John von Neumann's Work on the Theory of Games and Mathematical Economics." *Bulletin of the American Mathematical Society*, 64(3), pt. 2: 100–122.

Leonard, Robert (1994) "Reading Cournot, Reading Nash: The Creation and Stabilization of the Nash Equilibrium." *Economic Journal*, 104(424): 492–511.

Leonard, Robert (1995) "From Parlor Games to Social Science: von Neumann, Morgenstern, and the Creation of Game Theory, 1928–1944." *Journal of Economic Literature*, 33(2) (June): 730–761.

Leonard, Robert (2010) *Von Neumann, Morgenstern, and the Creation of Game Theory*. Cambridge: Cambridge University Press.

McGinn, Colin (1987) *Wittgenstein on Meaning*. Oxford: Basil Blackwell.

Menger, Karl [1934] (1979) "The Role of Uncertainty in Economics," with updated notes and revisions, in *Selected Papers in Logic and Foundations, Didactics, Economics*. Dordrecht: Reidel, pp. 259–278.

Mirowski, Philip (1986) "Institutions as a Solution Concept in a Game Theory Context." In Philip Mirowski (ed.), *The Reconstruction of Economic Theory*. Boston: Kluwer-Nijhoff, pp. 241–263.

Morgan, Mary S. (2012) *The World in the Model: How Economists Work and Think*. Cambridge: Cambridge University Press.

Nash, John (1950) "The Bargaining Problem." *Econometrica*, 18: 155–162.

Nash, John (1951) "Non-cooperative Games." *Annals of Mathematics*, 54(2): 286–295.

Neurath, Otto (1944) *Foundations of the Social Sciences*. Chicago: University of Chicago Press.

Putnam, Hilary [2001] (2012a) "Was Wittgenstein Really an Antirealist about Mathematics?." In Hilary Putnam, *Philosophy in an Age of Science*. Cambridge, MA: Harvard University Press, pp. 355–403.

Putnam, Hilary [2001] (2012b) "Rules, Attunement, and 'Applying Words to the World': The Struggle to Understand Wittgenstein's Vision of Language." In Hilary Putnam, *Philosophy in an Age of Science*. Cambridge, MA: Harvard University Press, pp. 404–420.

Rapoport, Anatol (1989) "Prisoner's Dilemma." In John Eatwell, Murray Milgate, and Peter Newman, *The New Palgrave: Game Theory*. Basingstoke: Macmillan Reference.

Rubinstein, Ariel (2000) "On the Rhetoric of Game Theory." In *The Economics and Language: Five Essays.* New York: Cambridge University Press, pp. 71–90.

Samuelson, Paul (1998) "How Foundations Came to Be." *Journal of Economic Literature* 36(3): 1375–1386.

Shubik, Marvin (1982) *Game Theory in the Social Sciences: Concepts and Solutions.* Cambridge, MA: MIT Press.

Sutton, John (1990) "Explaining Everything, Explaining Nothing?" *European Economic Review,* 34: 505–512.

Szpiro, George (2007) *Poincare's Prize: The Hundred-Year Quest to Solve One of Math's Greatest Puzzles.* New York: Penguin.

Turk, Michael (2006) "The Fault Line of Axiomatization: Walras' Linkage of Physics with Economics." *European Journal of the History of Economic Thought,* 13(2): 195–212.

Turk, Michael (2012) "The Mathematical Turn in Economics: Walras, the French Mathematicians, and the Road Not Taken." *Journal of the History of Economic Thought,* 34(2): 149–167.

Vanberg, Viktor J. (1998) "Rule Following." In John B. Davis,D. Wade Hands, and Uskali Maki (eds), *The Handbook of Economic Methodology.* Cheltenham, UK: Edward Elgar, pp. 432–435.

Veblen, Thorstein [1919] (1990) *The Place of Science in Modern Civilization*, with new introduction by Warren Samuels. New Brunswick, NJ: Transaction.

Weintraub, E. Roy (1988) "On the Brittleness of the Orange Equilibrium." In Arjo Klamer, Donald N. McCloskey, and Robert M. Solow (eds), *The Consequences of Economic Rhetoric.*Cambridge: Cambridge University Press.

Weintraub, E.Roy (2002) *How Economics Became a Mathematical Science.* Durham, NC: Duke University Press.

## Newspaper article

"Albert W. Tucker, famed mathematician," *Philadelphia Inquirer*, February 2, 1995: B7 (reporter: S. Joseph Hagenmayer).

# 5 Economics pursuing the mold of evolutionary biology

## "Accident" and "necessity" in the quest to make economics scientific

### Introduction

What makes economics scientific? For that matter, should economics, a discipline in the social sciences, be comprehended as a science akin to astronomy, biology, chemistry, or physics? This is a matter of some contention, as economics has long held out claims to having, or at least of aspiring to have, the form and rigor of the natural or physical sciences. To some degree a change in nomenclature captures this tension, as the study of "political economy," as the discipline was originally called, became the "science of economics" in the latter part of the nineteenth century. It was during this period that various groups of economists in England, France, Switzerland, and Austria known as the marginalists engaged in a rethinking of economics which led to the emergence of what came to be known as neoclassical economics and, over time, its increasingly mathematized and often highly abstracted treatment.

This quest to be scientific did not come without complications. The countervailing view of economics as fundamentally a social science, emphasizing the role of institutions, human agency, historical experience, or the interactive nature of human behavior in economic affairs, where the interpretation of events may itself influence the actions that follow, did not vanish. More often than not, advocates of this approach have been dissenters from the mainstream of economic thought over the last century, and they have spanned the range of ideological perspectives, bracketing the neoclassical mainstream from the left and the right.

Nor was the appropriate form, or even the measure of rigor, for a scientific economics clearly settled – or readily comprehended. For example, did the mathematization of economics offer up only the appearance of rigor, without necessarily establishing the substance or structure of a suitably scientific discipline? Moreover, if economics was to be understood as bearing some kinship with or resemblance to a "hard" natural science, which such science would best serve as the model?

It is this last question that brings into focus attempts that have been made to fit economics into the mound of evolutionary biology. At the outset there is a certain irony here, since if economics has borrowed from evolutionary biology, the reverse is also the case. One need look no farther than Charles Darwin's *Autobiography* to note the source cited as the origin of his idea of selective evolution arising from a struggle for survival that was won by those best adapted to do so, namely Thomas Malthus" *Essay on Population*, an immensely popular and influential, if also draconian and chilling work of political economy, first published in 1797:

> In October 1838, that is, fifteen months after I had begun my systematic enquiry, I happened to read for amusement Malthus on *Population*, and being well prepared to appreciate the struggle for existence which every-where goes on from long-continued observation of the habits of animals and plants, it at once struck me that under those circumstances favour-able variations would tend to be preserved, and unfavourable ones to be destroyed. The result of this would be the formation of new species. Here, then, I had at last got a theory by which to work.
>
> (Darwin 2005: 98–9)

Nor should any facile association of economic considerations with evolution be deemed sufficient to establish a solid, substantive link between economics and evolutionary biology. As the economist Kenneth Arrow cautioned twenty years ago, while contemplating the possibility of better results in economic theorizing: "The analogy between evolution and technological progress has been almost a commonplace since the time of Darwin … but has in fact not led to much" (Anderson, Arrow, and Pines 1988: 280).

## The "nomothetic paradox" in economics

An exploration of the basis for a possible fit of economics with evolutionary biology, as well as the limitations attendant upon that effort, requires a pre-liminary inquiry into the ways that economics might be seen as conforming to a structure, framework, or set of expectations generally associated with scientific disciplines, or as falling short in this regard.

The place to begin is in the realm of methodology. To a considerably extent the scientific claims of economics rest upon what might be termed its "nomo-thetic paradox." The tension between the nomothetic and the idiographic was derived from late nineteenth-century German idealist philosophy, primarily the work of neo-Kantians like Heinrich Rickert and Wilhelm Windelband, though the use of these two descriptives to sort out the scientific claims of eco-nomics was promoted only decades later by the Austrian-American economist Fritz Machlup, in articles with titles like, "The Inferiority Complex of the Social Sciences" and "Are the Social Sciences Really Inferior?"

Rickert and Windelband distinguished among intellectual fields of inquiry by positing an essential difference between universal rule-making or law-giving, characteristic of the nomothetic sciences, and individual fact gathering, the mark of idiographic disciplines. In Windelband's terms it was a distinction between sciences based upon laws, generally speaking the natural or physical sciences, and those built out of events, the human sciences. As a philosophical inquiry it had been prompted by concerns about the solidity of the foundations for all the "human sciences," informed as they are by human activity, interaction, and construction. For most of those engaged in this inquiry, economics, like history and political science, most likely belonged together as human sciences, though there was no unanimity on the subject.

However, a much sharper distinction between the generalizing quality of abstract principles and the more individuated amassing of facts figured centrally in the *Methodenstreit*, or "quarrel over method," waged between the Austrian economist Carl Menger and the German economist Gustav Schmoller in the early 1880s. By and large, Menger, one of the leading marginalists noted above, prevailed: economics as a science was conceived of as built upon deduced universal principles, and the power to abstract was embraced as essential to the method of economics. But this presented a paradox, for it meant that to be scientific economics would have to be decoupled from historical narrative and the daily economic affairs of humankind, from which it originally sprang, whether it be the accounts of British commerce or French agriculture that both formed and informed the first major writings in political economy.

How satisfactory was this result? And, if economics was to be regarded as essentially nomothetic, how were its laws to be determined? In particular, what place did individual facts and societal events have in establishing or confirming these economic laws? Further, what kind of laws were these? Were they inevitable and inexorable, like the law of gravitational attraction, or more on the order of universally recurring patterns, likely tendencies that might be discerned?

The assertion of the nomothetic character of economics led to an alignment of economics with classical physics, which was taken as the paradigmatic science of law-making. For economists so inclined this meant consciously emulating the achievement of Isaac Newton in classical physics in reducing the multiplicity of the actions and movements of all objects, both at close range as well as at astronomical distances, to the simplicity and great explanatory power of a few laws of motion with universal application. And while the lure of Newton had attracted economists from the earliest days of political economy, drawing in such diverse figures as Adam Smith and Karl Marx, it was especially strong in the period when economics came to be conceived of as a science. Among the marginalists perhaps no one was a more ardent champion of a linkage between economics and physics than the French-Swiss economist, Leon Walras, who envisioned an economics as structured by analogy with classical mechanics, but with its own – corresponding – fundamental principles and elementary elements. He espoused the use of mathematics in economics, which would make possible the resolution of markets by solving equations where the only critical variables were prices for and quantities of goods produced. While Walras' attempt to establish a general equilibrium across an economy on that basis has been widely critiqued, the turn to classical physics as a model for economics entered the mainstream of economic thought, and has remained there (Turk 2006).

## A possible model in biology

Even as this alignment of economics with physics took center stage in economic thought, though, there were alternatives posed by economists who still sought a suitable model to enhance the scientific legitimacy of economics through a correspondence of some sort with a broadly accepted scientific discipline, but had doubts about the aptness of the analogy of economics to physics. In particular, these economists tended to look toward biology as a model. One might in fact note that a biological model, specifically the flow of blood through the body, inspired the French Physiocrat, François Quesnay, a political economist, administrator, and court physician to Louis XV, in his adumbration of the circular flow of goods in the national economy, found in his *Tableau économique*. Quesnay's construction is now widely regarded as the first substantial effort at system-building in economics.

But it is with the emergence of evolutionary biology that the countervailing approach to align economics with biology took hold. The first step in this regard took place with the recognition of a kinship between economics and biology as both being subjects of complexity. The British economist Alfred Marshall, who was active in the late nineteenth and early twentieth century, is often seen as the first major figure in the era of the science of economics who favored a correspondence between economics and biology. Marshall is credited with adapting marginalist economics into the broader synthesis of neoclassical economics, and his textbook, *Principles of Economics*, shaped the general contours of microeconomics, as well as the graphical and mathematical techniques used in its analysis. These techniques clearly contributed to the comprehending of economics as akin to classical mechanics, a point acknowledged by Marshall himself.

Yet at the same time Marshall stated plainly in the *Principles* that economics more nearly resembled biology than mechanics, on at least two counts. First of all, economics, like biology, was concerned with living things; this immediately set it apart from physics. Second, the multiplicity of human activities could not ultimately be reduced to a few universal principles. Instead, economics was a subject whose phenomena and variables reflected the diversity of actions of living beings.

As Marshall noted in the *Principles of Economics*:

> [T]here are many [economic laws] which may rank with the secondary laws of those natural sciences, which resemble economics in dealing with the complex action of many heterogeneous and uncertain causes. The laws of biology, for instance.
>
> (Marshall 1898: 104)

Moreover, even if not stated, this also implied that economic phenomena might well be better comprehended as acting within a system.

Over the course of the twentieth century philosophical disquisitions about the nature of biology, whether by philosophers of science or evolutionary biologists, emphasized the central place of complexity in the framework of biology as a science. Thus herein lay a possible linkage between economics and biology.

A second strand in the thread tying economics to evolutionary biology can be found in the work of Marshall's contemporary and critic, the American economist Thorstein Veblen. Veblen faulted neoclassical economics for failing to take up the scientific challenge posed by Darwin's theory of evolution. Veblen saw himself, and was seen by others, as a "Darwinian" among economists. He felt that the universal principles enunciated by economists, classical or neoclassical, produced a self-contained and self-fulfilling system out of touch with the experience of everyday life, and effectively prevented economics from claiming the mantle of science. Instead, Veblen envisioned a far more dynamic approach to economics, where social and cultural phenomena were integrated into the depiction and analysis of economic life and where, crucially, changes in economic life took place as adaptations of current mores and practices, producing an evolution of economic experience over time. Veblen's critique of the failure of economics to comprehend evolutionary change and development was presented forcefully in a 1919 paper entitled, "Why Is Economics Not an Evolutionary Science?"

Veblen, and similarly minded economists, constituted a school of economic thought known as Institutionalism, which flourished in the United States in the first decades of the twentieth century. They dissented from the mainstream of economic thought in that period, often challenging the complacency of neoclassical economists in accepting the economic status quo, and evoked a general theme: changes in economies occur on a cumulative basis, as economies evolve over time.

As a school Institutionalism helped spawn an interest in and the development of an "evolutionary economics" for which dynamic processes, institutional changes, and cumulative effects were seen as inextricably linked. In recent decades this approach has to some degree taken on a more conservative cast, in line with a "new Institutionalism" largely reconciled to the virtues of the status quo.

A further variant upon the notion of an "evolutionary economics" took hold in the latter part of the twentieth century, influenced by the thinking of the heterodox economist Kenneth Boulding. In this instance the tack taken was fundamentally ecological, as economies were viewed as eco-systems, where, according to Boulding, "[e]ach economy is then seen as a segment of the larger evolutionary process of the universe in space and time" (Boulding 1991: p. 10). At this stage it is apparent that a more general idea of evolution, with only a tangential connection to evolutionary biology, informed this infusing of economics into the totality of the environment.

Overall, the notion of "cumulative change" constituted another possible point of contact between economics and evolutionary biology. For both these economists and evolutionary biologists the concerns were similar: how might one explain how changes, whether economic or biological, take place over time, and then how might one demonstrate, establish, or posit the connectedness of such changes through a process of adaptation. For economics this reintroduced the problem of reintegrating history into economic analysis.

In general terms, the effort to align economics more closely with evolutionary biology has drawn strength from the notion that both fields of inquiry might be viewed as relying more upon concepts than laws, Marshall's ready and expansive use of the term "law" across disciplines notwithstanding. The physicist and science popularizer Alan Lightman has provided a neat formulation for distinguishing how biologists think about science as opposed to physicists: while the former emphasizes concepts and complexity, the latter is built upon laws and simplicity.

"Physicists make simplifications and idealizations and abstractions until the final problem is so simple that it can be solved by a mathematical law ... Biologists think differently... [B]iology deals with living things, [a]nd life requires the interaction between elements in a system. Thus, biology usually deals with *systems*" (Lightman 2005: xii).

Lightman goes on to say:

> Where physics might ponder the electrical force between two electrons, biology would be concerned with how the electrical charges on both sides of a cell membrane regulate the passage of substances across the membrane and thus connect the cell to the rest of the organism. Roughly speaking, physics has laws, while biology has concepts.
>
> (Lightman 2005: xiii)

Hence, to place economics more directly in league with biology requires a rethinking, even a reconstruction, of economic laws by replacing them with economic concepts, but nonetheless derived from the same experiences and constructions as those economic laws.

This process would entail treating "equilibrium" and "maximization" as central concepts in economics, rather than as mathematically reached physical states, say as the result of constrained optimization, that reflected the resolution of economic forces obtained through the most efficient use of resources, as one might balance a lever. Equilibrium might then be regarded as a temporal state, of unstated duration, while maximization would be taken to be the most efficacious form of adaptation. In that form both equilibrium and maximization could readily be understood as corresponding to similar notions in evolutionary biology. One might, for example, see a parallel between the "punctuated equilibrium" of evolutionary biology, where a seeming stability in biological states holds for a considerable period of time, and the apparently smooth and uninterrupted growth of an economy, only for both to suddenly undergo rapid and transforming changes, the bases for which lay in more gradual, barely perceived events.

## The parallel provided by "accident" and "necessity"

There is another possible source of alignment of economics with evolutionary biology that can be found in their methodologies, which I believe is a more fundamental way of grasping the formative elements linking the two disciplines. This approach opens the way to establishing a more specific correspondence between the construction of the two disciplines rooted in the parallel between "accident" (or "chance") and "necessity" in evolutionary biology and the idiographic and the nomothetic in economics. Thus this correspondence would be formed from their natures as disciplines, and requires a discerning of the evolutionary mechanism in both.

In *Chance and Necessity*, first published in 1971, Jacques Monod recounted the broad implications of his research into the nature of the regulation of gene expression and through it the basis for evolutionary change in biology. Monod identified an evolutionary interplay between accidents, individual and effectively random events, which might produce genetic variations in biological development, and a more generally determined and adaptive means of selection that would lead to the permanent inclusion of those variations that would advance the species. Hence, the randomness of the particular was linked to an adaptive mechanism that acted in accordance with general principles.

Monod described the interplay of chance and necessity as the essence of the process of evolution:

> The initial elementary events which open the way to evolution in the intensely conservative systems called living beings are microscopic, fortuitous, and utterly without relation to whatever may be their effects upon teleonomic functioning.
>
> (Monod 1971: 118)

He then noted the "translation" of accident into necessity:

> But once incorporated in the DNA structure, the accident – essentially unpredictable because always singular – will be mechanically and faithfully replicated and translated ... Drawn out of the realm of pure chance, the accident enters into that of necessity, of the most implacable certainties. For natural selection operates at the macroscopic level, the level of organisms.
>
> (Monod 1971: 118)

In the last several decades of the twentieth century, nearly contemporaneous with the publication of Monod's work, a number of younger economists, like Brian Arthur, Paul David, and Paul Krugman, were grappling with the significance of scale effects, loosely speaking of the gains achieved by the concentration of economic activity and their impact upon the way that economies changed over time. The stakes involved in these inquiries were high. If scale or other concentrating effects, sometimes known as agglomeration effects, proved to be essential to the actual changing configuration of economic activity by region or country, over time, then the dominant model of purely competitive economic arrangements, abstracted from all historical experience and contexts, faced a serious challenge. It would mean that economics in time, that is, seen as occurring in a historical evolution would turn out to be largely a story of imperfect competition, with less than fully competitive markets playing the larger role.

Each of these economists drew upon the notion of a critical interplay between chance events and the general principles embodied in the laws governing economic activity, hence presenting at least implicitly a parallel with Monod's vision of an evolutionary interplay between chance and necessity in biology.

Indeed, one might see the appeal of this interplay of accident and necessity to both evolutionary biologists and historically minded economists presaged in Windelband's characterization of an ambiguous status for biology, posed somewhere between the nomothetic and the idographic, in light of evolution, which introduced events and historical time into the study of a natural science. Moreover, Windelband's depiction was effectively echoed a century later by Ernst Mayr:

> When a biologist tries to answer a question about a unique occurrence … he cannot rely on universal laws … [Instead] he constructs a historical narrative.
>
> (Mayr 1997: 64)

It is a similar matter ultimately driving the inquiry of these economists: how to set an economics based upon a science of general rules in real or historical time.

Nonetheless, there are differences in the focus of the three economists. In works like *The Spatial Economy* Paul Krugman was concerned with the nature of the spatial or geographic specialization of economic activity the resultant clustering of industry by region and patterns of international trade. Krugman identified the likely bifurcation of economic activity, say, between more heavily concentrated manufacturing regions and largely agricultural areas, on the basis of tipping points reached because of locational differentials in resources, price levels, or wages that had existed at an earlier time, or because of a set of initiating conditions or events that reinforced over time the advantages accruing to a certain region. Krugman referred to these events as the "accidents of history."

Arthur and David explored the connectedness of previous technological choices as events establishing the actual subsequent pathway of technological change and development. These pathways might inform a narrative of economic history, making sense of the past economic experience of the United States or various European economies, or be presented as a theoretical construct. For his part, Arthur emphasized the concept of technological "lock-in," where earlier events and decisions set a fairly rigid path for future development. David famously proffered the QWERTY thesis, whereby a combination of economic and historical circumstances led to the adoption, standard use, and long-term dominance of a particular typewriter keyboard, even in the face of technologically superior versions. Here economic change could be tracked along a pathway of adaptations constrained by previous events, though one might also conceive of the constellation of circumstances as a system or context within which technological changes are situated and interpreted.

There are also some significant differences in conceptualization among these three economists, even as they all sought to create an economics that was both historically minded and scientific in character or operation. Krugman stressed the importance of initial conditions as the accidents of history upon which economic forces, cast by analogy in physical terms as either centripetal or centrifugal, then act. This leads to a cumulative process, which may also be understood as an evolution that is ultimately a matter of distribution and configuration: to what extent does economic activity become concentrated or broadly dispersed? It would be a mistake to conceive of this approach as laying out a path, as Krugman has consciously constructed his spatial model on the basis of thresholds or tipping points.

By contrast, both David and Arthur do establish path dependence as central to their constructs of economic change occurring in time. For both a critical distinction exists between states of equilibrium and disequilibria, and it is with regard to the latter that positive externalities, in David's terms, or agglomeration effects, in Arthur's terms, are associated with economic changes unfolding in time. Path dependence is advanced through the instability – or uni-directedness – produced by events at each stage or step.

Such path dependence was analogized with physical states as they were described and categorized in thermodynamics. They applied the notion of ergodicity, derived from Boltzmann's hypothesis about an independent pathway of motion of gases for which past states were of no causal consequence, to two different sets of economic affairs. In the one that was ergodic, time – and certainly historical time – played no part; these produced a static equilibrium, consistent with neoclassical rules regarding the efficient allocation of resources. In the other, which was nonergodic, historical time held an essential part, for dynamic processes were at work, shaped by concentrating factors and effects of one sort or another.

### Arthur and Monod

In many ways Brian Arthur shows the closest – and deepest – affinity with Monod, and this is not altogether coincidental. While Arthur's work can be understood in one sense as a blending of economics with engineering in his pursuit of a mathematically based and scientifically sound model, his thinking on the subject of economics has been very much shaped by his reading of disparate and diverse writers from different fields, making for a substantially more heterodox outlook about the workings of economics. In the late 1970s Arthur was struck in particular by new ideas emerging from biology and their possible application to economic theorizing. His introduction to these new ideas came first from Horace Judson Freeland's *The Eighth Day of Creation*, which was published in 1979. This led Arthur to Jacques Monod's *Chance and Necessity*, which he himself described as formative to his thinking.

Economists like Arthur favored comprehending economics as a subject of "complexity," an approach advanced significantly by a multidisciplinary and cross-disciplinary institute, the Santa Fe Institute, among whose leading thinkers included the economist Kenneth Arrow and Arthur himself. They have tended therefore to look at least as much towards biology as physics as the source of a scientific model or set of correspondences. Thus, I think it is fair to say that Arthur was attracted to the pair of "accident" or "chance" with "necessity" at least in part because it came from the natural, but not the physical sciences.

Drawing upon the dichotomous pairing of chance and necessity, Arthur clearly set as foundational the distinction between the "accidental" as historical and the "necessary" as economic. Arthur called the accidents of history "small events," by which he was referring to choices among technologies. The necessity of economic laws refers to the rules governing economic agglomeration, like increasing returns to scale, where the magnification of inputs into production leads to an even greater magnification of output produced.

The process Arthur described was essentially evolutionary. In a seminal paper on "competing technologies, increasing returns, and lock-in," Arthur wrote: "Under increasing returns however, static analysis is no longer enough. Multiple outcome are possible, and to understand how one outcome is selected we need to follow step by step the process by which small events cumulate to cause the system to gravitate toward that outcome rather than the others" (Arthur 1994b: 28).

From Arthur's perspective increasing returns have certain salient characteristics:

> To the list of already known increasing-returns properties like potential inefficiency and nonpredictability, a dynamic approach adds two new ones: inflexibility, in that allocations gradually rigidify, or lock-in, in structure; and nonergodicity, in that small events early on may decide the larger course of structural change. The dynamics thus take on an evolutionary flavor, with a "founder effect" akin to that of genetics.
>
> (Arthur 1994b: 28)

There are two fundamentally complementary options: one in which the static analysis of equilibria holds; the other in which dynamic processes, shaped by agglomeration effects or other concentrating factors, like increasing returns, hold sway. Here "accidental historical order of choice," "geographical attractiveness" (Arthur 1994c: 51), and economic rules combine to establish the direction, or what Arthur calls the "course of structural change," owing to technology, that is seen as the economic counterpart of speciation.

Arthur acknowledges that the dichotomy presented by static situations, which are set in isolation, and dynamic processes, which evolve over time and – critically, from the perspective of economic theorizing – in time, that is, within the framework of historical experience and events, leads to two quite different conclusions:

> Our analysis of the validity of the historical-dependence viewpoint does not imply that the conventional viewpoint, the unique-equilibrium state one, is wrong. The two Weltanschauungen are complementary. The validity of each depends on the degree to which agglomeration economies are present or absent.
>
> (Arthur 1994c: 28)

## The flaw in the analogy

But does the correspondence with evolutionary biology, as sought by Arthur, actually work? Monod's necessity is that of a certain purposefulness of evolution itself: accidents that matter are those which advance the species, while those which do not remain inconsequential. Monod saw the mechanism of natural selection as progressive and purposeful by dint of its teleology, embodied in the "teleonomic apparatus." According to Monod "[i]t is the teleonomic apparatus ... that lays down the essential *initial conditions* for the admission, temporary or permanent, or rejection of the chance-bred innovative attempt" (Monod 1971: 119–20).

Further, "[i]t is teleonomic performance, the aggregate expression of the properties of the network of constructive and regulatory interactions, that is judged by selection" (Monod 1971: p. 120).

Thus, in the language of evolutionary biology advanced by Jacques Monod and his colleague François Jacob in the 1950s and 1960s, it was the "teleonomic apparatus" that served as the mechanism linking the accidental event to the necessary and general rule. From a more contemporary perspective one might think of it in terms of establishing the "fitness" of any possible variation. As Jacob noted in his own popular account of the nature and implications of evolutionary biology, *The Logic of Life*, this introduces a teleology into evolutionary biology (Jacob 1973: 8–9). Without such a teleology it would be necessary to adopt an instrumental hypothesis and assume that the results themselves demonstrate the fitness of the variations that were incorporated into the species.

Is there, then, a similar sorting out in economics, whether conceived of as a "teleonomic apparatus" or not, whereby historical, that is, "small-event" accidents, will either initiate a new economic pathway, or not? One might think of the possibility of an overarching economic efficiency as a grand rule, operating thereby as an evolutionary principle within economics itself. Yet economic rules do not express an inner, driving logic of their own; even when touted as universal, that is, without any limitation of time or place, they are applied to the situation at hand, typically on an ad hoc basis.

Elias Khalil, who has taken a strong interest in the philosophical under-pinnings of the idea of economic complexity, has argued that the "[economic process] is about the production of goods by purposeful activity" (Khalil 1990: 164); in effect, contending that a teleology along the lines suggested by Monod does obtain in economics. But Khalil then goes on to limit the scope of such a teleology by distinguishing the purposefulness of economic organi-zation from economic structures, like the business cycle. These latter "are unintended results of acting efficiently" as "response[s] to or ... anticipation[s] of" (Khalil 1994: 191) whatever such productive activity, or even the possibi-lities of such activities, might offer. Moreover, the persistence of the business cycle itself, with its turns towards vicious circles of decline through panics and recessions, as well as towards virtuous circles of growth and prosperity, is a signal of the inability of economies to proceed along an economic path in which the better outcome is always pursued and successfully attained.

What Arthur has done is graft Monod's dichotomy into the longstanding distinction between the nomological and the idiographic, substituting "necessity" for the former and "accident" for the latter; while at the same time seeking to establish the interrelation between the two. That may be one of Arthur's central insights and innovations for his work in economics, even though it follows from a flawed correspondence, as it lacks the critical element, akin to the "teleonomic apparatus," that would bridge the idiographic and the nomological by translating one into the other.

It is the case that in general the advocates for treating economics as a subject of complexity have met with mixed results in grafting this notion from evolutionary biology, and this includes many of those who have participated with Arthur in workshops at the Santa Fe Institute. Writing in *The Quark and the Jaguar*, first published in 1994, the physicist Murray Gell-Mann, who was also one of the collaborators in the Santa Fe Institute, offered up at best a tentative assessment of its success (Gell-Mann 1994: 320–4). Gell-Mann's description of the scope of the economics initiative at the institute is telling:

> a number of scholars ... have directed their efforts toward studying economies as evolving complex adaptive systems composed of adaptive economic agents endowed only with bounded rationality, possessing imperfect information, and acting on the basis of chance as well as perceived self-interest.
>
> (Gell-Mann 1994: 322)

The framework Gell-Mann sets forth is highly abstracted: if it is intended to allow for the depiction of, or an explanation for, economies evolving, it appears to be divorced from any historical experience, or history itself. It would produce a paradox of a new sort in economics: a nomothetic system that describes evolutionary processes out of historical time. Nor does it address the central concerns raised in the work of Krugman, David, or even Arthur in trying to mesh economic rules with historical experience.

Moreover, as a final note, often it has been matters of finance, especially in the estimation of stock options or the workings of financial markets, that have been deemed most suitable for treatment as subjects of complexity. Here the notion of a random walk is often invoked. In fact, there is a long history of such exploration, dating back more than a century, to the use of a model of dissipative motion like Brownian motion to track the movement of stock prices, preceding even the pathbreaking examination of Brownian motion in physics at the beginning of the twentieth century.

But, as the reference to the business cycle, noted above, shows, this approach has not extended to broader models capturing the pertinent elements in the workings of the economy as a whole. It thus leaves open to further question the significance and consequences of the fault line in economics between microeconomics, with its modeling of the behavior of individual economic agents through a set of basic postulates, and macroeconomics, where abstract models about the overall state of the economy share the stage with statistical characterizations and economic history. This presents yet another gap in the analogy drawn between economics and evolutionary biology, for Monod saw the link between chance and necessity as also bridging a parallel pairing in biology of the microscopic and the macroscopic. In the world of economics, though, notwithstanding all the efforts undertaken to establish the microfoundations of macroeconomics, no neat or seamless interweaving of the two has been effected.

## References

Anderson, Philip W., Arrow, Kenneth J., and Pines, David (eds) (1988) *The Economy as an Evolving Complex System*. Redwood City, CA: Addison-Wesley.

Arthur, W. Brian (1994a) *Increasing Returns and Path Dependence in the Economy*. Ann Arbor: University of Michigan Press.

Arthur, W. Brian (1994b) "Competing Technologies, Increasing Returns and Lock-in by Historical Events." In W. Brian Arthur,*Increasing Returns and Path Dependence in the Economy*. Ann Arbor: University of Michigan Press.

Arthur, W. Brian (1994c) "Industry Location Patterns and the Importance of History." In W. Brian Arthur,*Increasing Returns and Path Dependence in the Economy*. Ann Arbor: University of Michigan Press, pp. 49–67.

Boulding, Kenneth (1991) "What Is Evolutionary Economics?" *Journal of Evolutionary Economics*, 1(1): 9–17.

Darwin, Charles (2005) [1958] *The Autobiography of Charles Darwin, 1809–1882*, ed. Nora Barlow. London: Norton.

David, Paul (1985) "Clio and the Economics of QWERTY." *American Economic Review*, 75(2): 332–337.

David, Paul (1997) "Path Dependence and the Quest for Historical Economic." *Discussion Papers in Economic and Social History*, no. 20. University of Oxford.

Delorme, R. and G. Hodgson (2005) "Complexity and the Economy: An Interview with W. Brian Arthur." In J. Finch and M. Orillard (eds), *Complexity and the Economy*. Cheltenham, UK: Edward Elgar, pp. 17–32.

Fujita, Masahisa,Krugman, Paul, and Venables, Anthony J. (1999) *The Spatial Economy*. Cambridge, MA: MIT Press.

Gell-Mann, Murray (1994) *The Quark and the Jaguar*. New York: Holt.

Jacob, François (1973) *The Logic of Life*, trans. Betty E. Spillman.New York: Pantheon.

Khalil, Elias (1990) "Entropy Law and Exhaustion of Natural Resources: Is Nicholas Georgescu-Roegen's Paradigm Defensible?" *Ecological Economics*, 2(2): 163–178.

Khalil, Elias (1994) "Entropy and Economics." In *The Elgar Companion to Institutional and Evolutionary Economics A–K*. Aldershot, UK: Edward Elgar, pp.186–193.

Krugman, Paul (1991a) "Increasing Returns and Economic Geography." *Journal of Political Economy*, 99(3): 483–499.

Krugman, Paul (1991b) *Geography and Trade*. Cambridge, MA: MIT Press.

Lightman, Alan (2005) *The Discoveries: Great Breakthroughs in 20th-Century Science*. New York: Vintage.

Machlup, Fritz (1978) "The Inferiority Complex of the Social Sciences." In *Methodology of Economics and Other Social Sciences*. New York: Academic Press, pp. 333–344.

Machlup, Fritz (1978) "Are the Social Sciences Really Inferior?" In *Methodology of Economics and Other Social Sciences*. New York: Academic Press, pp. 345–367.

Marshall, Alfred (1898) [1891] *Principles of Economics*, 4th edn. London: Macmillan.

Mayr, Ernst (1997) *This Is Biology: The Science of the Living World*. Cambridge, MA: Harvard University Press.

Mayr, Ernst (2001) *What Evolution Is*. New York: Basic Books.

Menger, Carl (1963) [1882] *Problems of Economics and Sociology*, trans. Francis J. Nock, Urbana, IL: University of Illinois Press.

Monod, Jacques (1971) *Chance and Necessity*, 1st US edn; trans. Austryn Wainhouse. New York: Knopf.

Rickert, Heinrich (1921) *Kulturwissenschaft und Naturwissenschaft*, 4th edn. Tubingen: Mohr.

Turk, Michael (2006) "The Fault Line of Axiomatization: Walras' Linkage of Physics with Economics." *European Journal of the History of Economic Thought*, 13(2): 195–212.

Veblen, Thorstein (1919) "Why is economics not an evolutionary science?" In *The Place of Science in Modern Civilization and Other Essays*. New York: B.W. Huebsch.

Windelband, Wilhelm (1913) "The Principles of Logic." In Arnold Ruge (ed.), *The Encyclopedia of Philosophy*, vol. 1: *Logic*, trans. B. Ethel Meyer. London: Macmillan.

# 6   Economics as plausible conjecture

In the last decades of the twentieth century, methodological inquiries into economics took a linguistic turn, much as was the case for other disciplines, including, notably, history (Iggers 1997). This linguistic turn has clearly animated discussion of methodology in economics in recent times: economics has been recognized as a discourse (Samuels 1990), its disputes as to content recast as differences in rhetoric (McCloskey 1983; Klamer et al. 1988), its schools of thought seen as possible constructions of knowledge (Weintraub 1991), its models re-formed into narratives (Morgan 2002), its writings treated as literature (Henderson 1995). Those engaged in explorations of the literary or linguistic substratum of economics are among the major contributors to contemporary debates about economic methodology. Moreover, the focus upon the role of rhetoric or the possibilities of "emplotment" in economics, to borrow a term from the historian Hayden White (White 1973), offered a new vantage point to explore the boundaries between fact and fiction in economic modeling.

The linguistic turn in theorizing about economic methodology, though, also needs to be set in perspective. For example, one might well question whether, or to what extent, the practice of economics was changed by this heightened awareness of the place of language and literary form in it; that is, some measure of the broader impact of this linguistic turn upon the discipline. Did it alter the economic analysis applied, say, to contemporary issues, or affect the thinking underlying economic policy? Or, one might attempt to establish the common intellectual ground linking this type of inquiry across disciplines, and thereby to capture the wider intellectual currents shaping – potentially – economics as a field, much as economists have, in the past, linked economics to the physical sciences or psychology.

However, there is yet another tack that might be taken. One could invert the linguistic turn itself by setting the notion of a literary substratum to economics in historical context. Here one might begin by examining the relation between literary form, language, and literature, on the one hand, and economics, on the other, in the period when classical economics came into existence: the eighteenth century, in western Europe. This would give great weight to comprehending economics through its foundations, and is consistent with the notion of the primacy to be attached to a "classical" period, formulation, or framework.

On one level this would call for a recognition of the conscious role accorded literary forms, figures of speech, and the use of language in the writings of eighteenth-century political economists. This may be most evident among the most notable figures among them. For example, in his "Dialogue on the Work of Artisans" François Quesnay used the device of the dialogue to tease out the appropriate meaning of "productive" and "sterile" economic activity, a central component of his analysis of physiocracy (Quesnay 1963b). He also drew attention to the "ambiguities of language" (Quesnay 1963b: 223) and their effect upon the formulation of "abstractions" used to establish the relation between production and value and to determine the correct way to measure such value (Quesnay 1963b: 213–14).

For his part, Adam Smith, who had lectured on "belles lettres" and rhetoric, placed great emphasis upon the means of communication as the key to ordering and comprehending concepts, a point highlighted by Dugald Stewart, Smith's first biographer.

But this inversion of the linguistic turn would also require, more importantly, an effort to capture critical elements in the historical setting, be they social facts or currents of ideas, informing the emergence of political economy. By and large it has been literary scholars rather than economic methodologists or historians of economic thought who have focused attention upon an identifiable change in intellectual consciousness and social world over the course of the eighteenth century, centered primarily in western Europe, that would link the origins of economics to other literary phenomena of the day, notably the rise of the modern novel. This has meant, unfortunately, that the implications of such a connection in shaping the subsequent development of economics have not been explored or fathomed to any significant degree. In particular, rather than seeing this focus upon language simply lend a literary quality to economics as a field or to economic texts, one might find instead a central insight into the method of economic theorizing. It might serve to explicate why the blurring of lines between fact and fiction in economics, perhaps most vexing in the matter of economic modeling, remains problematic (Maki 2002), as does the recurring tension, as Wassily Leontief once phrased it, between "theoretical assumptions and non-observed facts" (Leontief 1971).

This, then, will be a methodological inquiry in economics that will introduce some measure of historical analysis in assaying the meaning and significance of eighteenth-century texts, economic and otherwise. But it is also premised on the notion that history matters on a formative basis: that how the field of political economy formed into classical economics is relevant to, even decisive for, the ways that economics and its method of inquiry would develop over the course of the next two centuries.

## Storytelling in and out of historical time

Mary Morgan (Morgan 2002) and Deirdre McCloskey (McCloskey 1990) have led the way in spotlighting the role of storytelling or narrative in economic thought and practice, but both place the narrative form fundamentally outside the bounds of historical time. For Morgan the actual practice of economists necessarily involves the introduction of a series of questions and answers in order to construct and use models. This series effectively takes the form of a narrative (Morgan 2002: 185). Overall, Morgan sees storytelling as playing an essential mediating role in linking the abstraction of models to the reality of economic life as perceived and experienced. The relation between storytelling and economic models is more formal than historical; moreover, Morgan draws all of her examples from the mainstream of twentieth-century economics.

McCloskey, who has focused upon the need to ground economics in and through its literary forms, sees the reliance of economists upon narratives as commonplace: "Economists, especially theorists, are forever spinning 'parables' or telling "stories" (McCloskey 1983: 503). Moreover, the choices made in storytelling capture better the apparent differences among economists than do the actual assertions of conflicting ideological claims or perspectives (McCloskey 1990: 65).

She distinguishes between metaphor and narrative in ordering all thought, including economic thought, where metaphors are timeless and universal, while narratives unfold at least implicitly in time (McCloskey 1991: 21ff.). However, time in this instance is parametric, which is not derived from historical experience, but may be imposed upon it.

Moreover, the distinction between metaphor and narrative is itself somewhat misplaced. One may extract a narrative which nonetheless purports to convey a universal theme; in short, a story that can be repeated over and over, and thus can be imposed at various and diverse times. At the same time, metaphors can also be rooted in historical circumstances essential for their meaning and use, and thereby be particularized.

Instead, from an historical perspective, one might ask if particular historical experiences or specific historical moments would affect the nature of economic storytelling. To see if this is the case entails setting the moment itself, where new forms of writing – and storytelling – appear.

One can discern several new approaches to the writing of fiction in the eighteenth century: the fictional imaginings of shorter prose forms to convey a heightened realism, pursued by Denis Diderot, among others; the reemergence of introspective examination as a secularized form of spiritual autobiography, most demonstrably brought to the fore by Jean-Jacques Rousscau; and, most significantly, the appearance of the modern novel itself, remarkable for its combination of subjectivity and deeply evoked social world. In addition, the eighteenth century witnessed a reinvigoration of the fable, the form of which was applied by Bernard de Mandeville in *The Fable of the Bees* to an economic tale of inverted morality. Fables had their own blend of fact and fiction. They were commonly understood to be "either corrupted ancient stories or the caprice of imagination," according to Voltaire's *Philosophical Dictionary* (Voltaire 1962: 266), and were regarded as conveying allegories, that is, stories with a message. In turn, allegories were commonly understood to be "diffused metaphors," as metaphors were "contracted allegories," as Adam Smith characterized them (Smith 1983: 30).[1]

Moreover, fictional forms might be used to broach political or philosophical ideas. This was most striking in Montesquieu's highly popular *Persian Letters*, first published in 1721. In his reflections on the *Persian Letters*, dating from the 1750s, Montesquieu himself pointed to the importance of using the literary form of the epistolary novel to present ideas about "philosophy, politics and ethics" (Montesquieu 1973: 11).

With David Hume, and then Adam Smith, economic narratives might draw upon history, but as likely as not, this was a "conjectured" history,[2] in which the fictional was accepted as providing a clearer – and better – sense of reality than any possible amassing of available facts; especially when these facts prove to be few and hard to glean. These "conjectured" histories represent early versions of economic thought-experiments, which invariably convey the sense that a fictionalized reduction of reality produces a heightened comprehension of that reality. Such thought-experiments typically begin with a leap of the imagination and an appeal, implicit or explicit, to the reasonableness of what is presented, akin to a request for a "suspension of disbelief." Thus, in certain critical respects reality itself is supplanted by a fictionalized version of it. This fiction appears as a picture or portrait, and even if it begins as an effort to compensate for the lack of historical evidence, it takes shape as the demonstration of an analytic principle whose persuasiveness, or plausibility, also allows it to serve as a heuristic device.

In this way I intend to show that what distinguishes economic theorizing is its ties to a new kind of narrative in the eighteenth century, with a somewhat fluid boundary between fact and fiction, a concomitant of the somewhat fluid boundary which then existed between the literary and the scientific domains of knowledge. It may then be possible to recast the question about the boundary between fact and fiction in economic theorizing by identifying as essential to economic method an analytical approach, which might be called "plausible conjecture," whereby a continuing interplay between fact and fiction enables fiction to offer up a route for elucidating fact. For, from a practical standpoint, the standard mode of inquiry in economic theorizing continues to be the construction of thought-experiments or, in their elaborated version, models, and these constructions are typically produced through the use of plausible conjectures.

## The new consciousness

In *Sources of the Self*, which first appeared in 1989, the philosopher Charles Taylor posits the emergence of a new consciousness in the course of the eighteenth century, involving a revolution in the notion of identity and self in European thought and letters. For Taylor this radical change is central to the advent of "modernity," and gave rise to a new set of cultural understandings.

He highlights this "culture of modernity" by noting two new "valuations" or signs of this new consciousness: the first concerns an expansion of commercial life accorded intellectual valuation in the new discipline of political economy; the second the rise of the novel, in the hands – and words – of Defoe, Richardson, and Fielding (Taylor 1989: 285–6).

One might look upon this twinning of economics and the novel as simply a matter of coincidence, as products, or by-products, of the Enlightenment and the rise of commercial capitalism, most especially in Great Britain. Or, along the lines suggested by Taylor, one might see these developments as cultural manifestations in the historical moment leading up to the Industrial Revolution and hence joined as phenomena on the basis of common characteristics. As such, both draw upon an enhanced sense of individualism and individual introspection, set against a social world increasingly infused by economic calculation.

This is a perspective and a theme that has long garnered the attention and interest of literary critics and scholars. Those from the mid-twentieth century, like Ian Watt in *The Rise of the Novel* (1957), have given great weight to the economic context for the emergence of the modern novel; moreover, they saw in the depiction of new protagonists, but especially Defoe's Robinson Crusoe, the appearance of "economic man" (Watt 2001: 63ff.).

Maximilian Novak, a literary scholar, saw the "economic meaning of Robinson Crusoe" as central to Defoe's purpose, fashioning what approximated an economic model:

> By isolating first his hero and then a small group of settlers and returning them to a primitive economic condition, Defoe was attempting to illustrate some of his basic economic concepts.
>
> (Novak 1962: 49)

More recent literary criticism, especially from the last decades of the twentieth century, drew more directly from linguistics and critical studies, often incorporating ideas and approaches from structuralism and deconstructionism, and has cast economics and the novel as "twinned discourses," revealing a new world of bourgeois relations through what are characterized as the complementary texts of economics and the novel.

For example, James Thompson, in *Models of Value: Eighteenth-Century Political Economy and the Novel* (1996), claims "to investigate … a nexus of ideas that spread across a wide variety of eighteenth-century British texts." Thompson takes "the early modern reconceptualization of money from treasure to capital" as an event "represented or thematized as a crisis in the notion of value" (Thompson 1996: 2–3).

He goes on to say: "The two new literary forms or discourses that pre-eminently handle or manage this crisis – political economy and the novel – are at the same time produced by this crisis and are inseparable from it" (Thompson 1996: 3).

One might see in this emphasis upon discourses and texts the evocation of a form of high theory that may, in the end, engage only superficially at best the economics of the economic texts, as opposed to the notion that economics itself is a text, and that in particular fails to address the economic content of the discussion of value in those texts. One is left largely with a reproduction of the earlier thesis about the emergence of a heightened sense of self and the rise of commercial capitalism.

A deeper effort to bridge the realms of economics and literature can be found in recent works by writers on economics like Vivienne Brown who have pursued a literary turn in the study of economic writing, especially the narrative in Adam Smith's work. Brown has drawn upon the insights of the semiologist Mikhail Bakhtin in identifying the distinctive and distinguishing characteristics of voice in Smith's two most notable works, *The Theory of Moral Sentiments* and *The Wealth of Nations*. For Brown the former would be comprehended as dialogic, producing a narrative akin to the novel, while the latter would hew more closely to the storytelling of scientific inquiry. She posits that this is so because only the former presents and is infused with a moral sense (Brown 1994: 23–54). But, as will be discussed below, the Smithian model presented in *The Wealth of Nations* clearly depends upon philosophical and moral judgments, where efficiency and productivity are virtues in the economic affairs of humankind, built out of stories like that of the pin factory. The narratologist Catherine Labio set Smith's labor theory of value in the context of ideas advanced by contemporaries like Rousseau, but expressly avoided an examination of the theory's economic content (Labio 1997: 135–6).

Like Charles Taylor, these scholars emphasized a congruence of valuation in the new consciousness in a social world characterized increasingly by bourgeois relations, with measures of value attuned more closely to the affairs of commercial capitalism.[3]

While the congruence I see as essential here is also one of consciousness, it has at least as much to do with intellectual currents, and it turns on a question of what knowledge consists of and how it may be apprehended. These intellectual currents may rightly be seen and understood as changes corresponding to the economic relations of the emerging commercial capitalism noted above. Nonetheless, the affinity between political economy and the novel is less about value per se and more about method, if complementary in nature, in the use of imagination to capture and provide an understanding of essential elements, or the essence itself, of the social world.

For both political economy and the novel the autonomous self engaged in, yet set apart from, society figures centrally. However powerful and promising an insight, it comes with one obvious limitation: the economics of such seminal figures like Smith and Quesnay, and hence that of the classical school itself, is severely truncated. Smith, for example, is effectively reduced to expounding the virtues of the "invisible hand"; in Taylor's words, this is to be found in a new emphasis upon "self-regulating systems" (Taylor 1989: 286). The import of the division of labor, which launches *The Wealth of Nations* and may reasonably be contended is the most salient idea in the text, is virtually neglected.

## Economists and their Robinsonades

For economists *Robinson Crusoe* has served as an archetypal tale to which they have repeatedly returned, referring to it as a story, fable, parable, or metaphor through which economic ideas might be presented in outline. If Karl Marx threw down the gauntlet, mocking the "fondness" of economists for what he called their "Robinsonades" (Marx 1976: 169), then Eugen von Bohm-Bawerk picked it up, offering a sprightly defense of the simplified picture the Robinson Crusoe story afforded, pointing thereby to its subsequent absorption into numerous economic models:

> Robinsonades and pictures of primitive circumstances are very good when the object is to present clearly the simplest typical principles – to give a kind of skeleton of economical procedure,–and to that extent, I trust, our Robinsonade also has done good service. But, naturally, they cannot give us an adequate picture of those peculiar and developed forms in which this skeleton clothes itself in the living actuality of a modern economic community. And it is just at this point that it becomes important to fill out the abstract formula with explanation and illustration taken from life.
>
> (Bohm-Bawerk 1923: 104–5)

Through the next century after Marx and Bohm-Bawerk one can take notice of a cascade of Robinsonades. These later generations of economists have looked back to Robinson Crusoe and found a key to comprehending, variously, the nature of marginal utility, production, general equilibrium, or even game theory.

Seen in greater detail, each of the following – selective – examples contributes to a well-rounded picture of the presence of Robinson Crusoe in economic text and thought. In writing about the work of Silvio Gesell in *The General Theory*, J. M. Keynes noted:

> [Gesell] shows how it is only the existence of a rate of money interest which allows a yield to be obtained from lending out stocks of commodities. His dialogue between Robinson Crusoe and a stranger is a most excellent economic parable – as good as anything of the kind that has been written – to demonstrate this point.
>
> (Keynes (1964) [1935]: 356)

For Jurg Niehans, Crusoe emerges as an artifact and critical reference in shaping the thinking of William Lloyd about an alignment of value with marginal utility that presages the work of the marginalists by several decades:

> Lloyd wanted to persuade his readers that marginal utility schedules have meaning even in the absence of markets. Utility, he argued, is more fundamental than exchange. Since he did not have firsthand knowledge of economies without markets, he searched in Defoe's novel for telling experiences of Robinson Crusoe as quasi-empirical evidence ... Lloyd was not quite satisfied with what he found, but Crusoe had thereby obtained his honored placed among the paradigms of value theory.
>
> (Niehans 1990: 122)

Meanwhile, in his text on microeconomic analysis, Hal Varian links Robinson Crusoe to the foundational model of production and consumption:

> There is an analog of the Edgeworth box that is very helpful in understanding production and general equilibrium. Supposed we consider a one-consumer economy. The consumer leads a rather schizophrenic life: on the one hand he is a profit-maximizing producer who produces a consumption good from labor inputs while on the other hand he is a utility-maximizing consumer who owns the profit-maximizing firm. This is sometimes called a Robinson Crusoe economy.
>
> (Varian 1992: 349)

Finally, in their pathbreaking work on the integration of game theory into economics, John von Neumann and Oskar Morgenstern seek to highlight the limitations of the Robinson Crusoe economy, in order to advance claims for the use of strategic game theory in what they call a "Social Exchange" economy:

> Thus the study of the Crusoe economy and the use of the methods applicable to it, is of much more limited value to economic theory than has been assumed heretofore even by the most radical critics. The grounds for this limitation lie not in the field of those social relationships which we have mentioned before – although we do not question their significance – but rather they arise from the conceptual differences between the original (Crusoe's) maximum problem and the more complex problem sketched above.
>
> (Von Neumann and Morgenstern 2004: 12)

Economic critics have tended to challenge these references to Robinson Crusoe on a literal basis. Echoing Marx, they show how Crusoe's island economy required and made use of all sorts of resources, like the tools available from the shipwreck, ignored by those citing the virtues of the Robinson Crusoe model. Jacques Sapir decries the "myth of Robinson," seeing the story mistakenly accepted as a realistic depiction of an economy abstracted into its simplest form (Sapir 2002: 180–2). While Sapir's case is compelling, it begs the question: why are economists so "fond" of this picture? Or, more generally, why are economists so ready to resort to such storytelling?

One answer would be that in *Robinson Crusoe* economics and the novel complement each other, whereby the novel presumes a basis in fact, as economics, an intellectual discipline examining, ultimately, the meaning of human affairs, creates fictions – be they conjectures that come to form thought-experiments or models – to better explore such affairs. In that regard it is noteworthy that in distinguishing Defoe's novels from earlier lengthy narratives, literary critics like Thomas Keymer are apt to cite their "particularizing solidity" (Keymer 2007: viii).

Moreover, Defoe's novels attained a remarkable capacity to convey fact through a fictional text. Keymer, citing Virginia Woolf, evoked Defoe's "genius for fact" (Keymer 2007: viii–x). That is, though a work of fiction, *Robinson Crusoe* is seen as providing a wealth of detail on two counts. First, the greater depth of depiction of the external world, or societal state and circumstances, conveyed a sense of reality, or realism, hitherto unexplored or even unimagined. Second, the internal state, or consciousness, of the protagonist far exceeded that found in earlier stories of venturing forth in the world, in what were often described as picaresque tales. This too brought with it a heightened sense of reality. One might regard Defoe's first novel as a fictionalized version of a nearly contemporaneous shipwreck involving one Alexander Selkirk in 1705. Nonetheless, Defoe himself obscured the fictional nature of his work, laying claim to historical veracity by stating in the preface: "The Editor believes the thing to be a just History of Fact; neither is there any Appearance of Fiction in it" (Defoe 2007: 3).

It is in this "particularizing solidity" that the new consciousness limned by Taylor makes its appearance. In the novel this leads to the development of a narrative that, while a story, seems to enter fully the social world it depicts. In economics this can be found in a greater reliance upon capturing the details of business affairs, or, more generally, economic actions and activities in the world, in accordance with generally recognized principles regarding economic behavior through an act of imagination, often as a simple picture or image, creating a visual analogy, or as a construction built out of seemingly compelling, if only probable facts. The details of the operation of Crusoe's island economy remain, for all intents and purposes, unknown, perhaps even unknowable. It is possible, though, to imagine what it might have been, just as it would be possible to take from the smallest parts known an image of how they be fitted together into a coherent picture, even if little more than a plausible sketch.

François Quesnay's "economic table," for example, is built upon the detailed account of and accounting for French agriculture first presented by him in a series of articles for Diderot's *Encyclopédie*, but is accompanied by, and ultimately informed by, the general maxims or principles which Quesnay posits as the requisite guide to the national economy. Quesnay himself saw his table as a "hypothesis," yet one that was "copied from nature" (Quesnay 1963a: 151–6).

Loïc Charles, who has pioneered the exploration of the visual dimensions of Quesnay's work, has pointed out the pictorial nature of Quesnay's "tableau":

> [T]he tableau économique is a work of art (a picture) as well as a work of science (a table). Indeed, it is essential to note that the word tableau in the expression tableau économique refers not to a table, as is commonly assumed … The word tableau designated a framed picture, usually a painting, or metaphorically, a vivid and artful synthesis of various elements that were united in a single piece, be it a spoken discourse, written discourse, a play, or a visual artifact.
>
> (Charles 2004: 456)

Thus, this new consciousness raises new questions. As with the novel, one may ask of economics: how much is factual detail; how much is based on, or depends upon, behavior – or principle – assumed?

Literary critics identified one other innovation in the novel of the eighteenth century that would also resonate with the emergence of the discipline of political economy: the moral lesson embedded within. As Virginia Woolf described the virtues of *Moll Flanders*, Defoe's second novel, after *Robinson Crusoe*, she pointed to Defoe's need to justify "the existence of the novel" by wedding "true story" to a "Moral" (Woolf 2002: xii–xiii). Economics too would advance in ways requiring, or at the least calling forth, a moral of its own.

## "Conjectural sciences," "conjectural," and economics

Charles Taylor's focus upon the emergence of a "new consciousness" or "sense of modernity" in eighteenth-century Europe may be shifted to a related matter: the changing boundaries ordering knowledge and forms of intellectual inquiry, especially in distinguishing what constituted the natural sciences and the social sciences in European thought. In the eighteenth century the boundaries between the natural sciences and the social sciences, if not altogether blurred, nonetheless differed markedly from the classification schemes that would arise in the nineteenth century and after.

For Margaret Schabas this opens up the possibility of envisioning the "history of economics" [as] "the history of science," a rooting of political economy in the phenomena and organization of the natural world explored in her *Natural Origins of Economics* (Schabas 2005: 2). But it might just as well open up other possibilities, bridging the scientific with the philosophical and the literary. Schabas herself notes the role of dominant eighteenth-century thinkers like Montesquieu and Voltaire as "moral philosophers," whose writings were intended to raise broad philosophical, political, or, on occasion, scientific themes, even if presented in the form of a fiction (Schabas 2005: 42ff.). As Montesquieu captured the popular imagination in the 1720s with his exploration of proper governance and cultural differences in the *Persian Letters*, so Voltaire interpreted and popularized Newton's idea, captivating the French literary elite in the 1730s.

This capacity to move between the literary and the scientific also marked the work and career of Denis Diderot, encyclopedist and author of "contes historiques." In *Le rêve de d'Alembert* Diderot spoke of the "sciences con-jecturales," those fields of inquiry drawn from human affairs and moral, ethical, or philosophical matters (Diderot 1971: 71). These sciences require the use and application of imagination in order to set in proper relief the relations that exist among seemingly disparate and unrelated events, ideas, or phenomena. It has therefore been remarked that Diderot's role as both a writer of stories and other fictional pieces and the leading organizer and editor of, as well as contributor to, the *Encyclopédie* can be traced back to that understanding of the elucidating power of the imagination, evidently crossing lines between the fictional and the factual. As Diderot himself put it: "I substitute art for nature, the better to judge it" (Ozdoba 1980: 168). Joachim Ozdoba then characterized Diderot's mission in the following way: "The truth of fiction and the imagination and the truth of science and philosophy paradoxically coincide in the end" (Ozdoba 1980: 168). For Ozdoba this meant that, in essence, fiction served as a heuristic for Diderot.

Early on in his career Adam Smith paid homage to the power of the imagination along lines none too dissimilar from Diderot's. In his "History of Astronomy," one of the few surviving philosophical or scientific essays which he wrote, Smith noted:

> Systems in many respects resemble machines ... A system is an imaginary machine invented to connect together in the fancy those different move-ments and effects which are already in reality may be more easily produced.
>
> (Smith 1980a: 66)

He went on to state:

> but it often happens, that one great connecting principle is afterwards found to be sufficient to bind together all the discordant phaenomena that occur in a whole species of things.
>
> (Smith 1980a: 66)

To this ability to find, through the imagination, the fewest but most encompassing principles Smith later applied the name, "Newtonian method."

How did Smith characterize the Newtonian system? It was based upon a limited set of connecting principles, derived from an act of imagination. In summary Smith found Newton's system to be one "whose parts are all more strictly connected together, than those of any other philosophical hypothesis" (Smith 1980a: 104) Over time Smith waxed even more expansively about the "Newtonian method." In his lecture on didactics from 1763 he stated: "[it] is undoubtedly the most Philosophical, and in every science whether of Moralls or Naturall philosophy etc., is vastly more ingenious and for that reason more engaging than the [Aristotelian method]," centered upon classification and taxonomy (Smith 1983: 146; see also Loasby 1999: 9).

One might take the general resemblance in Diderot's and Smith's ideas about the role of imagination in the formation of the sciences evidence of a commonality in consciousness, a mark of the intellectual currents, broadly understood, sweeping across western Europe in the course of the eighteenth century. Those established an environment in which the conjectural, imagined as such or even cast in the form of fiction, would be perceived as leading to the construction or expansion of defined fields of knowledge.

The connections, though, between Diderot and Smith extend well beyond a commonality of consciousness. In the 1750s Smith was perhaps the most enthusiastic supporter in the British Isles of Diderot's – and d'Alembert's – project of producing the *Encyclopédie*, evinced by the praise Smith heaped upon it in an article that appeared in the *Edinburgh Review* in 1755: "The French work which I just now mentioned, promises to be the most compleat [*sic*] of the kind which has ever been published or attempted in any language" (Smith 1980b: 246). Smith goes on to refer to the *Encyclopédie* as a "great collection of science and literature" (Smith 1980b: 248).

When Smith traveled to France in 1765 to 1766, he was able to meet with many of the leading figures in France's intellectual life of the period. In Paris he attended salons and encountered not only the Physiocrats, but also Diderot and d'Alembert.

But perhaps the most important direct link, especially as regards the development of economic thought and method, can be found in Smith's borrowings from the *Encyclopédie*. In his authoritative annotations of *The Wealth of Nations* in 1904, Edwin Cannan identified two articles from the *Encyclopédie* that appeared to play a crucial role in Smith's text as he laid out the case for the division of labor and the advantages accruing to it. From the article entitled, "Epingle," it appears that Smith drew critical pieces of the depiction of which he made use in describing the pin factory, one of the most memorable passages in the entire work, and, one might add, in the history of economic thought (Smith 1976: 8). In addition, he drew directly upon the insights provided in the article entitled "Art," which concerned the mechanical arts, in enumerating the advantages in production, or gains in productivity, following from specialization (Smith 1976: 11). Cannan also noted that these same articles informed an earlier passage, dating from 1763, and often taken as the first run of Smith's case for the division of labor, describing the advantages of the division of labor in Smith's lectures on justice, police, revenue, and arms (Smith 1896: 164–6).

In the *Encyclopédie* article "Art" there is also a discussion of the development of the mechanical arts which bears a striking resemblance to the method adopted by Smith, in which imagined suppositions supersede the facts in the case, if those facts might even be known or knowable.

In outlining the *Projet d'un traité général des arts méchaniques*, the author states: "Often one ignores the origin of a mechanical art, where one has only vague knowledge of its progress … On these occasions it is necessary to resort to philosophical suppositions, starting with certain plausible hypotheses, some initial and fortuitous event, and advancing from that until the art has been sprouted" (Diderot 1751: vol. 1, 714)

He goes on to describe the "advantages of this method": "In proceeding thusly, the progress of an art would be brought to light in a more instructive and clearer manner than through its true history, when one would come to know it" (Diderot 1751: vol. 1, 715).

What, then, is this matter of "conjectural history" as found in Smith's writings? Dugald Stewart's depiction of it situates "conjectural history" at the center of Adam Smith's mode of inquiry in all the disciplines in which he was engaged, and characterizes it as new, or, to put it more precisely, "modern," for the intellectual world of the eighteenth century (Stewart 1980: 292)

Stewart then describes in greater detail Smith's method of inquiry:

> In this want of direct evidence, we are under a necessity of supplying the place of fact by conjecture; and when we are unable to ascertain how men actually conducted themselves upon particular occasions, of considering in what manner they are likely to have proceeded, from the principles of their nature, and the circumstances of their external situation.
>
> (Stewart 1980: 293)

Stewart introduces the possibility of allowing conclusions, reached via speculation, to serve as the basis for confirming facts in question:

> In such inquiries, the detached facts which travels and voyages afford us, may frequently serve as land-marks to our speculations; and sometimes our conclusions a priori, may tend to confirm the credibility of facts, which, on a superficial view, appeared to be doubtful or incredible.
>
> (Stewart 1980: 293)

Finally, Stewart concludes by naming this method:

> To this species of philosophical investigation, which has no appropriate name in our language, I shall take the liberty of giving the title of *Theoretical* or *Conjectural History.*
>
> (Stewart 1980: 293)

Set in a somewhat more contemporary context one might conceive of this mode of inquiry informing what amount to thought-experiments, in which plausible, if hypothetical situations are envisioned, for which a few "detached facts" might, on occasion, be adduced, but for which, overall, the conjecture itself is crucial.

These thought-experiments might then be regarded as conjectured fictions, rather than as some form of conventionalism, which would more likely be introduced as a conceit by "as if." There is a narrow line here that might readily be crossed, as economists come to base their models, thought-experiments, and conjectures upon assumptions, which presumably afford the possibility of treatment as conventions. Yet if one looks closely as Smith's modus operandi, it is clear that he does not always assume outright; rather, he paints a plausible picture, which may be more reasonably be understood as a translation of a literary pictorialism. Indeed, the strength of Smith's writing rests very much with his ability to persuade his readers of the case he is trying to make in just this way. Such a pictorialism certainly evokes Bohm-Bawerk's later justification of his "Robinsonade."

Nor should Smith be regarded as alone among eighteenth-century political economists in sorting through the role of conjecture, supposition, or fiction in making a science. Quesnay addressed the matter of "fiction," as well as supposition, in concluding his remarks – and general maxims – about the "tableau économique." In doing so, though, he appears to treat the notion of fiction more pejoratively, contending that the detailed picture of the national economy he has constructed must conform to the principles he has outlined; otherwise, his entire construction will be nothing but a "fiction" (Quesnay 1972: 21). However, Quesnay goes on to state that this does not defeat or vitiate the principles themselves; accordingly, one might regard his approach as somewhat Platonic, or an early statement of realism in economic thought, where the ideas, or set of economic principles, exist apart from and are independent of, the world of facts. The more proximate source for these ideas about abstract principles and suppositions is Condillac's *Traité des systèmes*, which first appeared in 1749. In the event, in Quesnay's economics, paradoxically, the apparent wealth of detail, even accounting, is subordinated to principle. Such principles were described by Quesnay as "suppositions," but one could translate them into an imagined picture, as it was one that Quesnay felt had been realized, to a significant degree, in England (Quesnay 1972: 20–2). Indeed, Quesnay created a visual model of the economy in the *Tableau économique*, a matter discussed at some length by Loïc Charles, in which the artistic and the artful were blended with the scientific (Charles 2003).

## Plausible conjecture and the labor theory of value

One can see the operation of plausible conjecture in the emergence of the labor theory of value, a foundational matter in the recasting of political economy by classical economists as they rejected the precepts of the mercantilists. Wherein did wealth reside? If it was not to be found in the visible bullion of the mercantilists, then it might instead be formed out of the productive activity of the economy. What, then, was the appropriate source and measure of those productive activities? For the classical economists wealth and the possibility of economic growth had to inhere within the productive capacity of the economy, for which the infusion of resources, beginning with labor, was critical. Sorting out these concerns led first to the Physiocratic emphasis upon the productive capacity of agriculture, then the Smithian emphasis upon the productive capacity of all economic activities involved in the making of things. It also required establishing a coherent theory of value, based at first upon the most fundamental input, labor. In turn, this posed the problem of distinguishing between the nature of value in use and exchange.

In part, Quesnay had sought to distinguish different forms of value by reference to diverse physical settings and circumstances, suggesting a kind of empirical analysis or at least observation that in fact was more likely drawn from the general knowledge and conventional understandings of the day. From his perspective the "savages of Louisiana" (Quesnay 1972: 9) might exchange goods of various sorts, often those produced as a result of hunting, but such exchanges among primitive peoples did not give rise to what Quesnay called "*valeur vénale*," typically translated as "market value" (Meek 1963: 41). "*Valeur vénale*" did arise when those same goods were exchanged with European traders, as they now belonged to an economic world of market exchanges. Here Quesnay has, through a thumbnail sketch or simplified picture, posited certain essential principles for value and exchange, and imposed them on an imagined state of affairs.

With Adam Smith one moves from France's North American colonies to Britain's, but Smith's reliance upon an imagined state of affairs is, if anything, keener than Quesnay's. Smith's "primitive" labor theory of value was cast in the form of a conceit, or thought-experiment, whereby Smith imagines and then compares the labor–time required to capture a beaver, as opposed to a deer. In Smith's conjecture it would take twice the time to trap a beaver than to catch a deer, hence the resulting exchange value would be two deer for one beaver.

Leaving aside the question as to how plausible Smith's conjecture was, one may ponder the sources for it. Most likely Smith conceived of the comparison on the basis of a text, as was often the case for him;[4] this time it was a map originally produced by Lewis Evans of the hunting domains of the Indian tribes who inhabited the "middle colonies," generally in "countries" including, or just west of, the Appalachian Mountains. These domains were divided between those of the Ohio and Thuchsochruntie, devoted to "deer hunting" and those of the Couchsachrage and the Skaniadarade, devoted to "beaver hunting." Evans' map was first published in 1755, and was sold in London that same year, gaining wide distribution in England. A version of it can be found in Thomas Jeffery's "American Atlas," a text found in Smith's library.[5]

This elemental labor theory of value underpins Smith's discourse upon the commercial exchanges and relations in his own day and society, by establishing thereby the meaning of economic value. With value linked to production, Smith could project the growth of economies over time. This notion of economic value then held for classical economics in general.

What, in general terms, is the nature of Smith's conjecture? Should it be regarded as a form of historical explanation, supplying a "conjectural history" as J. G. A. Pocock would see it, for those earlier periods in which a "civil history" could not be constructed? Or, might it be construed as fundamentally analytic, along the lines of systemic inquiry, as a "natural history," because it may be explicated "by the operation of nature alone"? (Pocock 2006: 276).

In fact, it may include both, for the imaginative leap taken by Smith may entail imagining useful and pertinent events or developments from the past, drawing upon a narrative that is quasi-historical and quasi-mythical, or it might equally be built out of suppositions forming general principles or universal behavioral postulates that are timeless in scope. These all fall within the purview of the method outlined in the article in the *Encyclopédie* for the development of the mechanical arts, which combines the use of "plausible hypotheses" with "fortuitous events."

In this regard Smith's conjecturing, though far more literary and wedded to text, bears a striking similarity to Quesnay's heuristic approach in the *Tableau économique*, as Loïc Charles has noted, "to visualize an abstract concept" (Charles 2003: 537), "us[ing] ... visual and mechanical artifacts as scientific tools, as engines of learning or discovery" (Charles 2003: 533).

A century or so later, when Thorstein Veblen lambasted the "conjectural history" of classical economics, it was this image of primitive exchange created by Smith – and the ones that followed in its wake – that he had in mind:

> The ultimate laws and principles which they formulated were laws of the normal or the natural, according to a preconception regarding the ends to which, in the nature of things, all things tend.
>
> (Veblen 1919: 65)

He then makes his charge more specific:

> As instances of the use of this ceremonial canon of knowledge may be cited the conjectural history; that plays so large a part in the classical treatment of economic institutions, such as the normalized accounts of the beginnings of barter in the transactions of the putative hunter, fisherman, and boatbuilder, or the man with the plane and the two planks, or the two men with the basket of apples and the basket of nuts.
>
> (Veblen, 1919: 66)

The last of these examples constituted Veblen's contemporaneous swipe at Alfred Marshall (Veblen 1919: 66), whose lengthy note on barter, set amidst the discussion of the laws of supply and demand in his *Principles of Economics*, posited the direct exchange of apples and nuts, and ended with the conjecture of two countries devoted to the production of each (Marshall 1891: 395). Thus, Marshall represented for Veblen the latest avatar of the Smithian tradition, making use of a form of plausible conjecture, with its appeal to an earlier time or more primitive state, from which general principles and behavioral postulates might be extracted, but where in the end it is simply a matter of assumptions leading ineluctably to the desired conclusion.

Veblen's critique can be brought forward to the present. Samuel Hollander's contemporary treatment of "The Labour Theory of Value" in his examination of *Classical Economics*, provides striking evidence of the continuing appeal of the mode of plausible conjecture for the same subject, divorced from everyday experience with little, if any, empirical or historical basis, where "deer-producing beaver consumers" interact with "beaver-producing deer consumers" in a "competitive model of long-run price determination" (Hollander 1992: 71).

The context for Veblen's critique should not be ignored. It appeared in an essay in which Veblen made the case that economics had failed to attain the requisite threshold as an evolutionary science, held in check by a closed method whereby preconceived understandings and judgments inform and lead to the outcomes reached.

Veblen's critique thus raised the question to whether the broad acceptance and widespread use of the conjectural method tainted, or at least limited seriously, the scope of economic inquiry. The general argument can be phrased in terms of the following questions: how was the initial conjecture formed? How were the initiating assumptions made? Typically, as Jacques Sapir would have it, they were "emboîtées," that is, assumptions or conjectures that were based at least in part on the conclusions sought, "boxed in" by a version of the Duhem–Quine paradox, where assumptions not explicitly acknowledged proved integral to reaching the seemingly inevitable conclusion sought (Sapir 2005: 11).

## The place of the embedded lesson

As the discursive writings on political economy from the eighteenth century were grounded in a mixing of historical narrative with the literary and the philosophical, where the boundary between the fictional and the factual or historical was none too precise; either fact or fiction might serve to inform a moral lesson about economic life. Like the tale of economics' most enduring protagonist, Robinson Crusoe, these economic narratives were stories, with a tale to tell; but more importantly, they mattered at the level of higher interpretation – in literary terms, one might describe this as a higher level of exegesis. They too imparted a lesson, most plainly a moral lesson, as to how one should cope with and master the affairs, and the business, of the world.

The transmutation of moral lesson into a new form within the emerging discourse of political economy is exemplified by the work of Adam Smith, a point noted by James Tobin in his appreciation of Smith.[6] In *The Wealth of Nations* Smith engages in lengthy historical digressions to elaborate upon, and ultimately validate, the points he is trying to make.

These digressions into economic history supplement, if not complement, the references to historical events and developments that punctuate the arguments within Smith's extended essay in political economy. One might regard these historical passages, whether abbreviated or lengthy, as narratives providing a kind of historical proof in which the economic lesson is adjudged consonant with what actually transpired. The selection of apposite historical events and developments represented an ad hoc reliance upon historical circumstances to fit the argument at hand.

Moreover, the didactic reach of Smith's political economy extends beyond history and historical digression. Consider Smith's discussion of the advantages accruing to specialization and the division of labor: it is a vivid and masterful portrayal of an economic lesson. Who could challenge the virtue of the greatly enhanced productivity of the pin factory set against the valiant and skilled labor of the individual craftsman? (Smith 1976: 7–20). One could reasonably frame Smith's case for specialization as the "virtue" of efficiency, from which nearly all other economic benefits follow. Thus, the best way for an economy to operate in effect also drives the economic analysis.

Subsequently, the more intricate models in economics that seem so far removed from the philosophical tales, historical digressions, and conjectural histories of early political economy retain critical features of the tale to be told, that central characteristic of those older forms. How can a model ostensibly formed on the basis of universal principles or rules be said to provide a narrative of a possible history? One might take up as an example the highly influential Solow model of economic growth or development, first presented in the 1950s, that places great weight upon capital formation, and even greater weight on technological innovation, while balancing sufficient increases of capital with all other requisite factors of production. Herein lies the tale of the virtuous economy which obtained and used its resources wisely, and, owing to a higher steady state level of capital, was rewarded with a higher and more sustainable rate of growth than would have resulted otherwise, and was likely to grow along a smoother path, less subject to the vicissitudes of fortune – and misfortune – associated with the turns of the business cycle. Whether explicit or only implied, the virtues extolled here have an affinity with the moral lessons of Robinson Crusoe.

This is so for two reasons. First of all, the analysis that accords with the model is meant to have effect, and be interpreted, in a social world; such models tend to be put forward, and used, to evaluate economic situations that have occurred, or might. These applications come with at least a hint as to better or worse ways to proceed. In the domain of international trade, economists championing free trade draw diagrams of gains and losses in producer and consumer surplus, harkening back to Alfred Marshall, to demonstrate the deadweight loss produced by the imposition of a protectionist tariff, showing thereby the losses incurred by less than fully efficient use of resources. This is hardly the same sort of analysis about the physical state of the world on the basis of Newton's law of gravitation or Bernouilli's principles of hydrodynamics. In economics, laws, rules, and principles come with a message. The economist may pose as the engineer of "efficiency," purporting to work much as physicists might, but efficiency is laden with value that is as much moral as it is about use or exchange. As Joseph Schumpeter noted, economics, unlike physics, is informed by the "knowledge of the *meanings*" of human and social "actions" (Schumpeter 1954: 16). Such meanings are inseparable from interpretation, which weight the theory more or less favorably. Moreover, the existence of such meanings in economics, but not physics, casts doubt on

McCloskey's contention about the universality of narrative across all disciplines.

This also leads to a second resonance with Robinson Crusoe. While Defoe's tale is cast as a history, appearing to describe a particular cast of characters under a singular set of circumstances, it barely masks its universal aspirations and reach. It is in reality a philosophical tale, the center of which is its message or lesson; the particulars of the story help move the reader to a recognition of its central purpose. Once one perceives the thicket of detail for what it is, one can see in this type of narrative economic concerns that can be displayed in other ways. Words can be replaced by a graphical sketch, or other abstracted notation, a practice greatly advanced by the late nineteenth century British economists, especially Marshall and Edgeworth, and rendered commonplace in the twentieth century.

## Conclusion

What does it mean for plausible conjecture to emerge as a framework or mold for economic explanation? As a formative element of economic inquiry, it would establish a pattern or tendency that endures. At the same time it need not be all-encompassing; simply put, not all theorizers in economics would have to conform to it. Instead, it would represent a dominant approach of such force that all might find themselves contending with it, even if, like Veblen, they railed against conjectural history in economics.

As a corollary, by emphasizing the importance of the formative it would add considerable weight to the role that history ought to be accorded in both the construction and interpretation of economics. Moreover, it would help establish why it is that economics as an intellectual discipline is built around generalizing principles, its nomothetic distinctiveness, yet typically relies upon an episodic or even ad hoc resort to or application of such principles, in the manner of conjecturing.

Finally, plausible conjecture has implications for the role of mathematics in economics. While this role is a major topic onto itself, and certainly not a new one, it seems to me that in general when mathematics is used by economists, it tends to be regarded as a ready-made tool, applying the formulation of Tobias Dantzig, among others, that number or mathematics is "the language of science," so that the case for a mathematized economics would be based upon the provision of a clarity or a precision otherwise lacking.

However, there are other ways to conceive of the relation between economics and mathematics. For one, applying mathematics as a tool is not the same as thinking mathematically, where the ambiguities and conflicts within mathematics and mathematical reasoning would figure in economic thinking, as one might ponder, for example, the scope and nature of axiomatization. For another, the Smithian "imaginative intuition" cited by Tobin fails (Tobin 1992:128), and the place of narrative and plausible conjecture is called into question, where the use of mathematics is counterintuitive.

# Notes

1 Compare Smith's phrasing with that of Deirdre McCloskey: "Allegory is merely long-winded metaphor" (1983: 505).
2 Dugald Stewart links the method of Smith's "conjectural history," discussed in greater detail later in the text, with Hume's "natural history" and ultimately the French "histoire raisonnée" (Stewart 1980: 293).
3 Brown focuses upon the "ideological origins of liberalism" in examining the "emergence" of *The Wealth of Nations* (Brown 1994: 2ff.; 142ff.), while Janet Sorensen explores the parallel she sees between changes in the nature of "linguistic exchange" and "the rising form of commodity exchange" in "Defoe's economies of identity" (Sorensen 1999: 75–94).
4 Charles Kindleberger, in his examination of Smith's work, refers to Smith as a "literary economist," relying upon texts, much as Kindleberger saw himself (Kindleberger, 1976: 6).
5 One can ultimately trace the map, and its title describing the "deer hunting" and "beaver hunting" countries, to Smith's library. A short notice of the map was entered into the British literary publication, *Monthly Review*, in 1756. "Pirated" copies of Evans' map, as so described by Henry Newton Stevens and Lawrence Henry Gipson, found their way into the publications of a number of British cartographers, often without attribution to Evans. One of these "pirated" copies was included in the "American Atlas" of Thomas Jefferys, which was printed by Sayer and Bennett in 1775. This work is listed in the catalogue of Adam Smith's library. Crucially, the language originally used by Evans in the map title to describe the "deer hunting" and "beaver hunting" counties was retained by Jefferys. See Stevens (1905).
6 Tobin praises Smith in literary terms that Smith himself might have used: "*The Wealth of Nations* is a very down-to-earth book, with a simple thematic moral, a rudimentary theoretical model, an imaginative intuition, a vast collection of historical and institutional material, and a great deal of wisdom and common sense" (Tobin 1992: 128).

# References

Bohm-Bawerk, Eugen von (1923) [1888] *The Positive Theory of Capital*, trans. William Smart.New York: G.E. Stechert & Co.
Brown, Vivienne (1994) *Adam Smith's Discourse: Canonicity, Commerce and Conscience.* London: Routledge.
Charles, Loïc (2003) "The Visual History of the *Tableau* économique." *European Journal of the History of Economic Thought*, 10(4): 527–550.
Charles, Loïc (2004) "The *Tableau* économique as Rational Recreation." *History of Political Economy*, 36(2): 445–474.
Defoe, Daniel (2007) [1719] *Robinson Crusoe.* Oxford: Oxford World's Classics.
Diderot, Denis (ed.) (1751–65) *Encyclopédie, ou Dictionnaire raisonné des sciences, des arts et des métiers.* Paris: Briasson.
Diderot, Denis (1971) *Le rêve d'Alembert*, in *Œuvres complètes*, tome VIII, Edition Chronologique, Le Club Français du Livre.
Evans, Lewis (1755) "A General Map of the Middle British Colonies in America." In *Geographical, Historical, Political, Philosophical and Mechanical Essays*. Philadelphia: B. Franklin and D. Hall.
Gipson, Lawrence Henry (1939) *Lewis Evans*. Philadelphia: Historical Society of Pennsylvania.

Henderson, Willie (1995) *Economics as Literature*. London: Routledge.

Hollander, Samuel (1992) [1987] *Classical Economics*. Toronto: University of Toronto Press.

Iggers, Georg G. (1997) *Historiography in the Twentieth Century*. Hanover, NH: University Press of New England.

Keymer, Thomas (2007) "Introduction". In Daniel Defoe,*Robinson Crusoe*. Oxford: Oxford World's Classics.

Keynes, J. M. (1964) [1935] *The General Theory of Employment, Interest and Money*. San Diego: Harcourt.

Kindleberger, C. P. (1976) "The Historical Background: Adam Smith and the Industrial Revolution." In Thomas Wilson and Andrew S. Skinner (eds), *The Market and the State: Essays in Honour of Adam Smith*. Oxford: Clarendon Press, pp. 1–25.

Klamer, Arjo,McCloskey, Deirdre, and Solow, Robert (eds) (1988) *The Consequences of Economic Rhetoric*, Cambridge: Cambridge University Press.

Labio, Catherine (1997) "The Aesthetics of Adam Smith's Labor Theory of Value." *Eighteenth Century: Theory and Interpretation*, 38(2): 134–149.

Labio, Catherine (2006) "The Solution Is in the Text: A Survey of the Recent Literary Turn in Adam Smith Studies." In Vivienne Brown (ed.), *The Adam Smith Review: Volume 2*. London: Routledge.

Leontief, Wassily (1971) "Theoretical Assumptions and Non-Observed Facts." *American Economic Review*, 61(1), 1–7.

Loasby, Brian (1999) *Knowledge, Institutions, and Evolution in Economics.*London: Routledge.

McCloskey, Deirdre (1983) "The Rhetoric of Economics." *Journal of Economic Literature*, 21: 481–517.

McCloskey, Deirdre (1990) "Storytelling in Economics." In Don Lavoie (ed.), *Economics and Hermeneutics*. London: Routledge.

McCloskey, Deirdre (1991) "History, Differential Equations, and the Problem of Narration." *History and Theory*, 30(1): 21–36.Maki, Uskali (ed.) (2002) *Fact and Fiction in Economics: Models, Realism and Social Construction*. Cambridge: Cambridge University Press.

Mandeville, Bernard (1714) *The Fable of the Bees, or, Private Vices, Public Benefits*. London: Printed for J. Rororts.

Marshall, Alfred (1891) *Principles of Economics*, 2nd edn. London: Macmillan.

Marx, Karl (1976) [1867] *Capital*, vol. 1, trans. Ben Fowkes, intro. Ernest Mandel. Harmondsworth, UK: Penguin Books.

Meek, Ronald (1963) *The Economics of Physiocracy: Essays and Translations*. Cambridge, MA: Harvard University Press.

Mizuta, Hiroshi (ed.) (2000) *Adam Smith's Library: A Catalogue*. Oxford: Clarendon Press.

Montesquieu (1973) [1721] *Lettres persanes*, ed. Jean Starobinksi.Paris: Gallimard/ Folio.

Morgan, Mary (2002) "Models, Stories, and the Economic World." In Uskali Maki (ed.), *Fact and Fiction in Economics: Models, Realism and Social Construction*. Cambridge: Cambridge University Press.

Niehans, Jurg (1990) *A History of Economic Theory*. Baltimore: Johns Hopkins Press.

Novak, Maximilian E. (1962) *Economics and the Fiction of Daniel Defoe*. Berkeley: University of California Press.

Ozdoba, Joachin (1980) *Heuristik der Fiktion*. Frankfurt a.M.: Lang.

Pocock, J. G. A. (2006) "Adam Smith and History." In Knud Haakonssen (ed.), *The Cambridge Companion to Adam Smith*. Cambridge: Cambridge University Press, pp. 270–287.

Quesnay, François (1972) Extract from the Royal Economic Maxims of M. de Sully, 3rd edn. In *Quesnay's tableau économique*, trans. and ed. Marguerite Kuczynski and Ronald L. Meek. London: Macmillan, pp. 1–22.

Quesnay, François (1963a) "Analysis." In Ronald L. Meek (ed.), *The Economics of Physiocracy; Essays and Translations*. Cambridge, MA: Harvard University Press.

Quesnay, François (1963b) "Dialogue on the Work of Artisans." In Ronald L. Meek (ed.), *The Economics of Physiocracy; Essays and Translations*. Cambridge, MA: Harvard University Press, pp. 203–230.

Samuels, Warren (ed.) (1990) *Economics as Discourse*. Boston: Kluwer Academic.

Sapir, Jacques (2002) *Les économistes contre la démocratie*. Paris: Albin Michel.

Sapir, Jacques (2005) *Quelle économie pour le XXIe siècle?* Paris: Odile Jacob.

Schabas, Margaret (2005) *Natural Origins of Economics*. Chicago: Chicago University Press.

Schumpeter, Joseph (1954) *History of Economic Analysis*, ed. Elizabeth Boody.New York: Oxford University Press.

Smith, Adam (1976) [1904] *An Inquiry into the Nature and Causes of the Wealth of Nations*, ed., with notes and annotations, Edwin Cannan; pref. George J. Stigler. Chicago: University of Chicago Press.

Smith, Adam (1896) [1763] *Lectures on Justice, Police, Revenue and Arms*, ed., intro., with notes Edwin Cannan.Oxford: Clarendon.

Smith, Adam (1980a) "The History of Astronomy." In W. P. D. Wightman (ed.), *Essays on Philosophical Subjects*. Oxford: Clarendon, pp. 33–105.

Smith, Adam (1980b) "A Letter to the Authors of the*Edinburgh Review*." In J. C. Bryce (ed.), *Essays on Philosophical Subjects*. Oxford: Clarendon, pp. 242–254.

Smith, Adam (1983) "*Lectures on Rhetoric and Belles Lettres*." In J. C. Bryce (ed.), *Essays on Philosophical Subjects*. Oxford: Clarendon.

Sorensen, Janet (1999) "I Talk to Everybody in Their Own Way." In Martha Woodmansee and Mark Osteen (eds), *The New Economic Criticism*. London: Routledge, pp. 75–94.

Stevens, Henry N. (1905) *Lewis Evans, His Map of the Middle British Colonies in America*. London: Stevens, son, and Stiles, p. 18.

Stewart, Dugald (1980) [1793] "Account of the Life and Writings of Adam Smith, L.L.D." In I. S. Ross (ed.), *Essays on Philosophical Subjects*. Oxford: Clarendon, pp. 269–351.

Taylor, Charles (1989) *Sources of the Self: The Making of Modern Identity*. Cambridge, MA: Harvard University Press.

Théré, Christine and Charles, Loïc (2008) "The Writing Workshop of François Quesnay and the Making of Physiocracy." *History of Political Economy*, 40(1): 1–42.

Thompson, James (1996) *Models of Value: Eighteenth-Century Political Economy and the Novel*.Durham, NC: Duke University Press.

Tobin, James (1992) "The Invisible Hand in Modern Macroeconomics." In Michael Fry (ed.), *Adam Smith's Legacy: His Place in the Development of Modern Economics*. London: Routledge.

Varian, Hal (1992) *Microeconomic Analysis*, 3rd edn. New York: W.W. Norton.

Veblen, Thorstein (1919) "Why Is Economics Not an Evolutionary Science?" In *The Place of Science in Modern Civilization and Other Essays*. New York: B.W. Huebsch.

Voltaire (1962) [1752–1764] *Philosophical Dictionary A–I*, trans. and intro. Peter Gay. New York: Basic Books.

Von Neumann, John and Morgenstern, Oskar (2004) [1944] *Theory of Games and Economic Behavior*, 60th anniversary edn. Princeton: Princeton University Press.

Watt, Ian (2001) [1957] *The Rise of the Novel*. Berkeley: University of California Press.

Weintraub, E.Roy (1991) *Stabilizing Dynamics: Constructing Economic Knowledge*. Cambridge: Cambridge University Press.

White, Hayden (1973) *Metahistory: The Historical Imagination in Nineteenth-Century Europe*. Baltimore: Johns Hopkins Press.

Woodmansee, Martha and Osteen, Mark (eds) (1999) *The New Economic Criticism*. London: Routledge.

Woolf, Virginia (2002) "Introduction." In Daniel Defoe,*Moll Flanders*. New York: Modern Library.

# 7   Max Weber and the lost thread of historical economics

Max Weber has long been regarded as one of the preeminent sociologists of the twentieth century, yet his place in the history of economic thought remains obscured, despite his extensive involvement with economic subjects and the academic world of economics in Wilhelmian Germany. Beyond his writings on what he termed "social economics", Weber trained as an economist, taught as a professor of economics, played a significant role in the debates that roiled the younger generation of the German Historical School, and served as editor of what became the leading academic journal in Germany sorting through economic matters in the first decades of the twentieth century, the *Archiv fur Sozialwissenschaften und Sozialpolitik.*

Moreover, the recasting of Weber as a sociologist is further complicated by the fact that his writings reflect a deep concern with the relation of history to economics, the centrality of which was captured in his methodological essays, including those with which he launched his philosophical inquiries in the social sciences, "The Logical Problems of Historical Economics."

What has befallen historical economics since Weber may constitute a "lost thread." The "lost thread" of historical economics, though, is less a question about how to characterize Max Weber's approach or work, one of the major disputes that have animated a host of Weber scholars, among them Wolfgang Mommsen, Dirk Kaesler, Wilhelm Hennis, Friedrich Tenbruck, and Keith Tribe, and more a matter of the fate of historical economics itself, and, consequently, the extent to which Weber's grappling with it may afford some insight into what a historical economics might have become.

## Backdrop to Weber's shift from economics

Weber pursued a course of study in the latter decades of the nineteenth century that, in the German tradition, provided the requisite training in economics, typically through the faculty of law, while in his university appointments, including at Heidelberg, he taught courses in economics. Weber first gained notice in the early 1890s for his study of agrarian labor in Prussia, which fit well within the research aims and program of the German Historical School.

In 1904, after his career as a teacher had been shortened by a nervous break-down and related health matters, Weber assumed editorial responsibilities, along with Werner Sombart and Edgar Jaffe, of the *Archiv fur Sozialwissenschaften und Sozialpolitik*, where he made explicit his desire and plan for the journal to treat economic subjects, but conceived of in the broadest possible way.

Weber was also associated with, and participated in the meetings of the Verein fur Sozialpolitik, the leading organization for the workings of the later German Historical School, under the aegis of Gustav Schmoller, and played a significant role at its 1909 conference in Vienna, debating the nature and scope of economic productivity. Weber, in concert with his brother Alfred, put forward a spirited case for a "postulate of value judgment" that presented a challenge setting him apart from the German Historical School. As described and presented by Wilhelm Hennis, Max Weber published a report four years later about this challenge, noting that in rebuking "the blending of science and value judgements in Manchester liberalism" where "money-making" was taken as the sole pertinent economic "motivation," Schmoller and the later generation of the German Historical School had themselves "fused together" "scientific investigation and value judgement" (see Hennis 1991: 33).

But it was also the case that in the first decade of the twentieth century Weber had entered into a period in which methodological concerns, plumbing the foundations of economics from a largely philosophical perspective, took center stage. These included a set of critiques of two of the leading figures of the earlier German Historical School, Wilhelm Roscher and Karl Knies, on the problematic features of historical economics, the essay on "objective possibility" that launched Weber's notion of an "ideal-type" construction, and a critique of the logic of the cultural sciences that had been advanced by the economic historian Eduard Meyer, also associated with the German Historical School, so as to highlight "the different steps involved in the 'imputation' of causality in history (its 'logical structure')" (Colliot-Thélène 2006: 20).

Thus, by 1909 Weber's differences with the German Historical School had become evident. Weber had begun a disciplinary shift, participating in the formation of and first meetings held by the German Sociological Society (Kaesler 1984). His involvement with it did not prove to be altogether smooth, even as he produced several lengthy volumes of a pathbreaking *Grundrisse* on "Economics and Society," much of which was published posthumously. In the end his advocacy of an "economic sociology" encountered resistance that would, after Weber's death in 1920, lead to the virtual disappearance of such a disciplinary framework within sociology for the next half-century, until its revival – of sorts – in the 1980s through the efforts of Richard Swedberg and Mark Granovetter (see Swedberg 1998: 162–72).

### *"Conceptual foundations of economics"*

While Weber taught what would have been regarded as the standard curriculum in German universities of the day, one course that Keith Tribe has given special attention to involved economic methodology, and covered "the conceptual foundations of economics," the extant lecture notes from 1898–1899 from which Tribe was able to draw.

In examining these lecture notes Tribe has highlighted two critical aspects of Weber's treatment of the "conceptual foundations of economics": one that separates Weber from the dominant approach taken by the German Historical School; the other that sets him in opposition to the emerging neoclassical school of thought. As to the former, Tribes cites Weber's fluency in contemporary economic thought, and the mere fact of his attention to "methodological issues" as evidence of his interest in and recognition of the importance of economic theorizing, transcending the "systematic" recounting of the details of economic history, as Schmoller had done. Tribe extends this contrast further by attributing to Weber an apparent decoupling of economics and history: "The focus is thus upon the conditions of modern economic activity, [and] does not seek to grasp the nature of economic life as the product of a long process of historical development" (Tribe 1995: 90–1).

I regard this latter notion as gainsayed by much that occupies center stage in Weber's methodological essays and later writings on "social economics." One might consider in this vein Weber's description of what constitutes the "'systematic' approach" in economics in a letter to Heinrich Rickert, dated 28 April 1905:

> In *economics*, the 'systematic' approach – when it is not simply a classification of theorems for the purposes of *instruction* – is *either concept formation* (construction of ideal types), that is to say (logically speaking) *preliminary* historical work, *or* a *historical* cross-section of an individual stage of development. In the *latter* case, it is 'history' in the same sense as Jacob Burckhardt's *Culture of the Renaissance*.
>
> (Weber [1905] 2012: 381)

Moreover, in the outline of his lecture notes, Weber prefaced his enumeration of the assumptions underlying the "abstract theory of economics" with remarks that set such theory within a historical evolution, emerging within "modern Occidental culture" (Weber [1898] 1990: 29).

As to Weber's opposition to the abstract theory of neoclassical economics, Tribes sees it as rooted in Weber's objection to the mathematization of economics, and identifies Stanley Jevons as the exemplar. That was because mathematization deviated and deflected from the "science of man" that Tribe, following Hennis, sees as Weber's central pursuit.

To make this case Tribe cites the critique of "abstract theory" Weber presented in the outline of his lecture notes. The full text appears below:

> For this purpose it presupposes a *constructed* 'economic subject,' in respect of which, by *contrast* to empirical men, it

a.  *Ignores* all those motives not specifically *economic* in nature; considers, that is, among all those motives that influence empirical men, only those arising from the satisfaction of material needs and treats the remainder as *not present*:

b.  *Fabricates* the presence of specific qualities in empirical men, when they are in fact either *absent* or only *partially* present, to wit

   (i)    Complete *insight* into the prevailing *situation* – perfect economic knowledge;

   (ii)   Unfaltering selection of the *most appropriate means* for a given end – absolute 'economic rationality':

   (iii)  Exclusive devotion to one's own powers to the attainment of economic goods – unwearying economic endeavour.

It therefore argues on the basis of *unrealistic* men, analogous to a mathematical ideal.

(Tribe 1995: 91)

I take Weber's cautions and objections as forming a more complex critique of economic abstraction, beyond the question of mathematization, and linked to a host of concerns and considerations raised elsewhere by Weber and his contemporaries, but also not without its own contradictions. This emerges immediately in the first point raised, for the "ideal types" that Weber advanced as the way forward in relating theory to empirical evidence are realized as rational, if fictive constructs. As Weber stated in his essay on "objective possibility and adequate causation": "In order to grasp the real causal interconnections, we construct unreal ones" (Weber [1906] 2012: 182).

Thus, the turn to an idealized fiction need not be mathematical, even if analogized as such. Of course, in Weber's view the construct must then be gauged in relation to how closely, or how distantly, it comports with the facts, a matter that he noted required historical research (Weber [1904] 2012: 131–2). In consequence as well, historical perspective was reintroduced into Weber's construction of economics.

The challenge to the restriction of entertaining only economic motives fits rather neatly the terms of Weber's vision of a wider scope to the treatment of economic subjects, as expressed in his 1904 essay in the *Archiv*. By implication it accords with the impact of the historical school that Weber identified in that essay through Roscher, but had been made explicit even earlier in the critique of Roscher from 1903, where Weber faulted Roscher – and presumably the German Historical School more generally – for failing to grasp the need to establish fully the "causal *heteronomy*" of economic subjects (Weber [1903] 1975: 80).

Finally, the "fabrications" cited by Weber bear a striking resemblance to the cautions raised by Henri Poincaré in his correspondence in the early 1900s with Leon Walras over the possibilities of mathematizing economics. While Poincaré was generally supportive of Walras' aspirations, he took note of the limitations posed by both the lack of clairvoyance, what Weber called the lack of "perfect economic knowledge," and the circumscribed nature of "economic rationality" (Turk 2012). Thus, Weber's concerns here were attuned to the same ones voiced by the conventionalists of his day. By and large such concerns amounted to a "road not taken" in mainstream twentieth-century economics.

## Whither economic theorizing?

While deeply concerned with matters of methodology across disciplines and the formation of concepts within them, Weber appeared only minimally engaged with the content of economic theory in his writings. In 1917 Weber was compelled to respond to stinging criticism by his other *Archiv* co-editor Edgar Jaffe, cited below, even as Weber sought to affirm the importance of economic theory, a point emphasized by Swedberg (Swedberg 1998: 203):

> In spite of the extraordinary range of his knowledge and the extension of his work into a large number of adjacent fields (legal science, epistemology, sociology), [Weber] has completely neglected economic theory and also from time to time expressed a minimum of expectation with respect to the possible results of purely theoretical investigations.
>
> (see Weber [1917] 2012: 303)

In his early lectures on economics, though, this was not the case, as Keith Tribe has pointed out (Tribe 1995). On the other hand, in his methodological pieces and his lengthy disquisitions on economics and society, references to economic thinkers are few and far between. It is therefore striking to find among these rare references ones to Bohm-Bawerk's *Rights and Relationships* in Weber's methodological essay on the "materialist conception of history" (Weber [1907] 2012: 217f) and in his posthumously published *Economy and Society* (Weber [1921] 1999: 205).

Weber did produce a short piece that appeared in 1908 in support of the theory of marginal utility as an economic rather than psychological construction, a subject which otherwise seems far afield from his concerns in assaying historical economics. Extensive commentary suggests that this was more an effort on Weber's part to place himself in and above the *Methodenstreit*, defending Carl Menger's intellectual integrity, if not necessarily the full content of his program, against what Weber regarded as the unfair and unwarranted criticism of it by Lujo Brentano (see Weber [1922] 1988: 395–6, especially p. 396, fn. 1), occasioning a letter from Weber to Brentano (Weber [1908] 2012: 396). It also represented a means whereby Weber could assert his primary concern about methodology; namely, how economic theory might be constructed through the use of "fictive assumption[s]."

This essay in turn built upon Weber's longstanding methodological case against the grounding of economics or history in psychology. In his earlier critique of

Karl Knies, the second of his essays on historical economics, Weber rejected Wilhelm Wundt's claims for a scientific role for psychology (Weber [1905] 1975: 111), then challenged the notion put forward by Hugo Munsterberg about the existence of "subjectifying sciences" in the following way:

> There is a view which holds that 'psychology' in general or some as-yet-undeveloped special sort of psychology must be an indispensable 'foundational science' for history and economics. This is because all historical and economic processes pass through, and must 'traverse,' a 'psychical' stage. This view is obviously untenable.
>
> (Weber [1905] 1975: 140)

The linchpin of Weber's contention was that "[h]istory," and by extension economics, "does not treat inner processes ... as having intrinsic interest. On the contrary, its intrinsic interest is in the relation of man to the 'world,' its 'external' conditions and its consequences" (Weber [1905] 1975: 141). Hence, as Hennis has emphasized, Weber sought to advance a "science of man" (Hennis 1989).

In what might be taken to be a form of reciprocity in the realm of economic theorizing, Richard Swedberg notes that Menger, who actually outlived Weber, never mentioned Weber in his own writings, and Bohm-Bawerk alluded to Weber only once, and that with regard to the article on marginal utility (Swedberg 1998: 301, fn. 141).

Moreover, Simon Kuznets' notion of the "recalcitrant nature" of reality (see chapters 8 and 9) was a matter already taken up and addressed from a methodological standpoint by Weber in his critique of Karl Knies, where he focused attention upon the "irrational gap" between concept and object (or concept and reality). It is only a small step to treat a standard macroeconomic measure, like national income or gross national product, as a concept to be defined. How great, then, is the "gap" between such a concept and reality?

For all these concerns, though, a central thesis of Weber's inquiry into historical economics was the rejection of a disciplinary division based upon a distinction between the nomothetic and the idiographical, which had often been cited in distinguishing between the rule-making and regularities of economics and the amassing of detail associated with history.

Might one draw upon what disciplines seek to explain as the basis for distinctions among different disciplines, rather than the recurring notion of a division between the nomothetic and the idiographical? Weber saw the imperative of superseding such a division, and instead addressed the importance of discerning purpose or goal, introducing differences in the weight of meaning and interpretation, so this may serve as a possibility. This also leads to a rethinking of the question of the balance between the general and the particular; calling thereby for a broader examination of the methodological and philosophical concerns that propelled Weber's inquiries into the possibilities of a historical economics.

## Reconceptualizing the framework for economics

In his formulation of the nature and state of economics at the turn of the twentieth century, Weber made a striking pronouncement upon assuming the editorship of the *Archiv fur Sozialwissenschaften und Sozialpolitik* in 1904. The discipline, or the comprehension of that which is economic, had changed, been recast, or perhaps even transformed with the advent of two mid-nineteenth-century economic thinkers: Roscher and Marx. From the vantage point of continental – and most certainly central – Europe, economics at the turn of the twentieth century centered about three different and competing schools: Manchester liberal, Marxist, and German historical. The rise of the last of these schools in and after the 1870s was seen as a rejection of the ideology of free trade advanced by British interests and as a response to the radical claims of Marxian socialism; in effect, the creation of a "third way" in economics. What Marxist thought and the German Historical School had in common was a strong link between economics and history, even if the nature of that link differed markedly between the two. Marxists saw the "law of motion of capital" unfold through historical stages, with economic law as the classical school might have conceived of it effectively superseded by the laws of history. The German Historical school viewed any economic law with general or universal pretensions as suspect, and instead took the totality of culture, embodying social experience and historical background, often framed on a "national" basis, as the shaper of economic experience and understanding, different and distinctive for each nation.

What Weber's reference to Roscher and Marx can only mean is that, in some fashion and without necessarily choosing to pursue the approach taken by either of the two schools implicitly alluded to, any contemporary economic inquiry must contain a link between the economic and the historical. This would provide the basis for a "historical economics." While Weber moved outside the orbit of the German Historical School from which he originally began, he continued to draw upon certain aspects of it. In Weber's case one can discern an abiding concern for an interpenetration of history and economics, and a strong tendency to see culture, as idea, ideology, or social form, shaping in part – but not in whole– economic activity and action. Even in his defense of the theory of marginal utility as an economic construct rather than a grafting from psychological theory, Weber contended that it was ultimately based upon a "cultural/historical fact" that comports with a world in which capitalist relations have come to dominate (Weber [1922] 1988: 395).

Weber's approach was intended to situate economic activity as a part of "culture," whose understanding necessarily required a historical setting and perspective. As he stated in his disquisition on "the objectivity of knowledge," the second part of his introductory essay in the *Archiv* in 1904:

> To the extent that our science traces back and causally imputes economic cultural phenomena to individual – economic or non-economic – causes,

it seeks "historical knowledge." To the extent that it traces [the course of] one specific element of cultural phenomena – the economic one – as culturally significant or important through the most diverse cultural contexts, it seeks to *interpret* history from a specific point of view, and it provides a partial image – [in other words:] it makes a *preliminary contribution* to the complete historical knowledge of culture.

(Weber [1904] 2012: 110)

"Theory" itself is seen as drawing upon "cultural significations" or "cultural meanings" of an "empirical reality" to form "imaginary pictures," if "rational constructs," constituting what Weber called "ideal-types" (Weber [1922] 1988: 396; Weber [1906] 2012: 175).

At the same time, Weber saw the need to establish a coherent basis for gauging causes in historical explanation, relying upon causal imputation and the referencing of facts to values, all part of a methodological approach known as "objective possibility" that took Weber outside the realm of the historical school (Freund 1978: 170–2). Here Weber drew heavily from the work of the neo-Kantian psychologist Johannes von Kries, whose writings on "objective possibility" appeared in 1886 and 1888. The later work in fact was entitled, "Uber den Begriff der objektiven Moglichkeit und einige Anwendungen desselben" (von Kries 1888).[1]

## The "logical problems of historical economics"

In the essays tackling "the logical problems of historical economics" Weber initiated a critique of the philosophical framework underlying the work of two of the three dominant figures, rather than the specific content of their texts, from the early generation of the German Historical School, Wilhelm Roscher and Karl Knies (with the third being Bruno Hildebrand).

Weber's critique of Roscher, his first methodological essay, written in 1903, raises a raft of foundational questions about the nature of economics, most especially about what it seeks to explain. Weber sets the stage by conceiving the "institutions of economic life" as the result of a qualitative transformation of their constituent elements:

Clearly the economy is not a mere aggregate of single economic organizations, no more than its analogue, the human body, is "simply a mixture of chemical phenomena."

(Weber [1903] 1975: 80)

He then states:

Before as well as after Roscher, the fundamental substantive and methodological problem of economics is constituted by the question: how are the origins and persistence of the institutions of economic life to be explained, institutions which were not purposefully created by collective means, but which nevertheless – from our point of view – function purposefully?

This is the basic problem of economics for the same reason that the problem of the explanation of the 'purposefulness' of organisms dominates biology.

(Weber [1903] 1975: 80)

Weber then turns to a dissection of Roscher's failings in pursuing this problem:

At this point, we find the same contradictions in Roscher's methodological reasoning which we noted earlier in his philosophy of history. Roscher's intention is to conceive the processes of life historically: that is to say, in their full actuality. Therefore we should expect that – in accordance with the later conception of historical economics developed since the work of Knies and in opposition to classical economics – he should focus his investigation on the constant influence of *non*economic factors on economic action. That is to say, we should expect him to focus upon the *causal heteronomy of the human economy.*

(Weber [1903] 1975: 80)

The first of these considerations, it has been suggested, reflects the influence of Carl Menger and the Austrian school in relating the individual to institutions (see, variously, Swedberg 1998: 176, 284 fn. 15; Hodgson 2001: 117–18), yet the allusion to the "origins and persistence" of such institutions, indeed their centrality to "economic life," points to a greater need to examine the role of institutions as such. This in turn leads to the second concern, in which Weber challenged the historical school for failing to be sufficiently thorough-going in its incorporation of a wider net of human experiences, actions, and thoughts.

One might think in terms of the German philosophical traditions underlying and shaping Weber's comprehension and critique of the German Historical School and its goal of establishing a historical economics within the realm of the historical sciences. Both neo-Kantian and Hegelian perspectives had to be addressed. Weber's criticism of Roscher was based in significant part on the implicit "emanationist" approach Weber saw Roscher turn to in what Weber called an "involution" of Hegel (Weber [1903] 1975: 90–1) in order to explain how the accumulation of pertinent facts – economic, social, or otherwise – may lead to the forming of general, universal economic laws, where the concept of generality existed in inchoate form in the facts themselves. Here Weber struck a neo-Kantian pose, relying upon Heinrich Rickert's treatment of "concept formation," where the "irrational gap" between concept and object, or concept and reality, had to be acknowledged as essential to the construction of any intellectual discipline. Hence, Roscher's adherence to the idea that a historical economics would produce an emanating set of universal laws was fundamentally wrong-headed.

On the other hand, Weber dismissed the notion that the historical or cultural sciences could be distinguished by their idiographical quality, emphasizing the particular, as against the generalities of the nomothetic sciences, placing him thereby in opposition to Wilhelm Windelband and Rickert, the neo-Kantians of the Baden school, who had championed that distinction. Moreover, Weber clearly drew upon Wilhelm Dilthey's division of the natural and the cultural sciences, to the extent that he took up the notion of "Verstehen" as essential to the operation of the latter. In that last regard, it has been contended that Dilthey's division of the sciences was rooted in ontological considerations, that is, in its nature, while, following Rickert, Weber's was epistemological, a matter of perception and comprehension (Colliot-Thélène 2006: 33), and hence opened the way toward transcending that division, at least in part.

Weber's assessment of this division is laid out in the opening of his critique of Roscher:

> The philosophical sciences have the following aim: to order an extensively and intensively infinite multiplicity of phenomena by employing a system of concepts and laws. In the ideal case, these concepts and laws are unconditionally and universally valid.
>
> (Weber [1903] 1975: 55)

Note the emphasis here on both "concepts" and "laws," rather than a focus directly upon laws alone, as one might expect in the traditional disposition of the distinction between the nomothetic and the idiographical. "Concepts" could be regarded as definitional, aligned with analysis, in contrast to the pairing of description and explanation. Equally important, it brings to light the importance of "concept formation," which also must be comprehended in the context of reigning German philosophical traditions, active at the turn of the twentieth century through the work of Wilhelm Wundt and Rickert. So Weber went on to state:

> Their uncompromising logical commitment to systematic hierarchies of general concepts under other concepts still more general and their standards of precision and unambiguity commit the philosophical sciences to the most radical reduction possible.
>
> (Weber [1903] 1975: 56)

For the "sciences of concrete reality," "the definitive logical instrument of these disciplines is the formation of relational concepts which are increasingly rich in *content*. In consequence, they are of increasingly limited *extension*. Their definitive products – if they may be said to have any conceptual character at all – are concrete *substantive concepts* of universal – or, as we may say, 'historical' – *significance*" (Weber [1903] 1975: 58).

In the end he concluded:

> If Roscher did not succeed in following his path away from Hegel to its
> ultimate conclusion, then this circumstance is principally responsible; unlike
> Hegel, he failed to grasp the methodological importance of the logical
> problem concerning the relationship between a concept and its object.
>
> (Weber [1903] 1975: 91)

Its solution then became the central question before Weber.

Weber also saw Wundt's work on the classification of science, presented as a
disquisition on the nature of the logic of science, as one of the critical, contemporaneous benchmarks against which efforts to categorize the various
"sciences" or intellectual disciplines needed to be gauged. In certain respects
Wundt loomed larger in Weber's critique of Knies than Knies himself. For
Weber Wundt's categorization of the "socio-cultural sciences" as fundamentally
different from the physical sciences failed to account for the requisite interpretation and imposition of value judgments that underlay the operation of
all sciences. This led Weber to seek out and make plain "the *meta*historical
values on which history is based" (Weber [1903] 1975: 111).

Jean-Jacques Guinchard offers up another insight into the place Wundt
held for Weber, suggesting that in the late nineteenth century discourses of the
neo-Kantians and Dilthey pointed the way forward for the human or cultural
sciences which was to be found through one of the following exemplary or
paradigmatic pathways: the first was through the psychology advanced by
Wundt, "which moved beyond introspection to experimentation," while the
second was through the political economy advanced by Gustav Schmoller, the
dominant figure in the later generation of the German Historical School
(Guinchard 2006: 72).

As to the former notion, Guinchard is following in the footsteps of Julian
Freund, who, while treating Weber as a sociologist first and foremost, stated
that "[m]ore so than the incipient sociologies of other countries, only German
sociology was influenced at the start by psychologism," in part through the
*Volkerpsychologie* as "prescribed by W. Wundt" (Freund 1978: 151). As to
the latter, in Freund's analysis "historicism" played a significant but secondary
role (Freund 1978: 151).

It is also the case that Wundt not only presented a vision – or at least a
version – of psychology that might be pursued; he also devised a means of
categorizing science, or the various scientific disciplines, more generally. It is
also to this categorization, and the analysis that underlies it, that Weber reacted
and responded.

## Weber and Marx on "historical materialism"

Philippe Raynaud, introducing Weber's *General Economic History* to French-
speaking audiences, situates Weber's "project" as fundamentally rooted in

critical philosophy, where in significant part Weber sought to place historical materialism on a more solid philosophical footing (Raynaud 1991: II).

From that vantage point one can reassess Weber's relation to Marx. Weber is often seen as confronting or opposing Marx. This is often cast as a contrast between Weber's grounding of historical change in both economic and non-economic factors, manifested in "cultural significations" and represented through "ideal-types," and Marx's materialist history; or the ideational *Spirit of Capitalism and the Protestant Ethic* set against the materialist *Capital* or *Communist Manifesto*. As a parallel contrast, in the realm of sociology, Karl Lowith posed Weber's emphasis upon the centrality of rationalization in capitalism against Marx's emphasis upon self-alienation (Lowith [1932] 1982).

But even at the outset this picture needs some adjustment. Colliot-Thélène, like Swedberg, cites a reference in E. Baumgarten's work (published in 1964) to a conversation Weber had with Oswald Spengler, in which Weber "affirmed that every intellectual of his era had to recognize his/her debt to Marx and Nietzsche" (Colliot-Thélène 2006: 46)

Tribe also describes Weber's familiarity with Marxian writings from the 1898–1899 course outline of the "Conceptual Foundations of Economics." He notes that the section devoted to "'The Stages of Development of Economic Theory' is divided into pre-Smithian, classical, and socialist economics, in which the last interestingly enough contains twenty-three references including *Capital* and Engels' *Anti-Duhring*" (Tribe 1995: 93).

Among intellectual forebears mentioned in his methodological writings Weber devoted considerable attention to Marx, even when the greater part of his commentary was critical, intended to distinguish and differentiate his analysis and perspective from that of Marx. For example, Weber cited Marx as having produced the "most important" "ideal types", while distancing himself from the import of or world-view associated with Marxian ideas or analysis: "We have deliberately refrained from referring to what is (in our view) by far the most important case of ideal-typical constructions: th[ose made by] Marx."

He went on to state:

> Here we shall therefore merely point out that *all* specifically Marxist 'laws' are evolutionary constructions – provided they are *theoretically* correct – have an ideal-typical character.

Weber then followed with a warning:

> While these "concepts" have *heuristic* importance, it would be "dangerous" not to distinguish them clearly from being "empirically valid or even as *real*."
> (Weber [1904] 2012: 132–3)

This combination of distancing and embrace is evident in the way that Weber rejected the Marxian "world-view" underlying the "materialist conception of history" laid out by Marx and then sought to sustain and develop his own "scientific" conception of "historical materialism."

"Undoubtedly, the emphasis on the *socio-economic* aspects of cultural life leads to a severe limitation of the subjects with which we deal. It will be said that the economic or, in the imprecise terminology that has sometimes been used, the 'materialist' point of view from which cultural life will be considered here is 'one-sided.' Indeed so, and that 'one-sidedness' is intentional. The belief that scientific work, as it progresses, should assume the task of overcoming the 'one-sidedness' of the economic approach by broadening it into a *general* social science is flawed from the outset" (Weber [1904] 2012: 111).

He then set forth his own approach, intended to be "applied carefully and without dogmatic prejudice" (Weber [1904] 2012: 111):

> While we have abandoned the outworn belief according to which the totality of cultural phenomena can be *deduced* as a product or a function of 'material' constellations of interests, we for our part still believe that the *analysis of social phenomena and cultural processes*, from the particular perspective of their *economic* conditionality and implications, has been a creative and fruitful scientific principle, and will continue to be so in the foreseeable future … Conceived as a *'world view'* or as the common denominator of the causal explanation of historical reality, the so-called 'materialist conception of history' must be categorically rejected; [nevertheless] it is one of the principal aims of our journal to cultivate the economic *interpretation* of history.
>
> (Weber [1904] 2012: 111)

But even in so doing Weber continued to show admiration for Marx, referring to "the so-called 'materialist conception of history." in its old sense – as expressed crudely, but with genius in the *Communist Manifesto*" (Weber [1904] 2012: 111).

## Historical meaning, historical understanding

Thus, Weber's "historical materialism" was intended to infuse an economic interpretation into historical events and developments. Yet the "meaning" of those events and developments was, according to Weber's critique of Knies, necessarily "historical," requiring a further examination of the questions of causality attendant upon historical meaning as well as its nature:

> However, the fact that we ascribe historical 'meaning' to each of these events cannot be deduced from the circumstances of their causation.
>
> (Weber [1905] 1975: 108)

> On the contrary, in each of these cases, the meaning we ascribe to the phenomenon – that is, the relations which we establish between these

phenomena and 'values' – is a logically incongruous and heterogeneous factor which cannot be 'deduced' from the 'constitutive elements' of the event in question.

(Weber [1905] 1975: 108)

Hence, there is no inherent meaning that arises directly out of the facts themselves. Moreover, while this assessment can be found in what appears to be a set of abiding concerns about the "methodological problem of economics," economics, at least as a distinct subject, is nowhere in view, nor are any of the historical facts to which Weber alluded necessarily economic, like the often-cited interpretation of the significance of the battle of Marathon, a pivotal example raised by Eduard Meyer in his history of classical antiquity (Weber [1906] 2012: 176; also Weber [1919–20] 1978).

Elsewhere Weber did make the link between the historical fact and the economic statistic. In his correspondence with Ladislaus von Bortkiewicz Weber affirmed that such statistics should be regarded as "fact" when they are "historical," otherwise their role is an interpretive one.

The degree of frequency is [either] a 'historical' fact (because it is of historical interest) or a 'heuristic instrument' depending on the 'sense' of the cognitive aim, and the same is true of all other 'statistical' products of knowledge.

(Weber [1906] 2012: 385)

Recent efforts to explore Weber's conception of "a valid scientific explanation," set in the context of the philosophy of history, continue to give significant weight to the role played by "historical understanding" (Bevir 2007). According to Mark Bevir: "Weber … conceived of historical understanding as a part of (or even a species of) causal explanation" (Bevir 2007: 269). He began by noting:

For Weber, a valid scientific explanation is a causal one, but in the human sciences, causality has to assume a peculiar form in that it required an interpretive dimension … Consequently, causal explanation in the social sciences depends on demonstrating a concrete relation between a specific action and its subjective motivation, not on formulating general causal laws.

(Bevir 2007: 263)

Yet there are nuances and complications to all this, as well as questions as to the scope of any subjectivity entailed. Weber's emphasis upon the role of interpretation in the human or social sciences was meant, at least in part, to transcend the notion of a fundamental division within all the sciences between the nomothetic and the idiographical, and to set the contrast between the natural and the social sciences on a different footing, indeed a different foundation. Moreover, the emergence of "interpretation" at the center of any causal analysis in the social sciences brought forward a new set of problems and questions.

"What is the role of understanding within this causal epistemology? For Weber … [understanding] is built into the logic of the human sciences. Nonetheless, Weber also argued that … verstehen must be supplemented by causal analysis" (Bevir 2007, 263). Hence, "a proposed interpretation must satisfy a double criterion of 'adequacy'" (Bevir 2007, 263): one that is "subjective," the other "causal."

However, one must also account for what Weber comprehended more generally to be a "historical fact": something shaped by theory, whose significance is the result of a weighing of possibilities (or probabilities) and the attachment of different cultural values to them. According to Colliot-Thélène:

> Far from the 'historical fact' being an immediate given from experience prior to any theoretical elaboration, it is on the contrary molded by theory, to the extent where the historian can disentangle the real causal relations only by passing through the construction, implicit or explicit, of unreal relations (the possibilities not realized).
>
> (Colliot-Thélène 2006: 21)

These are the arrays of possibilities, some realized, some not, found within what might be termed "logical space." This notion seems likely drawn directly from von Kries' projection of the "range of possibilities" denoted as "Spielraum" (see Heidelberger 2001: 177–8), a term which Weber used in prefacing his description of abstract economic theory in his 1898 lecture notes (Weber [1898] 1990: 29) and then took up in his discussion of social action in *Economy and Society*, distinguishing "Nahrungsspielraum" from "Erwerbsspielraum" (Weber [1919–20] 1978: 46).

## Deciphering "ideal-types"

According to Bevir, to make this two-step process of causal attribution work required "the deployment of ideal types" (Bevir 2007: 264). These ideal types were intended to offer up theoretical constructs, largely of concepts, that could be matched, if not perfectly so, to a set of facts or empirical experience drawn from a "concrete reality" whose multiplicity or "extension" was unbounded.

But did this process adequately address the question of how one interpretation might be chosen over another? Put in other terms, was the "deployment" Bevir described more a matter of mental construction, as Fritz Machlup has suggested (Machlup 1978b: 236–9)? If so, the choice of model for construction needs to be reexamined, deciphered, and decoded in a new light.

To begin with, the notion of "ideal-type" is generally thought of in terms of grand concepts, rooted in history and economics, with sweeping explanatory power, like "feudalism" or the "city economy," though it is also the case that Weber included theories like "marginal utility" as "ideal-types" as well.

In certain critical respects the influence of the psychologist Johannes von Kries, already noted above, was decisive. As Weber himself remarked in a footnote to his essay on the "logic of science": "I am almost embarrassed by the extent to which v. Kries' ideas are 'plundered' here" (Weber [1906] 2012: 182f.).

Von Kries had sought to find a way of establishing what he called "objective possibilities" in human experience from among which, on the basis of a probabilistic standard drawn from criminal proceedings, a process known as "causal imputation," the most likely specific outcome could be identified. Weber adopted this two-step procedure of causal attribution, even drawing upon von Kries' terminology of "objective possibility." The array of possible facts, whose establishment constituted the first of the two steps, was shaped by theory, what von Kries and Weber both referred to as "nomological" knowledge. (See, for example, Heidelberger 2001: 178.) Independent of this was the determination of the most likely specific outcome, which Weber saw as a product of "historical understanding" or even historical research.

What is the exact place of theory in the process of constructing "ideal-types"? This is not altogether clear. On the one hand, as Weber wrote to his former student Robert Liefmann shortly before his untimely death in June 1920:

> I am supposed to claim that the epistemological value of theory is 'slight.' *Where* might that be? Theory constructs ideal-types and for me that is a most indispensable contribution.
>
> (Weber [1920] 2012: 410; see also Hennis 1991: 29)

In his earlier methodological essays, though, Weber took a somewhat different tack. In his essay on marginal utility Weber inverted the relation between theory and "ideal-types":

> The principles that constitute economic theory as such not only, as everyone knows … fail to represent 'the totality' of our science, they are moreover only one means for the analysis of causal relationships of empirical reality, albeit a means that is often underrated. As soon as we seek to grasp and explain causally this reality itself as a complex of cultural significations, then economic theory stands revealed as a summation of "ideal-typical" concepts.

He went on to state:

> That means that its principles represent a series of intellectually constructed processes that rarely, if ever, appear in an "ideal purity" in historical reality but which are on the other hand – since the elements of these principles are derived from reality and only intellectually accentuated as rational constructs – usable both as heuristic analytical tools and as a productive instrument for the representation of empirical variety.
>
> (translation provided by Hennis 1991: 30; text found in Weber [1922] 1988: 396–7)

Critically, if "economic theory stands revealed as a summation of 'ideal-typical' concepts," is there any overall structure to economic theory, or is it the episodic or even serendipitous collection of individual concepts, much as one might conceive through a kind of parallelism of strands of history or historical narrative? If at the same time these concepts are "constructed" by theory, does this represent a reflexive loop of theory both "constructing" and being "constructed" by concepts? After all, Weber also claimed that the "principles" of economic theory are ultimately "derived from reality," only "heightened" or "*accentuated.*"

Also noteworthy is the fact that Weber speaks in terms of principles and concepts rather than laws or rules. In fact, in detailing the nature and operation of "ideal-types" Weber stressed the dangers attendant upon the "reduction" of reality to laws (Weber [1904] 2012: 131).

At the same time, Weber's championing of the need to recognize the centrality of "value-judgments" in deciding among the various facts to be given probative weight might well lead one to a relativist perspective in which the "reality" presented reflects the "value-judgments"; and hence the "value-systems" of those constructing the history. This, for example, is evident in Freund's treatment of Weber's consideration of the relation of facts to values (Freund 1978: 173–4). Weber himself chose to make "value-judgments" on the basis of what was deemed "typical," as in the case of the concept of "economic exchange." Here he interpreted it in light of the "rational" behavior exhibited as "capitalist" practice, validating thereby the use of the notion of the "law of marginal utility" (Weber [1904] 2012: 131).

Thus there are two elements of which to take note: the probabilistic standard and the explicit identification of values, or value-judgments, underlying the selection of facts from the "soup" of reality (also metaphorically characterized as "concrete").

Moreover, it may be possible to give a more contemporary ring to the notion of "ideal types" as well. Recent efforts to examine and enhance the role of narrative in the model-building typically conducted by economists have included some significant focus on the matter of "fit", as in Mary Morgan's exploration of model-building as a critical entry into how economists think and work (Morgan 2012). Morgan noted that the narrative or story about which the model cohered provided only an approximate or imperfect fit. Weber clearly saw his "ideal types" as theoretical constructs, rather than narratives or stories, but also recognized a crucial concern in their "fit" as well, that is, their rough conformance to the "concrete reality" from which they had been abstracted, borrowing language from Rickert and ultimately Emil Lask about the "irrational gap" between "concept" and "object" (Colliot-Thélène 2006: 38).

Under these circumstances, what keeps the history being constructed from being no more than one of a multiplicity of possible histories? Is the probative weight of evidence in a courtroom sufficient to overcome and transcend the centrifugal effect of diverse "value-judgments" and make it possible to choose from any array of possible facts? While there is no reason to link directly Weber's immersion in central European thought with the philosophical inquiries of Ludwig Wittgenstein, it is nonetheless striking that both drew upon the model – or analogy – of the courtroom experience. According to Georg Henrik von Wright, Wittgenstein drew inspiration for his pictorial theory of language in the *Tractatus Logico-Philosophicus* by analogizing from the courtroom accident reconstruction of all "possible states of affairs" (von Wright 1955: 532–3).

Moreover, the philosopher of science Michael Heidelberger has suggested that Wittgenstein's *Tractatus* was significantly influenced by Johannes von Kries' elaboration of a "logic of probability." According to Heidelberger, von Kries' "perspective" would lead to "the concept of an elementary proposition in Wittgenstein" (Heidelberger 2001: 185). Heidelberger's characterization of von Kries' central notion about probability bears a striking resemblance to Weber's own structure of "objective possibility" and the need for the two-step form of causality noted by Bevir, though with the element of subjectivity removed:

> [As a neo-Kantian, von Kries] argues that probability must be based in some way or other in physical, objective features of reality and not on some degree of subjective certainty. The required foundation is to be introduced by way of the concept of 'objective or physical possibility.'
>
> (Heidelberger 2001: 177)

Weber, of course, was addressing a matter of concept or concept formation, drawing upon the work of Rickert in that regard, and so can be situated in his own historical moment. Yet some of the critiques of the more recent period may nonetheless apply, where matters of context, often through broader institutions, surface. Can the rules and courses of action be made comprehensible only on the basis of "community standards"? Moreover, does the probative standard itself call into question the primacy of individual motivation or action, as the courtroom proceedings are guided by a set of explicit rules communally agreed upon? But in the end Weber's grounding of such concepts seems rooted in the terrain of the German Historical School, in that they are meant to be related to cultural settings and historical facts.

And it may well be that in his last works, as Fritz Machlup has pointed out, Weber gave a more distinctly "sociological" cast to the notion of "ideal types," giving greater weight to their role in "generalizing sciences" like sociology (Machlup 1978b: 228). But does this not bring one full circle, as economics was regarded as well as a "generalizing science" in contrast to history, for which Weber sought to transcend just such a distinction?

All of this, though, still begs the question as to the place of economics – of some or any sort – in Weber's thinking about methodology. Weber first sees economic theory as "one means for the analysis of causal relationships of empirical reality" (Weber [1922] 1988: 396; translation provided by Hennis 1991: 30). Then he takes an additional step, by ordering reality as a complex of "cultural significations," which leads him to see economic theory transformed into a "summation of 'ideal-typical' concepts." Under these circumstances theory is supplanted by concepts, or, more precisely, the formation of concepts of "ideal types." Does economic theory wither away in consequence?

Weber appears to be of two minds about this. His initial statement suggests that economic theory has a considerable role to play in economic matters, yet his later infusing of the notion of "cultural signification" into explanations of economic phenomena and activity, a central element of his methodological and philosophical critique of the social sciences, would seem to point to a general supersession of economic theorizing for the construction of ideal types. That is, concept formation and construction from such concepts formed would delimit the boundaries of economic abstraction. In turn, these concepts would be rooted in an "empirical reality" that itself was part of, and comprehended as historical experience. Might that serve as the basis for a reformulated historical economics, linking economic concepts to the construction of models, but rooted in the interpretation of history?

## Weber, the Austrians, and the role of history

Swedberg, among others, contends that Max Weber observed and pursued a form of "methodological individualism," taking individual motivation, action, and belief as the starting point for his sociological inquiries, though tempered as "of a social rather than an atomistic nature, as in economic theory" (Swedberg 1998: 164). The text of Weber's letter to Robert Liefmann in March 1920 appears to bear this out:

> I want to put an end to the whole business … of working with collective concepts. In other words; sociology, too, can only be pursued by taking as one's point of departure the actions of one or more (few or many) individuals, that is to say, with a strictly 'individualistic' method.
>
> (Weber [1920] 2012: 410)

And he tended to receive a largely favorable reception from the second and third generation of Austrian economists for whom methodological individualism served as a cornerstone, even if the first generation of Austrian economists, notably Menger and von Bohm-Bawerk, essentially ignored Weber, and Ludwig von Mises, who had established a friendship with Weber, as quoted by Swedberg, thought "economics was alien to [him]" (Swedberg 1998: 204–5). Swedberg, citing Gottfried Haberler's recollections, noted that the L. von Mises seminar held in Vienna between 1920 and 1934 gave considerable attention to Weber's *verstehende* sociology (Swedberg 1998: 301–2 fn. 142). That would also suggest, though, an interest in other aspects of Weber's work and ideas. But all of this must then be gauged in terms of the similarities and differences between them and Weber, especially in elucidating the relation between economics and history.

Among the Austrian economists who delved into Weber's thought, Fritz Machlup took up the notion of "Verstehen" as underlying the social sciences, including economics. He also explored and attempted to set in perspective Weber's use of "ideal types," notably in two essays: "The Ideal Type; Bad Name for a Good Construct" (Machlup 1978a) and "Ideal Types, Reality, and Construction" (Machlup 1978b). Machlup's treatment of the notion of "ideal types" has the virtue of setting the idea in the context of central European thought, especially as he delineates the role played by such late nineteenth century figures like Dilthey, Wundt, Windelband, and Rickert (Machlup 1978b).

Of more questionable concern is the inclusion of precursors among economists, in particular von Thunen and Carl Menger. Machlup's notion that Menger offered up a complementary pairing of the "exact type" (Machlup translated this as "strict" type) and "real type" based upon "observables," is at variance with Weber's more nuanced reliance upon "fictive" or "unreal" elements in constructing "ideal types" to better capture reality, and weakens the complex interrelation between theory and fact so central to Weber's methodological explorations.

Even as Bruce Caldwell has attempted more recently to highlight the importance of Menger for Weber, he acknowledges an essential difference in their understanding of the nature and scope of "theoretical abstractions" (Caldwell 2004: 90):

> Menger had said that theory always looks at one side of a particular phenomenon and that exact theory examines its most typical, or generic aspects. Using Rickert's notion of concept formation in the face of an infinite and irrational reality, Weber went beyond Menger to claim that all description is theory laden.
>
> (Caldwell 2004: 91)

Moreover, Hennis' statement that Weber's concern for "cultural meaning" and "cultural significations" set him well apart from Menger is clearly on point (Hennis 1991: 31).

As for von Thunen, Machlup takes his imaginative reconstruction of the city (or town) and its agricultural hinterlands through abstracted assumptions, that greatly simplify, as an early version of the creation of an "ideal type" (Machlup 1978b: 224–6). One might well make the case that Weber's example of the "economy of the city" that characterized economic life in the later European Middle Ages, alluded to in Weber's 1904 essay on "objectivity" in the social sciences, comports rather well with von Thunen's "isolated state," at least at first blush.

Yet it is here that one of the central weaknesses in Machlup's analysis emerges. For one, there is the conflation of model, law, and concept, so that only the act of abstracting from reality to produce "a construct designed to explain ... social phenomena" (Machlup 1978b: 239), eliminating the rough edges in the process (what Weber referred to as "accentuating" certain elements in order to obtain a clear, discrete, and distinct separation of one concept from another) appears to matter, whereas all three notions may be regarded as conveying something different: (1) models built upon typically more than one element or assumption; (2) laws based upon "generalities" (hence, not necessarily abstractions) or "regularities"; and (3) concepts comprehended as "relations" more often than not, but in any event "definitional," built there-fore upon inclusions and exclusions, not things in and of themselves or mechanisms.

For his part, Ludwig Lachmann, another Austrian economist, recognized the influence of the German Historical School upon Weber (Lachmann 1970: 26), and also sought to dissociate "ideal types" from economic models (Lachmann 1970: 27). Instead, he proposed to use "plans" built around the "[p]henomena of human action" in place of "ideal types" as "mental con-structs" (Lachmann 1970: 29). It would appear that Lachmann has attempted to fit Weber's methodological approach into an Austrian mold, so that "human action" linked to "individual choice" would underlie all human institutions, the act of what Lachmann, drawing from Menger, referred to as "social forces" rather than "social design" (Lachmann 1970: 57).

Moreover, there is a historical cast to many of Weber's ideal types not to be found in von Thunen, and missing as well in Machlup's or Lachmann's treatment in general. This holds in the instant case, as Weber's "economy of the city" is linked to its period of efflorescence, and, crucially, as a concept "type" is set in opposition to the "capitalist economy" of the industrial world. Weber's penchant for situating ideal-types in broad historical and cultural moments also set him at variance with Friedrich von Hayek, who took issue with Weber's notion that "the need for 'calculability and reliability in the functioning of the legal order' was a peculiarity of 'capitalism' or the 'bourgeois phase' of society" (Hayek 1960: 455–6).

It is also true that there are certain ambiguities in Weber's approach to "ideal types" that might appear to support Machlup's claims. A potential lack of consistency notwithstanding, Weber does allow certain economic laws – better understood as tendencies or regularities – to serve as "ideal types."

For all that, though, Weber, unlike Machlup and the other Austrians tends to link the theory to a certain state of economic development, what might otherwise be seen as a historical moment or period. Indeed, Weber is adamant that its origins lie in certain "cultural, historical conditions", literally "facts" ("Tatsache"), rendering the theory as historically conditioned. Weber used a telling expression in the critique of Knies, making the system of competitive prices the reigning set of rules under current capitalist practice, called the "objective situation", for those "trapped within the market" (Weber [1906] 1975: 202; translated as "entangled in the market" in Weber [1906] 2012: 90).

It is noteworthy as well that von Thunen's model is based upon a set of simplifying assumptions rather than an oppositional contrast formed by opposing "exact concepts" that was favored by Weber. One might construct models in that way. For example, models of economic growth might be based upon constant returns to scale across all productive industries, or upon the dominance of increasing returns to scale. In this form model construction comes much closer to the sorting out of concepts that would be undertaken in a process of "concept formation", a matter dear to those engaged in intellectual endeavors in central Europe in the first decades of the twentieth century. An approach of this sort would produce what Weber saw as the differences in interpretation resulting from different associations of facts and values.

Weber's reference to the importance of the historical moment, his recognition of the existence of different socio-economic orders, and his focus upon the not always positive attributes of capitalism, all suggest, differences notwithstanding, a continuing and underlying influence of the German Historical School in his thinking, as it reflects Roscher's central tenet that economics should be concerned at the most basic level with "forms of [economic] organization" (A. and O. Neurath [1910, Vol. 1: 100).

## Weber and Braudel

Is there a distinction to be made between economic history and historical economics? This seems especially pertinent when it comes to those writers and thinkers whose work might, at first glance, appear to fall into either category. Moreover, if such a distinction does hold, to what extent does it depend upon the presence or strength of the role of economic theory or the philosophical balance between the general and the particular?

For Max Weber the boundary conditions that might exist between economic history and historical economics are particularly problematic, in that he has been categorized as an economist, historian, and sociologist, or seen as transcending all disciplinary limitations. Tenbruck, for example, has argued that Weber advanced from history to sociology (Tenbruck 1989: 235–42), while Hennis has countered that Weber could not be confined to any one discipline (Hennis 1989: 25ff.). Accordingly, one tack that might be pursued in exploring these boundary conditions would be to examine Weber's treatment of the nexus between economics and history in his methodological essays from the first decade of the twentieth century.

However, one might also engage in a textual comparison to gauge the distance, if any, between the approach taken by Max Weber in his late lectures, organized posthumously into his *General Economic History*, with English translation by Frank Knight dating from 1927, and that of Fernand Braudel in his multi-volume history of the transformation of the material world, but especially *The Wheels of Commerce*, with English translation dating from 1981 (Braudel [1982] 1992).[2] For, in many crucial respects this latter work covers the same territory, both by period and place, and, at least as importantly, by overarching theme. Each of these works explores the rise of capitalism in Europe, but the descriptions provided are also meant to suggest the causes of or bases for the emergence of capitalism (see Collins [1980] 1992).

Even at first blush one can note certain characteristic differences: Weber's work is more ideational and, one might contend from a certain perspective, "sociological"; Braudel's is suffused with historical detail intended both to impress the "concreteness of reality", always a central goal of Braudel's writings, and to convey through that "concreteness" the way that the economic transformation took place. Braudel appears to hurtle himself directly into, and immerse himself in what Simon Kuznets had referred to as the "recalcitrant nature" of reality, even as Kuznets had sought to establish standardized macroeconomic measures that transcended or obscured the complex relations and unique qualities that Braudel saw in the wealth of details. Will this weighing of the general versus the particular prove to be one of the keynotes in the distinction between economic history and historical economics?

Perhaps, but Weber's work may muddy the picture somewhat. While far less detailed than Braudel's, yet not without attention to crucial facts in the unfolding narrative, Weber conveys a similar attentiveness to economic life as broadly conceived, ensconced within a social world that forms the framework for economic activity to take place, and by which such activity is to be comprehended.

Braudel himself castigated Weber's comprehension of capitalism as fundamentally mistaken and antithetical to how historians in general have viewed it, although it should be noted that Weber's *General Economic History* was not widely known in France and translated into French by the publishing house Gallimard only in 1991. Even so, Braudel's critique of Weber is a more nuanced matter, with the lines between economics and history, and perhaps sociology as well, somewhat blurred.

In his *Afterthoughts on Material Civilization and Capitalism* Braudel began by stating:

> For Max Weber, capitalism in the modern sense of the word was no more and no less than a creation of Protestantism or, to be even more accurate, of Puritanism.
>
> (Braudel 1977: 65)

Braudel's case unfolds as follows:

> All historians have opposed this tenuous theory, although they have not managed to be rid of it once and for all. Yet it is clearly false. The northern countries took over the place that earlier had so long and so brilliantly been occupied by the old capitalist centers of the Mediterranean. They invented nothing, either in technology or business management.
>
> (Braudel 1977: 65–6)

Hence, "[w]hat was involved on each occasion was a shift of the center of gravity of the world economy, for economic reasons that had nothing whatever to do with the basis or secret nature of capitalism" (Braudel 1977: 67).

He concluded: "All things considered, I believe Max Weber's error stems essentially from his exaggeration of capitalism's role as promoter of the modern world" (Braudel 1977: 67). This, though, comes with a further twist: "But the basic problem does not lie there. Indeed, the real fate of capitalism was determined by its encounter with social hierarchies" (Braudel 1977: 67), a strikingly sociological perspective. Braudel then cited Werner Sombart, Weber's co-editor of the *Archiv*, with approbation in that regard.

## The lost thread

Two essential matters remain outstanding. First of all, how might Weber be better placed in the context of his own time, especially with regard to the intellectual and cultural currents in which he found himself, and as they pertain to what it meant for Weber to be an economist, as well as for the case for a historical economics? Second, what light does this exploration of the work and ideas of Weber shed on the current possibilities for a historical economics?

The first matter is a rather complex one. Here, for all the virtues, say, of Machlup's sketch of the broader intellectual context for Weber's notion of "ideal types", there is much more to attend to. One example may help put this in perspective. Weber, as it has been stated, based his methodological pursuits, in economics and elsewhere, on a form of methodological individualism. A close reading of his critique of Roscher shows that Weber took issue with an implicit version of Hegelian "emanationism" in Roscher's conception of historical economics, whereby the individual or particular facts or events were able to assume a general form, with the character of law, because of a guiding spirit that suffused them and could be divined as the distinct and distinctive nature of the "nation" or its "culture." Weber found this unacceptable, as he himself attempted to recast the problem of linking the particular to the general in some new way, a problem at the center of the philosophical ruminations of Wundt, Windelband, and Rickert. But it also represented a rebuke for what at the time would be taken to be a Romantic view of a unity "mystically" induced from the diversity of individual parts. Requiring that all intellectual inquiry be initiated from the vantage point of individual behavior, motivation, and action would provide a compelling alternative to any form of such "emanationist" views. Within the context of prevailing economic thought, such a form of methodological individualism would therefore be set against the notion of "nation spirit" or "cultural identity" found among many of the leading figures of the German Historical School and also against the collectivist approach advanced by Marxists who saw "classes" and "class struggle" as the key to comprehending the processes of economic development and transformation.

Swedberg notes another apparent tension in Weber's consideration of the nature of economics and especially economic theorizing, appearing to oscillate or perhaps even triangulate between the German Historical School and the Austrian economists. Hodgson suggests something similar (Hodgson 2001:

117–21). If it is the case that Weber, at least privately, took issue with Carl Menger's dismissal of the idea that there might be different applicable economic laws of development for different historical moments or states of economic development, then it would appear that he retained deeper intellectual ties to the German Historical School than is generally assumed, even as he seemed to have embarked upon a new course in making use of the historical approach.

This is evident as well in his 1904 essay that initiated his co-editorship of the *Archiv fur Sozialwissenschaften und Sozialpolitik*. There Weber spoke of the continuing tension between the theoretical and the historical in economics, citing with some approbation the role of the socialists and the historical school in sustaining the "historical" case against the wave of what Weber termed "naturalist" points of view that underlay both classical and neoclassical economics:

> This is particularly true as regards – the still problematical – relationship between "theoretical" and "historical" work in our discipline.
>
> (Weber [1904] 2012: 122–3)

In a more contemporary setting Weber's understanding of the role of history in his treatment of "objective possibility and adequate causation" opens a window on the possible means for "historicizing" the context for abstracted constructs, including economic ones. His "reference to rules of experience" conveys a turn-of-the-twentieth-century conventionalist perspective, not dissimilar from one that might have been forward by Poincaré.

> Every line of every historical account – indeed: every collection of archival material and documents destined for publication – contains 'judgments of possibility'; or, more correctly put: it must contain them, if the publication is to have 'value as knowledge.'
>
> (Weber [1905] 2012: 175)

> But what does it mean when we talk of several 'possibilities' between which those struggles are supposed to have 'decided'? In the first place, it means at least that we construct what we may safely call *imaginary pictures*: [we imagine] the absence of one or more of those components of 'reality' that actually existed, and we construct in our minds a sequence of events that is modified with respect to one or a few 'conditions.' This means that even the very first step toward a historical judgement is already – and this is what we want to stress here – a process of *abstraction*; it proceeds by means of analysis and intellectual isolation of the components of what is immediately given (viewed as a complex of *possible* causal relations), and it should lead to a synthesis of the 'real' causal interconnection. Consequently, even this first step transforms the given 'reality' in order to make it into a historical 'fact,' a *theoretical* construct. To quote Goethe: there is 'theory' in 'facts.'
>
> (Weber [1905] 2012: 175)

Thus, a judgement of 'possibility' – in the sense in which that term is utilized here – always implies a reference to rules of experience ... [the judgment of 'possibility'] here implies a reference to positive *knowledge* of 'rules governing events,' to our 'nomological knowledge,' as it is usually termed.

(Weber [1905] 2012: 175)

At the same time, in assessing the nuances in the distinction between a literary work of fiction and history built upon the conjunction of theoretical construct and historical facts, Weber makes the curious observation that points to the distance between Weber's stance and the intellectual currents in which he found himself, on the one hand, and the world of late twentieth-century relativism and postmodernism:

And when the historian presents the reader with the logical result of his causal historical judgements in the form of an account where he does not spell out the reasons underlying his findings and 'suggests' the course of events instead of 'reasoning' pedantically, surely that account would be a historical novel and not a [set of] scientific findings, unless there was a firm framework of causal imputation behind the artistically designed exterior.

(Weber [1905] 2012: 177)

Nonetheless, there are aspects of Weber's methodology that bear a real kinship with late twentieth-century insights about the nature of the production of narratives. Weber saw as an essential distinction between the natural sciences and the human sciences that in the case of the latter, and unlike that of the former, all "facts", "statements," and "relations" had a meaning attached to them, because they came out of a human context.

Moreover, one might also cast the matter of meaning in a more contemporary context, couched, to be sure, in different language but displaying underlying affinities. If what characterizes the natural sciences is a narrative or story on one level, then what distinguished economics as a social (or cultural) science are the multilayered narratives that it provides or sets forth. In other words, there is a message, subtext, or multilayered allegory in economics not found in the natural sciences. If this contention is correct, it would mean that Weber anticipated certain aspects of a narratology of economics, but on terms intelligible to the world of early twentieth-century thought. Weber's citation of Goethe, for example, was seconded a half-century later by the British linguist, J. R. Firth, who used it in his championing of the idea of "contextual meaning" (Firth 1968: 146). This would be the case as well for Weber's discussion of the gap between concept and object, with the concomitant introduction of the "irrationality" occupying the space. As these narratives might be conceived of as historical, it might make it possible to reintroduce history into economics in a philosophically, or at least methodologically consistent way.

## Notes

1 Writing in *History and Theory* Fritz Ringer emphasized the central role played by von Kries in shaping Weber's thinking about causation and "objective possibility," while downplaying significantly the influence of Heinrich Rickert (see Ringer 2002: 163ff.). As to this latter point, there are important differences between the two, noted in the text, but the correspondence between them, also referred to in the text, points to an abiding intellectual relationship whose effect should not be overlooked.
2 A comparison of Weber and Braudel was also noted by Philippe Raynaud when he suggested that Weber's work might be viewed as "historical" as well as "sociological" (Raynaud 1991: x).

## References

Bevir, Mark (2007) "Introduction: Historical Understanding and the Human Sciences." *Journal of the Philosophy of History*, I: 259–270.
Braudel, Fernand (1977) *Afterthoughts on Material Civilization and Capitalism*, trans. Patricia M. Ranum.Baltimore: Johns Hopkins University Press.
Braudel, Fernand (1982) *The Wheels of Commerce*, trans. Sian Reynolds (1992). Berkeley: University of California Press.
Caldwell, Bruce (2004) *Hayek's Challenge*. Chicago: University of Chicago Press.
Collins, Randall [1980] (1982) "Weber's Last Theory of Capitalism." in Mark Granovetter and Richard Swedberg (eds), *The Sociology of Economic Life*. Boulder: Westview Press.
Colliot-Thélène, Catherine (2006) *La sociologie de Max Weber*. Paris: La Découverte.
Firth, J. R. (1968) *Selected Papers of J. R. Firth, 1952–59*, ed. F. R. Palmer.Harlow: Longmans.
Freund, Julian (1978) "German Sociology in the Time of Max Weber." In Tom Bottomore and Robert Nisbet (eds), *A History of Sociological Analysis*. New York: Basic Books, 149–186.
Guinchard, Jean-Jacques (2006) *Max Weber: vie – œuvres – concepts*. Paris: Ellipses.
Hayek, F. A. (1960) *The Constitution of Liberty*. Chicago: University of Chicago Press.
Heidelberger, Michael (2001) "Origins of the Logical Theory of Probability: Von Kries, Wittgenstein, Waismann." *International Studies in the Philosophy of Science*, 15(2): 177–188.
Hennis, Wilhelm (1987) "A Science of Man: Max Weber and the Political Economy of the German Historical School." In Wolfgang J. Mommsen and Jurgen Osterhammel (eds), *Max Weber and His Contemporaries*. London: Allen & Unwin, pp. 25–58.
Hennis, Wilhelm (1991) "The Pitiless 'Sobriety of Judgement': Max Weber between Carl Menger and Gustav Von Schmoller – The Academic Politics of Value Freedom." *History of the Human Sciences*, 4(1): 27–59.
Hodgson, Geoffrey (2001) *How Economics Forgot History*. New York: Oxford University Press.
Kaesler, Dirk (1984) *Die frühe Soziologie 1909 bis 1934 und ihre Entstehungs-Milieu*. Opladen: Westdeutscher Verlag.
Kries, Johannes von (1888) "Uber den Begriff der objektiven Moglichkeit und einige Anwendungen desselben." *Zeitschrift fur wissenschaftliche Philosophie*, 12: 398–428.
Lachmann, Ludwig (1970) *The Legacy of Max Weber: Three Essays*. London: Heinemann.

Lowith, Karl [1932] (1982) *Max Weber and Karl Marx*, ed. with intro. Tom Bottomore and William Outhwaite; trans. Hans Fantel (1982). London: George Allen & Unwin.

Machlup, Fritz (1978a) "The Ideal Type: A Bad Name for a Good Construct." *Methodology of Economics and Other Social Sciences*. New York: Academic Press, pp. 211–221.

Machlup, Fritz (1978b) "Ideal Types, Reality, and Construction." *Methodology of Economics and Other Social Sciences*. New York: Academic Press, pp. 223–265.

Morgan, Mary S. (2012) *The World in the Model: How Economists Work and Think*. Cambridge: Cambridge University Press.

Neurath, A. and O. [1910] (1913) *Lesebuch der Volkswirtschaftslehre*, 2 vols, 2nd edn. Leipzig: Gloeckner.

Raynaud, Philippe (1991) "Preface." *Max Weber: Histoire économique*, trans. Christian Bouchindhomme. Paris: Gallimard.

Ringer, Fritz (2002) "Max Weber on Causal Analysis, Interpretation, and Comparison." *History and Theory*, 41(2): 163–178.

Schumpeter, Joseph (1954) *History of Economic Analysis*, ed. Elizabeth Boody Schumpeter.New York: Oxford University Press.

Swedberg, Richard (1998) *Max Weber and the Idea of Economic Sociology*. Princeton: Princeton University Press.

Tenbruck, Friedrich H. (1989) "Max Weber and Eduard Meyer." In Wolfgang J. Mommsen and Jurgen Osterhammel (eds), *Max Weber and his Contemporaries*. London: Allen & Unwin.

Tribe, Keith (1995) *Strategies of Economic Order: German Economic Discourse, 1750–1950*. Cambridge: Cambridge University Press.

Turk, Michael H. (2012) "The Mathematical Turn in Economics." *Journal of the History of Economic Thought*, 34(2): 149–167.

Weber, Marianne [1926] (1975) *Max Weber: A Biography*, trans. Harry Zohn. New York: John Wiley.

Weber, Max [1898] (1990) *Grundriss zu den Vorlesungen uber Allgemeine ('theoretische') Nationalokonomie*. Tubingen: J.C.B. Mohr.

Weber, Max (1919–20) *Economy and Society: An Outline of Interpretive Sociology*. Vol. 1, trans. Ephraim Fischoff et al., ed. Guenther Roth and Claus Wittich (1978). Berkeley: University of California Press.

Weber, Max (1981) *General Economic History*, trans. Frank Knight (1927). New Brunswick, NJ: Transaction.

Weber, Max (1991) *Histoire économique*, trans. Christian Bouchindhomme, pref. Philippe Raynaud.Paris: Gallimard.

Weber, Max [1922] (1988). "Die Grenznutzlehre und das 'psychophysisiche Grundgesetz.'" In Johannes Winckelmann (ed.), *Gesammelte Aufsatze zur Wissenschaftslehre*. Tubingen: J.C.B. Mohr, pp. 384–399.

Weber, Max [1903–6] (1975) *Roscher and Knies: The Logical Problems of Historical Economics*, trans. with intro. Guy Oakes.London: Free Press.

Weber, Max [1904] (2012) "The 'Objectivity' of Knowledge in Social Science and Social Policy." In Hans Henrik Bruun and Sam Whimster (eds), *Max Weber: Collected Methodological Writings*, trans. Hans Henrik Bruun. Abingdon, Oxon: Routledge, pp. 100–138.

Weber, Max [1905] (2012) "Critical Studies in the Logic of the Cultural Sciences." *Collected Methodological Writings*, pp. 139–184.

Weber, Max [1907] (2012) "R[udolf] Stammler's 'Overcoming' of the Materialist Conception of History." *Collected Methodological Writings*, pp. 185–226.

Weber, Max (2012) Letters (excerpts). *Collected Methodological Writings*, to: Heinrich Rickert, April 28, 1905: 381; Ladislaus v. Bortkiewicz, March 12, 1906: 385; Lujo Brentano, October 30, 1908: 396; Robert Liefmann, October 23–28, 1912: 404; Robert Liefmann, March 9, 1920: 410.

Weber, Max and Sombart, Werner [1917] (2012) "Declaration." *Collected Methodological Writings*, pp. 302–303.

Wright, Georg Henrikvon (1955) "Ludwig Wittgenstein, A Biographical Sketch." *Philosophical Review*, 64(4): 527–545.

# 8   Historical proof in economics

How might one go about "proving" something in economics? In particular, what role – and how large a role – should history play in affording the possibility of any such proof? First of all, this question prompts a preliminary inquiry about the nature and bases for proof itself. In turn, the matter of historical proof is inextricably linked to an explication of the relation between economics and economic history, since the source of proof of this sort must be drawn out of events and developments that took place in real time or from what is loosely described as "historical experience," though its exact meaning and connection to the world of economics are open to question.

It is the case that the writings of economic historians and economists highlighting the fraught relation between the two fields can elucidate the place "historical proof" might hold in economics. If one accepts Joseph Schumpeter's account of an emergent "Marshallian epoch" in economics at the turn of the twentieth century in which "economic history, amidst surf and breakers, established itself within the precincts of academic economics" (Schumpeter [1951] 1965: 241), several foci over the succeeding century offer up special insights in that regard. The "empty boxes" controversy of the 1920s between John Clapham and Arthur Pigou crystallized the tensions that existed between the two fields. The mid-century remaking of economics through a heightened mathematization and quantification, along with the blending of probability and statistics in econometrics, set in high relief questions about the differing scope of measurability in economics and economic history. Moreover, throughout the century there was an effort by economists and economic historians alike to comprehend and account for the place of "great events," in particular the Industrial Revolution, the Great Depression, and the recurrence of financial crises, in theorizing about economics, hence the goad of historical memory – or the lack thereof.

## The dilemma of proof

The categorization of forms of proof in economics might, at first blush, appear to track the methodological division between induction and deduction. In the case of the former, affirmation through or congruence with the facts holds the key; in the case of the latter, logical consistency in structure and derivation is paramount. Leaving aside for the moment what is meant by an "economic fact," one might reasonably regard the two corresponding forms of proof as either empirical or logical.

However, complications and complexities arise immediately. The "empirical" may be distinguished from the "historical," where the former is typically taken to be statistical evidence, and the latter something more or other, but in any event drawn from the past, laying the groundwork for a third, "historical," form of proof.

William Baumol and Robert Strom, while focusing in particular upon "the study of entrepreneurship" among economic topics, point to the virtues of history as a "source of evidence" vis-à-vis statistics or theory, as well as the difficulties inherent in such an approach:

> For empirical evidence, as one would expect, economists generally prefer statistics to history. Much as one can learn from historical circumstances and events, they are always complex, and their form and operations are subject to the interactions of an array of multi-faceted influences. History offers nothing that resembles the ceteris paribus cleanliness of a controlled experiment.
>
> (Baumol and Strom 2010: 527)

On the other hand

> "[S]tatistical analysis depends on the availability of a multiplicity of identical items that can be added together, averaged, or correlated with other variables." Where, in their view, a "fundamental heterogeneity" of activity or product exists, its "inherent diversity … remains a daunting obstacle to the econometric approach."
>
> (Baumol and Strom 2010: 527–8)

Schumpeter was even more explicit about the role of the "historical," giving primacy of place to "economic history" among the techniques of economic analysis, while identifying "statistics" and "theory," corresponding roughly to the empirical and logical categories noted above, as the other two central strands (Schumpeter 1954: 12–13).

The turn toward historical proof may be reinforced by philosophical considerations calling into question the possibility of either an empirical or logical proof being complete and free-standing. Since David Hume it has been recognized that an inductive proof cannot be all-comprehending and encompassing; rather, it provides a generalization that holds only until a contrary fact is established. A contemporary manifestation of this has surfaced in economic discourse regarding the emergence of a severe financial crisis in 2008, overturning the conventional wisdom of a "Great Moderation" in the business cycle in the late twentieth century, the shock of which was characterized as a "black swan" by Nassim Nicholas Taleb (Taleb 2007).

As to matters of logical proof, Kurt Godel's proof in 1931 of the "incompleteness" of any axiomatized arithmetic system undermined the possibility of constructing a logically deduced system, be it an economic structure defined by a set of mathematical statements and relations, that could stand alone, without the benefit of auxiliary assumptions, axioms, of hypotheses independent of that system (Nagel and Newman 1958). Acknowledging the need for such auxiliary elements would entail first identifying the pertinent ones, then assessing their validity and the rightfulness of their being added into the system as originally constructed.

In general, as a social science economics faces serious limitations in making use of the controlled experiment favored by practitioners of the physical sciences to establish the validity or explanatory range of any working hypothesis, for it appears impossible to isolate all the pertinent events necessary to make such a determination. As has oft been noted, of all the physical sciences economics resembles meteorology most closely, in that the number of variables to track is sufficiently large as to generate complexity and substantial ambiguity. In consequence, both fields suffer from deficiencies in terms of their capacity to predict.

This may pose a serious challenge to their "scientificality," following the conditions set out by Carl Hempel: "It is, therefore, of paramount importance for science to develop a system of concepts which is suited for the formulation of general explanatory and predictive principles" (Hempel 1952: 20), though Hempel's criteria for a nomological–deductive structure to any science have been challenged from many corners.

It is also the case that meteorology has benefitted in recent decades from a substantial increase in observations, especially through the extensive use of satellite reports, as well as the development of computer models relying upon such data.

For all that, along the lines of the changes brought to meteorology, one might see the case for an economics better buttressed through observable data in Simon Kuznets' assertion in his seminal 1941 article in the first issue of the *Journal of Economic History* that quantitative data and statistical analysis opened the door to a greater level of objectivity and a broader potential for verification in economic history (Kuznets 1941a). It would also provide economists with a much more fully substantiated basis for proving the generalizations and general statements that pervade economics. In fact, Kuznets' work has been lauded by Robert Fogel, a champion of the "New Economic History" who, with Douglass North, was the first economic historian to win the Nobel Prize in economics in 1993, as "pivotal ... in the transformation of economics ... into an empirically based social science" (Fogel 2001: 3). However, as one will see below, reliance upon quantitative data and statistical analysis would – and could – have only modest success, as it did not directly address the need for reasoned criteria underlying historical proof.

Kuznets himself noted the difficulties entailed in the forging of standard macroeconomics measures notwithstanding the signal role he had played in their creation and in establishing their broad credibility and use, invoking concerns more often associated with critics of quantitative approaches to economics:

> There is no escaping this subjective element in the work, or freeing the results from its effects. In consequence, all national income estimates are appraisals of the end products of the economic system rather than color-less statements of fact; and, like all appraisals, they are predetermined by criteria that are at worst a matter of chance, at best a matter of deliberate choice.
>
> (Kuznets 1941b: 3)

The matter of interpretation extended to the meaning of "market" in any such accounting:

> But if the market is considered as a complex of social relations of a certain type, and marketability as the characteristic of goods involved in them, it must be recognized that there are different kinds of market expressive of significantly different underlying social relations.
>
> (Kuznets, 1941b: 8)

There is a second vein of concerns regarding the nature of proof in economics that goes to the core of its relation to history. The grounding of economics in worldly matters, whether conceived as business, social or societal, or human, also raises difficulties in making assumptions informing hypotheses or techniques that require continuity of action or movement. It was Benoit Mandelbrot who pointed out in *The (Mis)Behavior of Markets* that the notion of randomness built into the "degrees of freedom" associated with statistical mechanics depended upon the essentially unbounded number of interactions involved. This in turn allowed for the assumption that the physical process was a con-tinuous one. By contrast, economic events were far more delimited by number, even – at least at times – discrete. This alone challenged any ready acceptance of continuity of action, or randomness, in economics (Mandelbrot 2004: 235–8), a thesis that had first been explicitly advanced by Louis Bachelier at the turn of the twentieth century (Bachelier [1900] 2006).

Moreover, and this was not taken up by Mandelbrot, the kind of events likely to matter in economics took place in historical time, while those con-stituting a physical process were likely to occur instantaneously (so many in any arbitrarily short "moment" in time), set in an abstracted understanding of time. Economists as dissimilar as Oskar Morgenstern and Robert Solow have noted that the data used by economists represent a moving target, unable to offer up an "isolated" (Morgenstern 1937: 8) or a "stationary" (Solow 1985: 328) set of points upon which a controlled test might be made.

Historical periodization, an essential part of the metier of historians, also constituted a not insignificant barrier to any unreflected reliance upon the assumption of continuity. Kuznets saw in the role of the historian in defining and thereby delimiting periods in history the provision of essential "differences," if not outright "discontinuities," a milder version of this critique of continuity, acknowledging that it might be of service to economists (Kuznets 1941a). Charles Kindleberger, who saw himself and was widely regarded as "an historical economist, [but] not an economic historian" (Kindleberger 1989: ix), expressed the need to account for discontinuity more strongly in assessing critically theories of economic growth: "Nothing grows geometrically at a steady rate for very long ... Discontinuity is endemic" (Kindleberger 1989: 3). And as Paul Bairoch, who held the chair in economic history at the University of Geneva, perhaps the oldest such position specifically designated as such, noted:

> To a very large extent, modern history is characterized more by economic discontinuities than continuities.
>
> (Bairoch 1993: 176)

However, the overhang of discontinuities in economic affairs figures perhaps more significantly in another way that history enters into economic explanation. For, it is the essence of historical agency to signal shifts or deviations from a prevailing course or direction previously set upon, by dint of the involvement of historical agents who then reshape and remake the flow of events and developments.

Only a passive version of historical agency, which effectively subsumes and subordinates any such agency to the purported inexorability of historical laws, operating with the same force as general or universal laws, as in certain interpretations of Marx's "law of motion of capitalism," might appear to be consistent with the implied assumption of continuity. Paradoxically, Marx's "law of motion of capitalism" can hardly be deemed an exemplar of continuity, since it sets forth an explosive and dramatic transformation that conforms to the notion of discontinuity through "coupure" or "break," whereby a critical turn in history occurs. Moreover, there is the contrasting Marxian emphasis, in which the variability of the "class struggle" gives rise to a quite active version of historical agency.

More generally, the extent and scope of "historical agency" in economic matters will help determine whether history may be viewed as the "driver" of pertinent economic events and developments, and thus how central "historical agency" is to any construction of "historical proof" in economics. The tension between historical agency and the assumed continuity of economics would, obviously, pose a serious challenge to any capacity to predict the future. It was Alfred Marshall who recognized that a century ago, for in his view both the capacity to explain and predict were predicated upon a belief in the "continuity and unity in economic development" (Marshall 1920: 7). In fact, his discussion of the scope of economic explanation follows upon his assertion as to the special force with which continuous evolution holds for economic phenomena.

## Economic facts and historical time

What are economic facts? It would appear to be the simplest of questions, and yet much may hinge upon its answer in demarcating the line between empirical evidence and historical evidence. This may be viewed as a translation of the tension between "in (real) time" and "out of (real) time" with which a few economists, like John Hicks and John Robinson, have sought to grapple. Are "economic facts" necessarily "historical," in that they must take place in time and, further, that they would be subject to the kind of testing associated with the separating of "fact" from "fiction" often invoked as one of the keys – perhaps the major one – in the historian's craft?

There are at least two considerations, though, that complicate this notion of testing as either sufficient or even pertinent. First, "facts" do not stand in isolation, but emerge only in context. Hence, the selection of the appropriate context or narrative is crucial, and economists have often – and rightly – been faulted for the ad hoc way in which facts are adduced in support of economic generalizations or theories. In part this calls for standards, criteria, or "theory" itself to be applied to determine the "value" or "weight" of various facts. Moreover, this suggests that the distinction between "fact" and "value" seen as underlying the difference between positive and normative economics is hardly clear-cut and discrete, but, on the contrary, may be understood better as an intertwining of the two. Furthermore, the inclusion of certain facts and the exclusion of others makes clear that the basis for selecting those for inclusion matters as much as the facts themselves.

Second, there is some contention by both economists and economic historians that economic statistics are not necessarily to be comprehended as "historical facts". How can this be the case, if such statistics are cobbled from circumstances or events occurring in time?

On the one hand, M. M. Postan posed a challenge from the perspective of economic historians:

> For though in a sense all facts are historical facts, and all historical facts are social evidence, the data which the economists and sociologists now accumulate are seldom employed in a way which an economic historian would recognize as historical.
>
> (Postan [1939] 1971: 25)

This obscuring of the "historical" might be seen in Kuznets' treatment of historical statistics. For his part, Kuznets identified three elements involved in the "statistical analysis in economics ... [in] relation to economic history":

(a)   the adjustment of data to fit analytical categories;
(b)   the analysis of different patterns of temporal change;
(c)   the measurement of theoretically formulated relations, largely of the short run.

(Kuznets 1941a)

Only the second of these directly makes reference to historical time. Those understood to conform to "analytical categories" or "theoretically formulated relations" fall under abstract time, purely sequential for purposes of ordering data or parametric for constructing economic models.

Yet the contrary case is difficult to gainsay, especially when one considers policy implications. For example, the rate of unemployment represents a datum for a particular moment in time, and is characterized as such. Observers might be attuned to the rate found for each preceding month at the start of the next month. The "history" of such statistics, where the changing, or at least evolving goals of the state gave rise to the collection of different kinds of data organized into various and diverse categories, reinforces their "historical" character. Obviously, whether economic statistics are taken to be "historical" or not has a significant impact upon the extent to which economies relies upon, or requires, historical proof.

## Law-making: Kepler vs. Newton

The nomothetic attribute of a scientific discipline refers to its law-making quality or capacity. What this would mean for a social science like economics has varied; in particular, the exactness and inexorability of physical laws, expressed in mathematical relations, may give way to likely tendencies, as Marshall saw it, in which deviations from them need not, or at least will not, be taken to refute the designated law.

Where economic laws are based solely on empirical data, as is the case for such varied "laws" as Engel's law and Zipf's law, they are typically acknowledged to be lacking a certain theoretical ballast, suggesting that whatever weight and shape one might accord economic laws, they require a theoretical grounding separate from any conformity with empirical evidence. This would appear to relegate empirical laws, like those noted above, to a lesser status. One might deem them "Keplerian," as they are fundamentally descriptive rather than analytical or causal.

As Keplerian, the analogue for such laws in the realm of classical physics would be found in kinematics, in contrast to the dynamic principles associated with the kinetics of Newton's laws of motion. In the construction of classical physics over the course of the seventeenth century, one might view Kepler's mathematical formulation of the elliptical pattern found in the cyclical rotation of planets as a foundational achievement in kinematics, while Newton's law of gravitation is almost invariably taken as the exemplar of classical kinetics (leaving aside the criticism of those, like René Thom, who saw purely quantitative laws of this sort as devoid of causal explanation) (Thom 1993: 69ff., 93ff., 104ff.).

It was Newton's laws that established the paradigm for what made laws scientific for classical economic thinkers from Smith to Marx – and beyond. In Newton himself economists would find an exemplar of scientific vision aspired to, as Samuelson saw in proclaiming Walras to be "the Newton of economics" (Samuelson 1961: 836). At the same time, one can see in the notion that it is possible to produce economic laws, conceived as broad generalities, from empirical or historical data alone a strand of thought from the German Historical School, especially as associated with Wilhelm Roscher.

Yet the ready translation of accounting identities into economic relationships capable of elucidating cause and effect raises the possibility that many of the economic laws fashioned thereby may be more Keplerian than Newtonian. For example, the first of Thomas Piketty's "laws of capitalism," while at first blush appearing to bear a certain kinship with Marx's rather Newtonian "law of motion of capital," essentially begins as an accounting ratio, a measure of the return on capital (Piketty 2014: 52–5). Piketty's thesis is then constructed on the basis of a secular, that is, long-term historical, comparison of the size of this rate of return in relation to the size of the rate of growth of incomes.

Piketty is hardly alone in this regard. In the realm of economics it is not at all unusual to "invigorate" accounting identities into dynamic relations relating causes and effects. One might think of such use of the identity of saving and investment at equilibrium in informing macroeconomic models from Wicksell through Keynes to Harrod and Domar and Solow, and the equivalence of money in circulation and the economic activities (or exchanges) for which such money is expended in Fisher's equation of exchange.

Yet there is an additional nuance to this distinction between Kepler and Newton. The mathematician Morris Kline engaged in a rather strenuous, even somewhat long-winded effort to show how Kepler's laws could be derived from Newton's (Kline 1977: 613–21). Allowing that to be the case, one needs to establish its underlying methodological or philosophical basis and import. For Robert Aumann the shift from Kepler to Newton signified a broadening of explanatory power, to which he likened the scope of game theory in relation to previously enunciated theories of oligopoly (Aumann 1989: 17–18). Kline's focus was less on matters of explanatory power, where the more expansive theory or law is taken to be the more fundamental in a hierarchy or ranking of theoretical postulates or "primitives" (as one might have spoken of Euclid's axioms or Newton's laws), and more on the theoretical limitations of Kepler's laws themselves, that is, as fundamentally descriptive.

Does this make the case for empirical laws to be, potentially, something other, awaiting a grander or more encompassing set of principles that might provide the seemingly missing theoretical base? Would this then allow for a multiplicity of Keplerian laws in economics to be regarded as theoretical way-stations?

And, of course, one cannot overlook the fact that, whatever the aspirations of economists, a century ago physicists came to reject the universality of the model of Newton's laws. As Hans Reichenbach, the logical empiricist, noted at mid-century regarding "historical research":

> What has hampered historical research, and the logical analysis of such research, is the ambition to find causal laws comparable in strictness to

the laws of planetary motion. The physicist has abandoned this ideal of a law in several of his fields of research. Why should the historian adhere to it, since it is so obviously unattainable?

> (Reichenbach 1951: 124)

Might one characterize the research program associated with Kuznets to be fundamentally Keplerian in its aims: an "empirical science" whose generalities and regularities are formed out of a mass of carefully accumulated data? Data organized into various and divers categories, reinforces their "historical" character. Obviously, the extent to which that is so will depend once again on whether economic statistics are taken to be "historical" or not.

## Into the fog of economics and economic history: "empty boxes" revisited

Writing in the *Economic* Journal in September 1922, John Clapham, the first to hold a chair in economic history at Cambridge University, delivered a blistering critique of what he regarded as the conceptual vacuousness of economics as a discipline, calling its abstractions "empty boxes."

Arthur C. Pigou, who had succeeded Alfred Marshall as professor of political economy at Cambridge University, felt obliged to respond to, and defend against, the charges laid down by Clapham. From Pigou's perspective, the historian was distinguished by his central and overriding concern with the facts. By contrast, the economist dealt much more with what Pigou characterized as "implications." His case ran as follows:

> There are two broadly distinguished sorts of knowledge: "pure" knowledge about implications, such as is sought in mathematics and logic; and realistic knowledge concerned with a subject-matter presumed to be actual, such as is sought by physicists.
>
> (Pigou 1922: 458)

He then goes on to state, somewhat defensively, "[b]ut knowledge of implications is just as much knowledge as knowledge of matters of fact" (Pigou 1922: 459).

So far it appears that the pertinent contrast is between mathematics and logic, on the one hand, and physics, on the other, whereby the former consists of rules and forms while the latter is concerned with "actual" content. Nonetheless, a shift now occurs, such that economics, it would appear, is aligned with the former, while history stands with the latter. Pigou offers up the following example of this new contrast, distinguishing economics from history:

> That, *if* certain conditions as to increasing or diminishing returns prevail, and *if* a tax of so much is imposed on a given article, such and such an

effect will follow, is a piece of truth, just as it is a piece of truth – if it is one – that a certain English king died from a surfeit of lampreys.

(Pigou 1922: 459)

This draws Pigou to conclude that "[t]he historian is interested in matters of fact; but the logician is interested in implications" (Pigou 1922: 459). At this juncture one must wonder whether the economist is meant to be a suitable and ready substitute for the logician. In fact, it is these shifts in contrasting pairs of disciplines that should garner the most interest. Does history bear a special kinship with physics? Is "pure" economics essentially a matter of logic?

Pigou's case is complicated further by his injection of causality as an essential feature of economic method:

A central problem of economics, from the time of Adam Smith downward, has been to disentangle and analyse the causes by which the values of different things are determined.

(Pigou 1922: 460)

It is worthwhile setting this statement by Pigou next to the depiction of Clapham's intellectual framework and frame of mind by M. M. Postan in 1946, on the occasion of Clapham's death. Postan, who succeeded Clapham in the chair in economic history at Cambridge University, noted Clapham's training and tutelage in economics under Alfred Marshall who, Postan claimed, may well have regarded Clapham as his "favourite" student (Postan 1946: 57). Clapham went on to write a monograph about the woolen and worsted industries in England.

But, as that study clearly shows, Clapham's work was rooted too deeply in facts; he was too interested in the past cause of things – in fact was too much of an historian – ever to have remained an economist (Postan 1946: 57).

In one crucial sense Postan's view is in accord with Pigou's: central to the work of historians is the exploration and examination of facts. But Postan's appreciation also sets up a certain and hardly insignificant disjuncture with Pigou's characterization of the method of the historian, for Postan sees the historian engaged in a search for "causes" rather than facts alone. If both historian and economist have as their central mission the search for "causes," if of different sorts, then both have had need, in Pigou's terms, "to disentangle and analyse," what one might think of as matters of hypothesis-making and interpretation. Under these circumstances the boundary between economics and economic history would become quite murky.

The critique, even disparagement of economics by economic historians continued well past Clapham's labeling of the product of economic theorizing as no more than "empty boxes." Postan's comments evince both a continuation as well as a tempering of Clapham's critique into the next generation of economic historians:

But if some of [the] conclusions [of economics] are capable of illuminating real problems of economic life, and economics as a whole is something more than a soufflé of whipped postulates, it is because even the most theoretical of economists sometimes manage to mix their theorems with a little social observation.

(Postan [1939] 1971: 24)

Decades later Postan wrote scathingly of the misapprehension of the Industrial Revolution by economists, and the concomitant impact of that misapprehension upon both the theory of economic development and its practice in the 1950s and 1960s. The lack of attention to the transformation of agriculture in the course of the Industrial Revolution – or even the extent to which such a transformation propelled the Industrial Revolution forward – resulted in a too narrowly focused emphasis upon industrial transformation.

For those countries [in which agriculture is still overwhelmingly the most important pursuit], as for England in the eighteenth century, development of agriculture is, and must for some time remain, the source of industrial development – its *sine qua non*.

(Postan [1965] 1971: 110)

Postan's case of course raises the proposition – and concern – that the theoretical constructs of economists draw rightly or wrongly upon historical patterns, based in turn upon a mistaken or hazy selection of facts. If so, this would mean that rather than immersing themselves in empty boxes, economists embarked upon constructing subfields on the basis of faulty historical patterns. But who formulates these patterns: historians or economists? Postan puts forth the notion that this task should fall to the historian, or dangerous misapprehensions or misinterpretations will ensue:

By refusing to connect the evidence of the past with the discussion of today, the economic historian does not thereby banish all such connections; all he does is merely to abandon them to non-historians. This is perhaps one of the reasons why modern economic and sociological debate is crowded with questionable deductions from past experiences. These deductions are not always offered as historical propositions, but they are nevertheless inferences from what certain non-historians have understood or misunderstood to have been the evidence of history.

(Postan [1965] 1971: 104)

Postan's cautionary tale also differs from the case laid out by Eli Heckscher, who bridged the fields of economics and economic history in the course of his academic career in Sweden in the first decades of the twentieth century. Heckscher saw the need to draw upon historical statistics to gain an accurate picture of what had transpired in the past, as well as the bases for it. At the same time Heckscher was scathing in his criticism of the main thrust of economic theorizing, echoing in part Clapham's objections of a failure to attend to the facts:

> Especially unfortunate, I think, is the construction of theories which do not admit verifications at the hands of facts, being frequently not related even to any given state of society. In spite of its lavish use of mathematical formulas, such a form of study is poles asunder from that of the natural sciences.
>
> (Heckscher 1939: 168–9)

Heckscher adds

> [M]y objection to economists is not that they are theorists, but that they are nothing else, and that their theory is often of a very unhelpful type.
>
> (Heckscher 1939: 139)

Where Heckscher comes closest to Postan is in his own version of the misapprehension by economists of the Industrial Revolution, thus presenting a factual critique underlying the challenge to economic theory, though Heckscher's criticism is most specifically leveled at Marx. For Heckscher the central, formative, and then transformative role accorded the cotton textile industry in the Industrial Revolution was misplaced, as it diminished significantly changes in the iron industry (a point that might have registered more deeply with Heckscher, in light of his background and interest in the economic history of Sweden, one of the leading producers of iron in that period).

While Postan emphasized the dangers of undergirding economic theory with a mistaken or wrongheaded economic history, Heckscher saw a disconnect between theory and history, to the detriment of economic theory.

Fifty years after Heckscher derided the weaknesses of economic theorizing, the relation between economics and economic history remained rocky. As a postscript to the Clapham–Pigou controversy one might look to the far more recent concerns and criticisms from two different historians: one, Paul Bairoch, who actually trained as an economist; the other, Eric Hobsbawm.

As an economic historian Bairoch decried the "myth-making" drawn from economic theorizing, whether put forward by neoclassical economists or their radical critics, fundamentally challenging the standard cases or conventional wisdom these different groups championed. Protectionism, it turned out, fostered more rapid economic growth, while the ascendancy of "free trade" was associated with period of slower growth. The industrialized, "more developed" states of Europe and North America did not drain the resources of the "developing world" in order to attain their level of economic activity and development. Here Bairoch set the "facts," meaning the historical data mined for the pertinent times and places, against the misleading and ultimately wrong-headed historical patterns economists sought to find as a result of applying theoretical economic constructs or concepts. This is then a case of theory applied to economic history, without the requisite attention to what the facts actually showed; effectively a case of history ignored. In Bairoch's caustic phrasing: "To paraphrase Leo Tolstoy, economic history is a deaf man answering questions no economist has put to him" (Bairoch 1993: xiii).

Hobsbawm presented his own critique in two lectures to the economics faculty of Cambridge University in 1980 and 1996 about the relation between economics and history.

Hobsbawm began by expressing his Clapham-like dismissal of the arid abstraction of economics:

> I am not an economist and, by the criteria of one school among my col-
> leagues, not even a proper economic historian, though of course those
> criteria would also have excluded Sombart, Max Weber, and Tawney. I
> am neither a mathematician nor a philosopher, two occupations in which
> economists sometimes seek refuge when hard pressed by the real world,
> and whose propositions might seem relevant to them.
>
> (Hobsbawm [1980] 1997: 94–5)

Hobsbawm then establishes a distinction between a history that explains and an economics that analyzes, which follows from the notion that historians are fundamentally concerned with "why" an event or development took place – "What we would like to know is why situation A was followed by situation B and no other" (Hobsbawm 1997: 111), while economists focus upon "how," that is, by what mechanism an economic activity or phenomenon took place.

This, though, has further consequences. It would appear to relegate matters of causality to history, and places a premium upon "historical understanding." Casting back over the past century of intellectual history, one might see in this heightened role for history the emergence, or re-emergence, of a form of methodological inquiry associated with Max Weber, with at least one crucial difference. For Weber, and in Weber's time and place, the line between historian and economist would seem quite fluid, a product in part of the emphasis upon "historical economics" in the German Historical School, for all that Weber found limitations to it. As noted above, Hobsbawm aligned himself as an "economic historian" with Sombart and Weber, even if just rhetorically, both linked to the historical school.

In fact, for Hobsbawm economics without history was, metaphorically, "dead-in-the-water":

> My argument implies that, divorced from history, economics is a rudderless
> ship and economists without history have not much idea of where it is sailing
> to. But I am not suggesting that those defects can be remedied simply be [*sic*]
> getting some charts, that is by paying more attention to concrete economic
> realities and historical experience. As a matter of fact, there have always

been plenty of economists ready and anxious to keep their eyes open. The trouble is that, if in the mainstream tradition, their theory and method as such has not helped them to know where to look and what to look for. The study of economic mechanisms was divorced from that of the social and other factors which condition the behavior of the agents who comprise such mechanisms.

(Hobsbawm 1997: 106)

If Hobsbawm is correct, economics requires history in order to form a coherent intellectual discipline, though this in itself does not establish the nature of historical proof in economics. Hobsbawm's contention that "attention to concrete economic realities and historical experience" does not suffice draws upon his Marxist perspective, reinforced by his grounding the case on the insights of Maurice Dobb. Yet his concern speaks to the broader question raised by both Marxist and non-Marxist historians, as well as other heterodox economists, namely the means by which or form through which the connection between "economic mechanism" and social world might be determined. Somewhat ironically, the mechanism driving economics in general to which Hobsbawm refers comports rather neatly with Pigou's characterization of economics offering up "knowledge by implication," which Pigou had presented as the core of his defense against Clapham's claims.

Robert Solow put forward his own disappointment at the state of affairs that existed between economics and economic history in his 1985 address to the American Economic Association:

For better or worse, however, economics has gone down a different path, not the one I have in mind. One consequence, not the most important one, but one that matters for this discussion, is that economic theory learns nothing from economic history, and economic history is as much corrupted as enriched by economic theory.

(Solow 1985: 328)

## "Barren results," "plausible rather than proven"

It might appear that the critique of economic abstraction as "empty boxes" was essentially a critique from without, by those identifying themselves primarily as economic historians. There is, though, a second contemporaneous vein of criticisms from economists that echoed the concerns of Clapham and others.

Perhaps one might view Wesley Mitchell's remarks in introducing Simon Kuznets' first major work in the mid-1920s, where he laments the century-long paucity of advances in economic theorizing about business cycles since the time of Malthus and Sismondi, as reflective of his Institutionalist perspective. Nonetheless, his contention that economics had so far failed to place its theorizing on a solid footing holds serious weight.

Mitchell's remarks were rather strongly worded:

> This problem [of business crises] has not lost its interest in the hundred years since Sismondi and Malthus discussed it … Many explanations have been offered.
>
> (Mitchell 1926: iii)

> All of these explanations are plausible, and perhaps no two are incompatible with each other. But our knowledge of business cycles is most unsatisfactory so long as it consists of an unsystematized collection of hypotheses which are plausible rather than proven. The present need is for testing every explanation to find how well it accords with the relevant facts. Such testing requires close study of the inter-relations among the fluctuations of all the processes involved. To study these inter-relations closely, we must have measured observations, covering a wide range of activities.
>
> (Mitchell 1926: iii–iv)

Conceiving of a heightened role for economic statistics to break through the existing limitations of empirical proof, Mitchell concludes: "Hence the theoretical significance of the recent progress in compiling and analyzing economic statistics" (Mitchell 1926: iv).

Mitchell's commentary needs to be set in comparison to the scathing remarks of a decidedly non-Institutionalist economist, Paul Samuelson, in the introduction to his path-breaking work, *Foundations of Economic Analysis,* which sought to remake the relationship between economics and mathematics by elevating the application of a broad array of mathematical techniques, thought of as tools, to a wide range of economic problems and questions:

> The majority [of economists] would have been glad to enunciate meaningful theorems if any had occurred to them. In fact, the literature abounds with false generalization.
>
> The economist has consoled himself for his barren results with the thought that he was forging tools which would eventually yield fruit. The promise is always in the future; we are like highly trained athletes who never ran a race, and in consequence grow stale. It is still too early to determine whether the innovations in thought of the last decade will have stemmed the unmistakable signs of decadence which were clearly present in economic thought prior to 1930.
>
> (Samuelson 1947: 4)

One can certainly argue that for both Mitchell and Samuelson their disparagement of the past or current state of economic theorizing served as a vehicle for the introduction and development of something rather new and different: in Mitchell's case the far more comprehensive use of statistics – but not probabilities, as one might encounter in econometrics – in furthering economic analysis and the "empirical science" associated with Kuznets; in Samuelson's the transformation of economic analysis through a broadened and more systematic use of mathematics in economics. It is certainly the case that Samuelson and Kuznets both could lay claim to firming up the "scientificality" of economics, recipients in succession in 1970 and 1971 of the newly created Nobel Prize in economics.

Nonetheless, one might ask if the tacks taken by Kuznets and Samuelson effectively responded to, or overcame, Clapham's challenge of an economics replete with empty abstraction. These "tacks" differ in certain essential ways. In constructing economic facts from historical statistics, Kuznets had to address the choices made among assumptions and emphases that would determine and perhaps even shape the data to be used. By contrast, Samuelson, while pragmatically introducing a host of mathematical techniques into economic analysis, was searching for the structural similarities in economic relations across economic subfields, to all appearances an ahistorical project.

Yet even here history, in some fashion, makes an entrance. Consider Samuelson's portrayal of causality in a mathematical system constructed with economic variables:

> The only sense in which the use of the term causation is admissible is in respect to changes in external data or parameters. As a figure of speech, it may be said that changes in these cause changes in the variables of our system.
>
> (Samuelson 1947: 9)

In other words, causality, whose philosophical form or basis is held in abeyance, matters only in time, though left unstated is whether this is real, that is, historical time through "changes in external data" or an abstracted version of it through "changes in ... parameters."

Hence, in establishing the framework for the treatment of economic problems through static optimization, Samuelson's reference to "external data or parameters" may bear a certain similarity to Kuznets' declared effort to separate out "the invariant element in the variable economic universe" (Kuznets 1941a: 28), so that, in the end, "Those irregular changes that remain, and cannot be analyzed further in general terms, are interpreted as far as possible in association with historical events or are treated as random" (Kuznets 1941a: 28). But in Samuelson's case there may also be a dynamic element associated with the external data, whereas for Kuznets historical events, notwithstanding his own deep interest in tracing the development of economies over time, may be relegated to background or "white noise". If such external data, though, is both the "driver" of changes to the economic system and the product of historical circumstance, then history looms larger in this schema than might have originally been contemplated.

## Historical proof and empirical evidence

Do historical proof and empirical evidence provide different notions and expectations about the nature of proof itself? In the case of proof through empirical evidence, one may apply a test of falsification: was the theory borne out by the factual evidence adduced? To simplify, one might pursue a specific example. Posit that, to succeed, all firms must be profit maximizers. Then, evidence that one successful firm did not take that route should negate the theory in question. As is evident, though, in the field of economics the more likely response is that of complicating complexity, noted at the outset, where other factors or elements not initially cited are seen as producing, or at least potentially producing, the unexpected outcome. Nonetheless, there is at least the possibility of establishing a correspondence between theory and empirical evidence.

In the case of historical proof, the capacity to falsify, though seemingly capable of being measured against historical facts, "wie es eigentlich geschehen," as Ranke put it, essentially vanishes. The advancing of historical statistics as economic facts does not, in and of itself, make for a historical proof; rather, they are the "stuff" of empirical evidence, providing statistical support to the case being made. Historical proof entails the embrace of narratives, which necessarily requires selecting among alternatives. Hence, historical proof is fundamentally a matter of heuristics. It is also true, as has been oft noted, that even the choice of historical statistics or economic facts calls for latching onto one story or narrative, or another, but these individual storylines do not have the force and primacy of those invoked in the full-blown making or claiming of historical proof. In this latter case any attempt at forecasting the future, a key element in any schema of falsification, gives way to a broad interpretive reconstruction, allowing instead the past to conform in some fashion to an extant theory. This makes economics less a science, certainly in the way that Hempel would have characterized it (Hempel 1952), and more the subject of, and subject to narratology.

This also creates a certain duality in the linkages between economics and economic history. On the one hand, economic history serves as the well-spring for historical proof in economics, making the two disciplines appear inseparable. On the other, the downgrading of "scientificality" associated with the more literary and subjective nature of narratology can serve as the springboard for asserting the countervailing notion that economics appears stronger as a field by setting it apart through its greater reliance upon quantitative measures and its capacity to produce general statements of "invariant relations." As Kenneth Arrow noted at the mid-twentieth century in distinguishing the more mathematical, if still somewhat circumscribed, approach of economics to mathematization in contrast with other social sciences: "These arguments seem logically irrefutable, and yet, outside the realm of economics, very little use has been made of mathematical and symbolic methods [in other social sciences]" (Arrow 1951: 130).

Overall, this led to the effort to recognize the work of those economists whose resort to quantification and mathematization was central to their achievements in the field when the "Nobel Prize" in economics was first ushered into existence in 1969.

Moreover, the heuristic nature of historical proof suggests that "proof" under those circumstances constitutes conformity with a certain narrative. As such, such concerns recall the mathematician David Hilbert's list, at the turn of the twentieth century, of the leading mathematical problems to be solved, if in transmuted form. What, after all, is understood to be a proof? What relation does and can any such proof bear to the "truth"? Narratology and the reflexivity of the principle of conformance lend an air of postmodernism to the discussion, with an objective truth somewhat beyond reach. But if the thesis of "Economics as Plausible Conjecture" is correct, then the intertwining of literary form and economics has its roots in the Age of Enlightenment, in the eighteenth century. Furthermore, the recognition of failed congruences amidst heightened rigor that emerged in and through Hilbert's challenges indicates that the late nineteenth and early twentieth century crisis in mathematical thinking offers up another and separate marker for the terms of this philosophical debate in economics.

Does economics require historical proof in order to explain? Whatever the strengths of logical or empirical proof, these succeed only in advancing economic analysis, a presentation or display of mechanisms that comports with the Pigovian notion of "knowledge by implication." If there is a desire to get at or reach for causes, an examination of the past must ensue. But this examination leads to a new set of questions, which turn on the primacy of either economics or economic history: whether "theory is matched to facts," or "facts are matched to theory."

## On macroeconomics and history

First, though, it is necessary to turn to the economists' take on the relation between macroeconomics and history. It is fair to say that the transformation wrought by the Industrial Revolution and the advent of the Great Depression constitute the two events (or developments) that have occupied a special place in the long-term interplay between history and macroeconomic theory and policy, with financial crises, when separated from the Great Depression, the nearest third. As Barry Eichengreen introduced his 1986 essay "Macroeconomics and History": "The modern subdiscipline of macroeconomics can trace its origins to the profound economic and intellectual disturbance occasioned by the Great Depression" (Eichengreen 1986: 43).

Eichengreen's treatment of economic history in this article was geared to respond to the question raised by Alexander Field about the future of economic history. Eichengreen's work is quite curious, in that he displays a keen sense and awareness of how various and apparently conflicting theories in economics might serve to explain certain major economic developments in Europe over the last several centuries, ranging from the sixteenth-century "price revolution" in Spain to the onset and persistence of the Great Depression of the 1930s. In this overview Eichengreen is clearly of two minds about the pertinent criteria for such explanations. On the one hand, he favors quantitative models, preferably econometric models, to explain the events, circumstances, or patterns that occurred. Yet at every turn he finds these efforts wanting, sometimes because no model is actually "specified" as the basis for the explanation, other times because relevant portions of the historical experience are missing. In this latter instance the failure to comprehend fully may be due to the circumscribed nature of the economic theories invoked, a fault in the construction or application of such theories, where critical historical elements or factors are treated as given, a form, in essence, of ceteris paribus applied, fairly broadly it must be said, to historical experience itself. While not stated, it may also result from a certain "recalcitrance" to quantification, to invoke Kuznets' caveat about the standardization of quantifiable measures. These concerns have been raised more recently by Baumol and Stern, as noted above, among others.

On balance Eichengreen appears to have sought to establish the underpinnings of choices made about economic policy and its impact through "historical experience." Exploring the possible causes of the Great Depression, he labels "historical experience" the "predetermined variable required to pin down differences in both policy's formulation and effects in the 1930s" (Eichengreen 1986: 76). In this way he sets forth a broader claim for the place of history in economics, differing in certain crucial respects from his effort to match up economic facts to economic models or to see economic history as a source of analogies for economists:

> [T]he use of history to facilitate integrated analysis of economic policy is a general proposition whose relevance extends well beyond this example and examples that resemble it. If macroeconomists are to move beyond partial equilibrium treatments of their subject which then take the most interesting aspects of the problem as given, they must develop an historical perspective that extends beyond the merits of long time series to include the role of historical experience as an influence on the characteristics of institutions and the attitudes of individuals in both private and public sectors.
>
> (Eichengreen 1986: 76)

The real puzzle, though, in Eichengreen's work is his own understanding of what constitutes economic history. The greater part of "Macroeconomics and History" is devoted to an explication of economic events in and over time on the basis of economic theories of varying sorts, with Keynesians effectively doing battle with monetarists or advocates of rational expectations (this was, after all, a work written in the 1980s), and with "explanation" following from, typically, econometric testing.

He proceeds to detail what he described as the "symbiotic relationship" between economic history and macroeconomics:

Nowhere is the symbiotic relationship of economic history and macro-economics more evident than in the literature on the causes of the Great Depression. Proponents of Classical, New Classical, Keynesian, and Monetarist theories of macroeconomic fluctuations, while far from notorious [*sic*] for the range of issues on which they concur, agree that their preferred interpretation should provide a satisfactory explanation for the onset, depth, and duration of the Depression.

(Eichengreen 1986: 68)

He goes on to state:

The vigor with which rival interpretations of the Depression have been advanced and the sustained attention devoted by macroeconomists to this juncture in twentieth-century history raise questions about the role of the economic historian in the analysis of such episodes. Should historians permit their investigations to be organized around the competing para-digms of the economics profession? Or is there a distinctly historical approach to the analysis of such events that transcends doctrinal disputes among economists?

(Eichengreen 1986: 68–9)

It appears then that under certain circumstances economic history may be applied economics, yet this may be contradicted, or at least thwarted, by two concerns raised by Eichengreen. One, as noted above, is the way that these economic, perhaps, better, econometric models fail to account for what are likely the most interesting – and most incisive – elements of historical experience. The other is implicit in the inability to transcend the theoretical suppositions of competing theories as they seek to explain. When histo-rical facts or data are adduced, they tend to support competing visions, to the extent that such theories appear to be self-contained, though there are occasional breakthroughs challenging the initial premises or assumptions. While one may overstate the virtues of falsification, there is a sense that such self-contained or referencing theories may not actually explain, but rather display an "if, then" mechanism. Again, one might think of this as a more recent instantiation of Pigou's "knowledge by implication" rather than "knowledge by fact," but with the added and not insignificant complication that there are contested understandings.

What, then, is one to make of "economic history"? Eichengreen's turn to the need to encompass a broader "historical experience" suggests another pathway to be pursued. His concluding notion that "economic history" would then fall somewhere between economics and history sounds a theme taken up more fully by Carlo Cipolla in *Tra due culture* (Cipolla [1988] 1991). But it is also the case that Eichengreen casts his essay and argument in terms of what he calls "macroeconomic history," whereby the rebirth of macroeconomics in the wake of the Great Depression (or, alternatively, the birth of modern macroeconomics) informs a new understanding of and perspective on economic history. This is certainly consistent with Eichengreen's view of the explanatory role played by economic theory in elucidating the past from an economic standpoint, and it conforms to the notion that events like the Great Depression have been crucial to the shaping of economic ideas and ultimately theory.

However, does it ring true for economic history as it has generally been comprehended over the years? In that regard. Schumpeter's introduction to his history of economic analysis is enlightening, in that he posits the emergence of economic history in the Marshallian era, from 1890 to 1920, thus predating the Great Depression. Eichengreen might well counter that works like Marshall's *Industry and Trade* are fundamentally microeconomic in character, focusing upon various industries rather than the economy in aggregate. Yet there is no question that Marshall's work presents a cross-country comparison assaying what we might regard as the pattern and pace of economic growth. What is missing from Marshall's inquiry are the macroeconomic tools for analysis developed only later. Thus, Eichengreen's contentions would hold, but only if economic history is comprehended on the basis of the economic analytical tools available, that is, on the basis of theoretical economics, which emerged out of what Eichengreen characterized as "historical experience."

One might set this in relief against the longstanding interest in the origins, strength, and sustainability of the Industrial Revolution, a matter like the Great Depression engaging both economists and historians. From Eichengreen's perspective, would a narrative of the emergence of the Industrial Revolution be adjudged to be a work of history, but whose subject matter was first and foremost the economy? And what of the notion that historical events and developments spur the advent of new or contrary economic theories, as indeed Eichengreen himself acknowledged was the case for the Great Depression, and may now result anew in the aftermath of the financial crisis of 2008 and the "Great Recession" that followed? In short, might the history drive the theory, perhaps even more so than the theory affords an explanation of the historical experience?

One need only turn to Arthur Burns' vision of a Ricardian age and a Keynesian age in economic thought, each shaped by the historical experience of the period in question, to see history frame the economics that for the time seems most compelling. Burns, who succeeded Mitchell as head of the National Bureau of Economic Research, nicely captured the importance of these two historical moments for economic theorizing and policymaking:

> I have taken this excursion into history because we are living in a time of bold and vigorous theoretical speculation, the only close parallel of which is the Ricardian age. The principal practical problem of Ricardo's generation was whether the state should foster the economic power of the landlords or the rising manufacturing class …The principal practical problem of our generation is the maintenance of employment, and it has now become – as it long should have been – the principal problem of economic

theory. This transformation of economic theory is due in large part to the writings of John Maynard Keynes.

(Burns [1946] 1954: 4)

But what exactly is meant or entailed by "historical experience"? Does this validate essentially an Institutionalist approach, of some sort, to any capacity of economics to "explain"?

For example, the notion that pivotal historical developments should be incorporated into any exploration of economic theory and policy could be linked to the idea that a broader net around what constitutes economic activity would transform the "market" from a universal, timeless "given" into a changing, evolving historical phenomenon. This may be regarded as the hallmark of the thought and approach of the Institutionalists.

It is also true of the work of Karl Polanyi. It turns out as well that the two sets of events that frame Polanyi's *The Great Transformation* are the emergence of the "market economy" in the nineteenth century and the Great Depression, though Polanyi sought to anchor all economic activity within a broader social network or fabric. So he cited Frank Knight's dictum that "no specifically human motive is economic" as applicable to "economic life itself" (Polanyi [1944] 2001: 258). And thus for Polanyi economic history provided the foundation for economics, as demonstrated in the advent of the market economy, with great weight given to historical agents:

> Economic history reveals that the emergence of national markets was in no way the result of the gradual and spontaneous emancipation of the economic sphere from governmental control. On the contrary, the market has been the outcome of a conscious and often violent intervention on the part of government which imposed the market organization on society for noneconomic ends.
>
> (Polanyi [1944] 2001: 258)

Polanyi was in fact cited by Fernand Braudel in what at first appears to be an inspiration for his own critique of the "market." For what emerges out of commercial capitalism is what Braudel calls the antithesis of the market: the "anti-market," and the market itself is treated as an "endogenous" factor, subject to change. There are, though, serious differences between the two, which will be explored more fully below.

As for a Marxian understanding of the nexus between economics and history and its implications for economic history, one may turn to the lectures provided on the subject by Eric Hobsbawm, noted above, as well as his characterization of the ascent of economic history in his autobiography, *Interesting Times*. Hobsbawm's case entails going well beyond the grounding in "concrete reality" advanced by Weber, seeing that as inadequate to the task, requiring instead a theoretical structure which, according to Hobsbawm, could be found only through a Marxian perspective. It is also noteworthy, though, that there is an acknowledgment on Hobsbawm's part that economic history came to the fore in the mid-twentieth century on two fronts: one led by Marxist historians, the other through the French and non-Marxist *Annales* school (Hobsbawm 2002: 285–8). Of course, as economics evolved, so did economic history. Perhaps Hobsbawm's take on the ascendancy and subsequent decline of economic history – to be succeeded, in his view, by the purveyors of and advocates for social and cultural history – should be comprehended in relation to that evolution. It is also true that there were other claimants advancing the case for a better integration of economics and history, like M. M. Postan, who were decidedly anti-Marxist, as Hobsbawm himself noted (Hobsbawm 2002: 282–3).

## Variations in matching fact and theory

Finally, there is the continuing complexity associated with the need to grapple with the interplay of fact and theory in the relations – and tensions – between economics and economic history. One can trace significant aspects of these tensions in Barry Eichengreen's work, beginning with his essay from the 1980s on "Macroeconomics and History," then taken up more recently in a piece entitled, "Economic History and Economic Policy" (Eichengreen 2012). In his most recent book, entitled *Hall of Mirrors*, Eichengreen is concerned with "the uses – and misuses– of history" by economic policymakers in responding to the macroeconomic difficulties posed by the Great Depression and the financial crisis of 2008, as their interpretation of past events forms and frames a narrative that guides the thinking and actions taken by policymakers.

In the 1986 essay Eichengreen assessed how different historical explanations, say of the causes of the Great Depression, did or did not comport with the terms of diverse theoretical economic models. Similarly, in *Hall of Mirrors* the guiding narratives can be, and in fact are, fundamentally influenced by economic theorizing, even shaped by theoretical perspectives, so that the framework for such narratives may be Keynesian or neoclassical (or some combination of the two). History would then serve economic theory, though with the caveat that what was extracted from past experience, say the particular nature of bank failure in the 1930s, would be accepted and understood as the pertinent set of facts upon which policymakers would build their response to the banking crisis of the late 2000s, however different and distinctive the current circumstances actually were (Eichengreen 2015).

In the 2012 piece, Eichengreen modified his position somewhat, treating economic history as offering up analogies from which policymakers in particular might draw. Eichengreen lays out a curious set of criteria for the introduction of what he calls "analogical reasoning":

> The question is under what circumstances individuals on their own and as members of groups rely most heavily on analogical reasoning. The literature on cognitive science and organizational learning suggest two situations.
>
> (Eichengreen 2012: 293)

He goes on to state:

> First, when there is limited time to reach a decision and those reaching it have limited information-processing capacity. Second, the literature suggests that individuals are likely to rely on analogy when they disagree on the principles needed for deductive reasoning.
>
> (Eichengreen 2012: 293).

Eichengreen's second consideration does raise a crucial point about the limitations of the deductive, or logical approach in economics. What happens when there is no fundamental agreement upon or acceptance of first principles or assumptions, as is the case in economics? While Eichengreen, in focusing ultimately on the bases for formulating economic policy, highlights the differences between "saltwater" and "freshwater" economists in the United States over the course of recent decades, one might readily extend this concern to the entire trajectory of the history of economic thought. If, as has been the case over the course of the history of economic thought, there are differing notions about the foundational nature of "value" – or price – in economics, then the resort to logical deduction in economics is highly circumscribed, complicated further by disagreements and differences as to how such terms may be defined as concepts.

But does the resort to "analogy" fill the gap? Eichengreen's reliance upon "cognitive science" and "organizational learning" casts the matter into the realm of psychology and behavior analysis. In any sorting through "historical experience" as recollected or constructed from historical materials, though, one is more likely to find the "likenesses" or the "likening" of analogies in historical patterns, discerned – perhaps – as Alexander Gerschenkron has described the nature of "historical research" for matters of policy more than half-a-century ago:

> Historical research consists essentially in application to empirical material of various sets of empirically derived hypothetical generalizations and in testing the closeness of the resulting fit, in the hope that in this way certain uniformities, certain typical situations, and certain typical relationships among individual factors in these situations can be ascertained.
>
> (Gerschenkron [1952] 1992: 111)

Consequently, however inchoate, the analogies produced would follow from "generalizations" about experience rooted in theoretical constructs themselves – or, if one prefers, theoretical predispositions.

Here the assumed relation between economics and economic history is the central matter under consideration. A set of facts and/or a narrative are fitted to economic theoretical strands, possibly drawn from economic models. Does this process conform to or comport with notions of proof, and, if so, of what sort? First of all, unless one accepts Marshall's thesis of continuity and unity in economic development, one can dismiss any notion of proof linked to prediction, as one might seek through controlled experiments, since the facts adduced, and the explanatory narrative provided, are drawn from the past rather than the future. Nor can one rely all that much upon what are effectively logical or axiomatic proofs, in which the "recurrent" or "invariant" relation is found to transcend the vagaries of historical proof. For Eichengreen proof, such as it is, does require a corroboration of some sort with a set of specific facts, so that his approach might be described in shorthand as theory confirmed by a given set of facts.

Yet this misses the essential mark. It is really the facts that are fitted to match the theory, not the other way around. In effect, facts are adduced to constitute a narrative that comports with, or justifies a given economic theory. Without further steps being taken, each such narrative has at best a post-modern claim as proof, since other narratives will "justify" other theories. As Solow pointed out in his short but insightful address to the American Economic Association:

> The competing [economic] hypotheses are themselves complex and subtle. We know before we start that all of them, or at least many of them, are capable of fitting the data in a gross sort of way.
>
> (Solow 1985: 328)

Moreover, the qualification "at best" is not insignificant, for it is based upon the standard of internal consistency or conformity to a given set of (theoretical) rules, a threshold which Eichengreen noted was often – perhaps almost always – difficult to attain.

These considerations lead in two different directions. One might pursue the tack taken by Marshall in laying out the philosophical framework for his amalgam of economics and economic history, *Industry and Trade*, in which explanations drawn from the past, the justification through narrative described above, serve effectively as "predictions" for the future, and thus carry economics over the threshold so as to sustain its credibility as a science. Marshall's framework, though, depends upon his foundational notion that there are no "leaps in nature," an assumption of evolutionary continuity.

On the other hand, the notion that proof consists in conformity to certain principles has an unmistakable Hilbertian ring to it. What was the Hilbertian dilemma portrayed here? David Hilbert's second problem, among those he presented as the great challenges in mathematics at the dawn of the twentieth century, concerned the "consistency" or "compatibility" of arithmetic axioms, essentially a matter of establishing a proof of internal coherence of an axiomatic system or structure on the basis of the axioms alone (Gray 2000). Thirty years later, Kurt Godel showed that such a proof was not possible, revealing a gap between that which was "true" and the ability to "prove" such.

Ironically, from this vantage point the matter of historical time, so essential to the relation between economics and economic history, appears less central to the case under consideration, in that it suggests a more general problem with proof, beyond a grounding in historical references, where proof, truth, and completeness all are subject to rigorous challenge – with less than fully determined results.

As applied to economic theory this would mean that even a seemingly "consistent" or "compatible" set of assumptions would fall short in providing proof, whether logical, empirical, or historical. A recognition of this limitation would seem to lead naturally to the use of additional or auxiliary assumptions from outside the given system, structure, or historical picture.

To complete a historical picture a narrative or plotline would have to be formed, and the only way that could occur would be through the introduction of "auxiliary" elements, assumptions upon which a "story" might take shape. Among the alternatives in creating or choosing a particular plotline is a reliance upon some form of colligation, in that the "incompleteness" of the historical picture may be seen and comprehended through the necessity of "setting the stage" in some way, where the present can be understood only through its relation to the past.

In the matter of historical proof, then, much depends upon a determination of primacy: does economic theory rest fundamentally upon a foundation built from economic history, whether verified or conjectured, or does economic history follow as an application of economics, that is, economic theory? Are the "causes" sought out either economic or historical in nature?

If, for example, "causality" comes under the purview of history, it might be inferred that any inquiry into the causes of the Great Depression is necessarily first and foremost a historical matter. By contrast, pursuing Eichengreen's logic, it would be the various economic theories that serve as causes, with a matching of selected historical facts to a set of theoretical or hypothesized constructs. To the extent that economic statistics enter the picture, they assume the role of historical data, as in the case of trade figures or the numbers of unemployed.

Heckscher appears to make a further distinction in this context in assaying the explanatory power of economic history and economics, by setting apart matters regarding the current state of affairs. Like Hegel's "owl of Minerva," economic history, in Heckscher's view, affords a retrospective glance from which the significance of events may be ascertained, or at the least asserted, ascribing a certain causality in the process. Heckscher speaks of this as the incorporation or the elucidation of "social change" within history:

> Since for all earlier periods of human history we know not only what took place but also what came after it, we have possibilities of choosing our facts, not only in relation to the actual situation in the period in question but also with regard to the significance of those facts, their relation to later developments, which is of course impossible when we are concerned with our own day.
>
> (Heckscher 1939: 168)

Without the ability to reference and draw upon the past, meaning (or significance) and causality are limited. Explanation, if not historical proof, flows from this. Hence, in stressing both "significance" and "choice," Heckscher was making the case for a version of historical proof in which claims for potentially competing explanations are drawn from the past; in fact, are necessarily so. His position thus represents the converse of Marshall's, as looking backward is infused with meaning and the ability to interpret rather than any capacity to predict the future.

## References

Arrow, Kenneth J. (1951) "Mathematical Models in the Social Sciences." In Daniel Lerner and Harold D. Lasswell (eds), *The Policy Sciences: Recent Developments in Scope and Method*. Stanford: Stanford University Press, pp. 129–154.

Aumann, Robert (1989) "Game theory." In John Eatwell,Murray Milgate, and Peter Newman (eds), *The New Palgrave: Game Theory*. Basingstoke: Macmillan.

Bachelier, Louis (1900) *Louis Bachelier's Theory of Speculation: The Origins of Modern Finance*, trans. with commentary, Mark Davis and Alison Etheridge (2006). Princeton: Princeton University Press.

Bairoch, Paul (1993) *Economics and World History: Myths and Paradoxes*, New York: Harvester Wheatsheaf.

Baumol, William and Strom, Robert J (2010). "'Useful Knowledge' of Entrepreneurship: Some Implications of the History." In David S. Landes, Joel Mokyr, and William Baumol (eds), *The Invention of Enterprise*. Princeton: Princeton University Press.

Burns, Arthur F. [1946] (1954) "Economic Research and the Keynesian Thinking of Our Times," *The Frontiers of Economic Knowledge*, for NBER. Princeton: Princeton University Press.

Cipolla, Carlo (1988) *Tra due culture*, trans. Christopher Woodall (1991). New York: Norton.

Clapham, John (1922) "Empty Economic Boxes." *Economic Journal*, 32(127): 305–314.

Eichengreen, Barry (1986) "Macroeconomics and History." In Alexander J. Field (ed.), *The Future of Economic History*. Boston: Kluwer-Nijhoff.

Eichengreen, Barry (2012) "Economic History and Economic Policy." *Journal of Economic History*, 72(2): 289–307.

Eichengreen, Barry (2015) *Hall of Mirrors*. New York: Oxford University Press.

Fogel, Robert W. (2001) "Simon S. Kuznets 1901–1985: A Biographical Memoir." Washington, DC: National Academy Press.

Fogel, Robert William et al. (2013) *Political Arithmetic*. Chicago: University of Chicago Press.

Gerschenkron, Alexander (1952) "Economic Backwardness in Historical Perspective." In Mark Granovetter and Richard Swedbergs (eds) (1992), *The Sociology of Economic Life*. Boulder: Westview Press, pp. 111–130.

Gray, Jeremy J. (2000) *The Hilbert Challenge*. Oxford: Oxford University Press.

Heckscher, Eli (1939) "Quantitative Measurement in Economic History." *Quarterly Journal of Economics*, 53(2): 167–193.

Hempel, Carl (1952) *Fundamentals of Concept Formation in Empirical Science*. Chicago: University of Chicago Press.

Hobsbawm, Eric (1997) *On History*. London: Weidenfeld & Nicolson.

Hobsbawm, Eric (2002) *Interesting Times: A Twentieth-Century Life*. New York: Pantheon Books.

Kindleberger, Charles (1989) *Economic Laws and Economic History*. Cambridge: Cambridge University Press.

Kline, Morris (1977) *Calculus: An Intuitive and Physical Approach*, 2nd edn. New York: Wiley.

Kuznets, Simon (1926) *Cyclical Fluctuations: Retail and Wholesale Trade United States, 1919–1925*, prefatory note, Wesley C. Mitchell.New York: Adelphi.

Kuznets, Simon (1941a) "Statistics and Economic History." *Journal of Economic History*, 1: 26–41.

Kuznets, Simon (1941b) *National Income and Its Composition, 1919–1938*, vol. 1. New York: NBER.

Mandelbrot, Benoit and Hudson, Richard L. (2004) *The(Mis)Behavior of Markets: A Fractal View of Risk, Ruin, and Reward*. New York: Basic Books.

Marshall, Alfred (1919) *Industry and Trade*. London: Macmillan.

Marshall, Alfred (1920) *Principles of Economics*, 8th edn. London: Macmillan.

Morgenstern, Oskar (1937) *The Limits of Economics*, trans. Vera Smith. London: W. Hodge.

Nagel, Ernest and Newman, James R. (1958) *Godel's Proof*. New York: New York University Press.

Pigou, Arthur C. (1922) "Empty Economic Boxes: A Reply." *Economic Journal*, 32 (128): 458–465.

Piketty, Thomas (2014) *Capital in the Twenty-First Century*, trans. Arthur Goldhammer. Cambridge, MA: Harvard University Press.

Polanyi, Karl [1944] (2001) *The Great Transformation*, 2nd Beacon paperback edn. Boston: Beacon Press.

Postan, M. M. (1946) "Obituary Notice: Sir John Clapham." *Economic History Review*,16(1): 56–59.

Postan, M. M. [1939] (1971) "The Historical Method in Social Science." *Fact and Relevance: Essays on Historical Method*. Cambridge: Cambridge University Press, pp. 22–34.

Postan, M. M. [1965] (1971) "Agriculture and Economic Development: A Lesson of History." *Fact and Relevance: Essays on Historical Method*. Cambridge: Cambridge University Press, pp. 103–118.

Reichenbach, Hans (1951) "Probability Methods in Science." In Daniel Lerner and Harold D. Lasswell (eds), *The Policy Sciences: Recent Developments in Scope and Method*. Stanford: Stanford University Press, pp. 121–128.

Samuelson, Paul (1947) *Foundations of Economic Analysis*. Cambridge, MA: Harvard University Press.

Samuelson, Paul (1961) *Economics: An Introductory Analysis*, 5th edn. New York: McGraw-Hill.

Schumpeter, Joseph [1951] (1965) *Ten Great Economists: From Marx to Keynes*. New York: Oxford University Press.

Schumpeter, Joseph (1954) *History of Economic Analysis*, ed. Elizabeth Boody Schumpeter.New York: Oxford University Press.

Solow, Robert (1985) "Economic History and Economics." *American Economic Review*, 75(2).

Taleb, Nassim Nicholas (2007) *The Black Swan: The Impact of the Highly Improbable*. New York: Random House.

Thom, René [1991] (1993) *Predire n'est pas expliquer*. Paris: Flammarion.

# 9 The fraught relation between economics and economic history
## Matters of measurement and method

The fraught relation between economics and economic history extends to, and is informed by, perceived differences in method that include differing notions about the scope and form of measurement. While much of the tension between the two fields of inquiry may be attributed to claims built around notions of the particularist character of history, with its emphasis upon the "facts," and the generalizing nature of economics, with its focus upon laws and rule-making, there is a related set of tensions arising out of the amenability to and capacity for quantification. Yet the interpenetration of theory and fact may call into question any reliance upon the neo-Kantian distinction between the idiographical and the nomothetic, and at the same time blur any bright line between what is taken as quantitative and qualitative.

### The conundrum of measurability

To what extent are history and economics distinguished by the criterion of "measurability"? One might begin with the reflections on this matter of Simon Kuznets, who had to grapple with the implications of making use of historical data to reframe what economics could measure and hence what it might be as a discipline.

Kuznets' comments in the inaugural issue of the *Journal of Economic History* suggest that economic history and an economics informed by statistics differ in matters of "measurability," that is, according to Kuznets, "the historian utilizes … information not expressible in measurable units" (Kuznets 1941a: 32). He sought to capture the nuances of "measurability," qualifying it in the following way:

> [E]conomic history seeks primarily to set down a specific record of qualitative changes in the structure and characteristics of economic institutions, and that it deals only rather incidentally with the quantitatively measurable magnitudes of these institutions and of their substantive performance – most frequently using these data as illustrations of qualitative statements relating to marked changes or differences, and almost never subjecting

them to analysis designed to segregate the common and persistent from the different and the variable.

(Kuznets 1941a: 32)

Presumably this last statement reveals several other dimensions to the pairings of distinctions separating history (here, economic history) from economics. Kuznets appears to be making the case that the common threads and generalizations attributed to and sought by economists are the product of "analysis," aligning his view of causation with that of his mentor, Wesley Mitchell, who treated it in a fundamentally heuristic way, a guide in effect to possible interpretations. It would also comport generally with Eric Hobsbawm's notion that history explains, but economics analyzes, effectively melting away the explanatory elements associated with assaying cause and effect (Hobsbawm [1980] 1997).

For Kuznets "the basic purposes of economic inquiry are to distinguish in the flow and interrelation of economic activities among the common, persistent elements and those that are diverse and variable" (Kuznets 1941a: 32), while "economic history is concerned with a concrete account of the changes in the historical unfolding of economic reality" (Kuznets 1941a: 33), not precluding at the same time the "select[ion] for treatment [of] only those events that appear ... important as determinants of the temporal flow of economic reality" (Kuznets 1941a: 33).

Not all economists would concur with Kuznets' trumpeting of the virtues of quantitative measures. Writing several years before, Oskar Morgenstern asserted that "the facts of economic life cannot be comprehensively described in terms of statistics" (Morgenstern 1937: 13). He attributed this to the inchoate nature of change in economic life: "There are always forces at work which are masked, mainly by the time factor, and which, immediately they begin to operate, are already shaping the present and the future without yet having given any tangible manifestation" (Morgenstern 1937: 13).

Writing in 1969, as he constructed his own "theory of economic history," John Hicks offered up a modulated position on the relative importance of quantitative measurement in economics and economic history, introducing what amounts to an evolutionary – and hence historical – argument into the differences found in the degree of quantification:

> In spite of the vogue of "Quantitative Economic History," economics historians are under less temptation than economists to see their subject as purely quantitative.
>
> (Hicks 1969: 1)

He adduces two reasons for this:

> This is not only for the reason that as we go back in time the figures become so patchy; there is a deeper reason, too. We are bound to find, as

we go back into the past, that the economic aspects of life are less differentiated from other aspects than they are today. Economic history is often presented, and rightly presented, as a process of specialization; but the specialization is not only a specialization among economic activities, it is also a specialization of economic activities (what are becoming economic activities) from activities of other sorts.

(Hicks 1969: 1)

Why is this reliance upon the measurable as the quantifiable not simply an expression of the circular or impredicative construction of the language and concepts of economics, borrowing from Henri Poincaré's conventionalist critique of science? Kuznets himself provides a good example of this problem in construction when he presented his definitions of "economic good" and "market." According to Kuznets, "[e]conomic goods" are those which are "a source of satisfaction, relatively scarce, and disposable" (Kuznets 1941b: 6–7), but also marketable, that is, "bought or sold," as this last condition simplifies, even makes possible, their measurement. This appears all well and good, except that markets are understood to be arenas or sites, physically or metaphorically, where economic goods (and by extension services) are exchanged. Hence, markets become forums or mechanisms whereby marketable goods are bought or sold.

Any analysis limited to "information … expressible in measurable units" (Kuznets 1941a: 32) must remain in the thrall of the measures devised for its operation. In this way the ideology of measurement enters the picture, on two counts. First, there are the differing choices made as to the pertinence and importance of various and diverse measures, contrasting, for example, a Keynesian focus upon the level of employment or rate of unemployment with a monetarist one centered upon the size of the money supply. Second, there is the underlying notion that reduction to the quantitative itself is a crucial prerequisite for economics to proceed, conflicting thereby with another of Henri Poincaré's notion, laid out in *Science and Hypothesis,* of the validity of "non-measurable magnitudes," which challenged the bifurcation of "qualitative" and "quantitative" (Poincaré 1905: 25–8).

Nonetheless, Kuznets sought to build a bridge between the two fields, through changes in the way that practitioners in both would approach "secular trends" and "business cycles." "In the field of secular movements, broad questions (for example, how to determine a homogeneous period of development) have not been explored in the light of the experience of historians who have attempted to set limits to relatively homogeneous historical eras in the development of society" (Kuznets 1941a: 37).

Kuznets lays down one other caveat about the uses of history by economists:

Recourse to economic history in most such controversies all too often means merely that the economist will plunge for a brief moment into the vast sea of potential information and emerge with a few historical facts in support of the hypothesis he favors, without regard to the possibility that other facts, of equal or greater weight, might bolster a different thesis.

(Kuznets 1941a: 38)

Moreover, Kuznets' careful assessment of how one might cobble together the foundational statistical measures in economics contains cautions that harken to the language and contrary notions of the critics of the unreflected use of such measures. Kuznets noted that:

> When carefully examined, estimates of national product are seen to be compounds of statistical data of varying accuracy based upon assumptions concerning the purpose, value, and scope of economic activity. These assumptions must be kept clearly in mind since they affect the estimates and their meaning much more than do inaccuracies in the statistical data.
>
> (Kuznets 1945: vii)

Kuznets then pointed to "the conflict between the aim of the investigator and the recalcitrant nature of reality" (Kuznets 1945: vii), such that:

> No matter what assumptions are adopted, so long as they are stable in space and time violence is done to the complexity and heterogeneity of the aspects of social activity that are essentially economic.
>
> (Kuznets 1945: viii)

Under changing economic conditions, especially those exacerbated during wartime, Kuznets found great difficulty in establishing "unequivocal" results, noting:

> To the degree that the [conceptual] problems are not resolved and the statistical analysis yields several variants rather than a single estimate, this report is merely a halfway house from which we cannot as yet remove the scaffolding of alternative assumptions and estimates.
>
> (Kuznets 1945: ix).

Does the "easy" reliance upon such measures over time represent a "suspension of disbelief" initially imposed to allow for the tentative use of new measures or concepts that, in time, comes to be the accepted practice, with all reservations either buried or forgotten?

A half-century later, Angus Maddison drew a distinction between the role of history and economics "[i]n assessing the nature of capitalist performance" that echoes many of the considerations raised by Kuznets, only now couched in terms of forms of causality. History offered up "ultimate" causes, while economics revealed or displayed "proximate" ones. One might contend that Maddison's set of distinctions is fundamentally reductionist, setting a weaker and more qualitative form of causality in history against a firmer and more quantitative such form in economics, extending to a broader range of explanatory power.

As for history:

> The investigation of ultimate causality involves consideration of institutions, ideologies, pressures of socio-economic interest groups, historical accidents, and economic policy at the national level. It also involves consideration of the international economic "order," exogenous ideologies, and pressure or shocks from friendly or unfriendly neighbours. These "ultimate" features are all part of the traditional domain of historians. They are virtually impossible to quantify and thus there will always be legitimate scope for disagreement on what is important.
>
> (Maddison 1991: 10–11)

Economics, in Maddison's view, provided a greater measure of objectivity:

> "Proximate" areas of causality are those where measures and models have been developed by economists and statisticians. Here the relative importance of different influences can be more readily assured. At this level, one can derive significant insight from comparative macroeconomic growth accounts which try to "explain" growth of output, output per head, or productivity by measuring inputs of labour and capital, availability of natural resources, influences affecting the efficiency with which resources are combined, and benefits derived from transactions with foreign countries. The most difficult problem at this "proximate" level of explanation which interacts in a myriad ways [*sic*] with other items included in the growth accounts.
>
> (Maddison 1991: 11)

One can see the conundrum posed by measurability in a contemporary example drawn from urban economics, where the evident lack of real advancement in conceptualization is supposedly offset by the insights afforded by changes in the capacity to quantify, that is, to measure economic phenomena.

One is struck by the extent to which Stuart Rosenthal and William Strange's survey of the economic thought underlying the "economics of agglomeration" in the 2004 volume of the *Handbook of Urban and Regional Economics* has its conceptual roots in Alfred Marshall's *Principles of Economics*, whose last edition was published nearly a century ago (Marshall 1920). The host of externalities identified by Marshall, including matters of labor pooling and spillover effects, provides the foundation for the exploration and analysis of the characteristics of urban economic life and dynamics that follows.

What has changed over the course of nearly a century, according to the authors, are the quantitative tools available to either display or prove the results of such theorizing. They include what they deem the older or more traditional approach in urban economics, namely the use of case studies. These rely upon a narrative and the selective incorporation and presentation of historical data or events; hence the criteria for selection become crucial. By contrast, though, Rosenthal and Strange emphasize a more quantitative approach, which typically entails the construction of models of some sort. Here what is noteworthy is the fact that such construction requires more than greater access to sources of data, whether economic or historical, or the introduction of more advanced mathematical techniques; rather, some version of an "auxiliary hypothesis" must be introduced, whether through the assumption of profit-maximizing behavior or the identification of a rent differential to explain the relative attractiveness of various sites or locations, almost invariably cast within an economic world of supremely efficient and competitive markets. That is, quantification is not simply a matter of the capacity to measure and the collection of pertinent data, but has conceptual ramifications as well.

As "auxiliary hypotheses" these might be seen as informing a methodological critique along the lines laid out by Otto Neurath (see Neurath 1913). Or, one might take up Carl Hempel's notion of the need to introduce "appropriate nondefinitional sentence[s]," "called justificatory sentence[s]" to prevent contradictions from arising in scientific theories (Hempel 1965: 18–20). As an alternative, one might conceive of these mathematically enabling assumptions as "supplementary hypothetical equations" to a given "structural system," along the lines suggested by Ragnar Frisch in his defining piece on "the notion of equilibrium and disequilibrium" in 1936 (Frisch 1936: 103–4). All of these approaches contemplate the necessity of supplemental elements, whether as assumption, statement (or proposition), or equation, to construct a system.

This in itself represents a serious qualification to efforts to separate neatly economics from economic history, as it calls into question the notion of the possibility of pure quantification, undertaken without conceptualizing about the nature and type of measure and a structure within which such measures might be interpreted. And a reading of Kuznets' effort to bridge the two fields (economics and economic history) is consistent with that understanding.

### Historical comparison and the nature of measurability

"Historical proof" surfaces in a whole other way in matters of "historical comparison", in that much of what emerges in and through historical proof is comparative, with the not unreasonable supposition that only such comparisons accord meaning and significance to the history. How are such comparisons made in economics? Are tables of data over time, or for more distant periods, constructed as one might reconstruct any economic or social history, with conjectures of various sorts, elaborating upon that which is available from sources? These pose difficulties that are laid out more fully by Carlo M. Cipolla in his *Tra Due Culture*. As the title of Cipolla's work suggests, he envisioned economic history perched as if over a chasm dividing economics and history, adopting and adapting decades later the notion of a vast gap between the sciences and the humanities popularized by C. P. Snow in *The Two Cultures and the Scientific Revolution*, first published in 1959 (Cipolla [1988] 1991).

Cipolla focused upon the problems presented by suggestive yet incomplete sources, like medieval cartularies, for economic historians, giving particular attention to pre-industrial Europe. Among those one might also consider in that regard are the tables produced by economic historians like B. H. Slicher von Bath to establish changes in crop yields and agricultural productivity in western Europe over the course of centuries (Slicher von Bath 1963) or the "family reconstitution" conducted by E. A. Wrigley (Wrigley 1997). While older source materials like the observations of Arthur Young in the eighteenth century have been utilized by many economic historians, other forms of historical evidence have included documents like probate inventories and early censuses. More generally, the "Cambridge studies in population, economy, and society in past time" exemplify the exhaustive work entailed in this regard over the last several decades. To translate and transform these into historical narratives typically requires what are often imaginative reconstructions.

Under these circumstances, it will be important to establish the scope of "historical comparison" in economics. Cross-country comparisons figure significantly in both practical discussions of policy and theoretical constructions of economic growth and development across a range of times and places, but most commonly where the age of industrialization had taken hold. The data construction and synthesis produced by Kuznets and later Maddison, consisting of wide-ranging multi-century construction of rates of economic growth, often concentrating upon, but not limited to, states during the time of industrialization, have been viewed as underlying any meaningful theory of economic growth and development. (See, for example, Maddison 2001.)

For both Kuznets and Maddison there is a tension between the statistical evidence adduced, using standardized measures, and interpretive synthesis undertaken to render possible explanations embodied in working hypotheses. Nonetheless, Maddison put forward the case for making quantitative comparisons built around "comparative macroeconomic growth accounts" (Maddison 1991: 11).

For his part, Robert Solow, in conjunction with his MIT colleague, the economic historian Peter Temin, advanced a similar standard, with a theoretical "twist": that the abstraction required to "account for" the role of factor inputs in economic growth and, consequently, the reliance upon measures of economic growth to gauge best the changes wrought by the Industrial Revolution, paved the way for making cross-country "historical comparisons" (Solow and Temin 1985). Paradoxically, then, such comparisons depended upon those aspects of economics seen, positively or critically, as characteristic of its ahistorical nature.

In setting upon economic growth as the critical measure for comparing national economies, Solow and Temin also ruled out the use of measurements of welfare as too broad or industrial structure as too narrow for making meaningful historical comparisons. The former holds because of the implications of the lack of "means to disprove such a theory," while the latter possibility fails on account of "[t]he diversity of historical experience" (Solow and Temin 1985: 76). In part their quest goes to the problem of measurability: the mainstream view among economists that only that which can be conveniently quantified is suitably measurable in economics, and thus worthy of a more complete examination and analysis.

Other approaches have introduced additional nuances into the matter of "historical comparison." In *The General Theory* (1936) John Maynard Keynes, writing before the full advent of national income accounting, espoused a rather cautious view on what economics can realistically measure (see the section "The Choice of Units"). He emphasized the importance just two such units: money and labor. The circumscribed scope of macroeconomic measures affected Keynes' perspective of what historical comparisons might consist:

> reserving ... the use of vague concepts, such as the quantity of output as a whole, the quantity of capital equipment as a whole and the general level of prices, to the occasions when we are attempting some historical comparison which is within certain (perhaps fairly wide) limits avowedly unprecise and approximate.
>
> (Keynes 1936: 47)

Here Keynes appears to identify the problem at hand as a fuzziness in the capacity to measure but also a similar lack of precision or clarity in the economic concepts themselves.

In an address from 1967 entitled, "Discipline and I," Alexander Gerschenkron asserted that historical cross-country comparisons necessarily entailed counterfactual elements. This appeared to open the door to the more general use of counterfactuals in economic history, at just the time when cliometricians had stepped forward to make claims for the possibility of a new mode of quantification in historical study; for some this constituted a "new revolution in economic history."

And even more recently Joel Mokyr, in surveying ways of measuring the impact of technological change in advancing the Industrial Revolution, touted the virtues of "counterfactual analysis." In line with the New Economic History:

> Counterfactual analysis has to be resorted to, at least implicitly, to assess the indispensability of the various elements.
>
> (Mokyr 1993: 28)

For his part, Gerschenkron saw the matter somewhat along the lines of Keynes, in that there was the difficulty presented by the appropriate scope of measurement. And, in fact, the barriers to establishing cross-country comparisons were sufficiently high for Wesley Mitchell, an indefatigable amasser of economic facts, to doubt its possibility, warning Kuznets against embarking upon such a task (Fogel et al. 2013: 112).

Gerschenkron, though, framed the matter in terms of "opportunity costs." If, pursuing the example Gerschenkron raised in the address, one claims that the British and German economies were of equal size in 1910, or even that the German economy now exceeded that of Great Britain, how in fact was that calculation to be made? As no standard, abstracted measures existed apart from the economic experience of both countries concerned, was it not the case that one economy needed to be measured in terms of the other, hence requiring some form of imputation? A version of "opportunity cost" would serve that task. But Gerschenkron did not spell out how one might actually proceed in using this sort of opportunity cost. Left unanswered as well was whether this would make reliance upon macroeconomic "opportunity cost" measures a form of counterfactual construction?

Thus, if the purpose of an economic inquiry is to draw meaningfully upon cross-country comparisons over time, the awkward question of measurement looms large. Keynes' and Gerschenkron's concerns about the limitations to such measurements appear on the mark. One might envision an analogy with the measures used to value the exchange of goods or services across international borders. Is it acceptable to rely upon existing currency exchange rates, whether established as fixed or flexible? Or, is it necessary to create a more complex measure, like purchasing power parity, to make for a more effective accounting? Realistically, the task appears to be more complicated and roundabout. There is a reflexive element here that must be taken into account. A is measured in terms of B, but B itself is not fixed, and is in need of outside measures to gauge its value. Crucially, it may only be effected if this work is more engaged with matters of history, if only to make intelligible in context the situations to be compared.

## Counterfactuals, econometrics, and the Weberian perspective

Does the introduction of econometric models change, in any way, how economic models ought to be comprehended, especially from a methodological perspective? Couched in other terms, might one posit that the mechanism put forward by A. C. Pigou of "knowledge by implication," and consistent with Hobsbawm's notion that economics engages in analysis rather than explanation, still holds for econometric models, only with this difference: the "if, then" relation of causality is gauged in terms of probabilities rather than definite outcomes?

Yet there are further complications here. Econometric models do not necessarily establish or display "causal" relations; rather, they present correlations. To the extent that cause and effect is attributed to any such correlation an interpretation, which is external to the workings of the model, must be summoned and applied, that is, through a heuristic intervention. It is, of course, conceivable that in the reflexive nature of all constructions, choices were made in the structuring of the model that were based upon the interpretation most likely sought.

All of the above was predicated on the assemblage of econometric models using empirical data, without reference to whether such data should be understood as either more statistical or historical. What would it then mean to employ econometric models to construct an historical case, assaying cause and effect, as the "New Economic History" attempted to do? These cliometricians adopted a method to weigh and evaluate historical causation through a form of counterfactual analysis. In effect, the econometric model constructed would demonstrate the significance of a given set of circumstances or state of affairs by gauging the deviation from what actually occurred had said circumstances or state of affairs been eliminated. Mokyr rightly referred to this as a measure of "indispensability."

When such methods ended up demonstrating that canal-building in the nineteenth century was at least as economically advantageous to the growth of the US economy as railroad networks, gainsaying the notion that the railroads held the key to the expansion of the US economy in that period, the thesis of Robert Fogel's *Railroads and American Economic Growth* (1964), or that slavery in the American South in the mid-nineteenth century was a profitable, productive, and hence sustainable enterprise for the future functioning of the Southern economy, the thesis of Fogel and Stanley Engerman's *Time on the Cross* (1974), one was left with more than a bit of wonderment at the extent of the challenge posed to prevailing interpretations of US economic history. Was the economic significance of two of the most central developments in nineteenth-century US economic history the product of a vast misreading of the past? Might this mean instead that these developments were shaped more by non-economic factors than economic ones, along the lines of the "causal heteronomy" advocated by Max Weber? Or, were these simply correlations that took the form that they did as a result of the interpretive elements that gave rise to the particular way in which the model was constructed, thereby calling into question the matter of causality altogether?

There is another perspective that might be brought to bear in this discussion. Weber himself had a criterion for gauging the indispensability of historical events. In part it appears to be an impressionistic, even intuitive take on what the elimination of a particular set of circumstances might have had on the historical outcome. To the extent that it might be rendered more objective, Weber drew upon a probabilistic standard that comported with the weighing of evidence in a courtroom proceeding. That is, rather than construct a mathematical structure, Weber chose a juridical one. Weber's approach has two advantages over that taken by the cliometricians. First of all, it is more open to the introduction of non-economic as well as economic factors amenable to quantification. Second, it appears to offer a quick check on a result that seems drastically at variance with a general understanding of the course of events, and so would allow for a conscious rethinking and reworking of the likely result as the process unfolds.

## A bridge or a breach?

Geoffrey Hodgson has noted the breach between economics and history as a new mainstream in economics took hold at the turn of the twentieth century, describing the attenuation of the efforts by heterodox schools, but especially the German Historical School and the Institutionalists, to integrate a historical perspective into economics, while in the main neither historical perspective nor understanding can now be found amidst that mainstream (Hodgson 2001).

When economists who do not belong to these heterodox schools have consciously sought to build a bridge between economics and history, how far does the bridge extend? More specifically, is it completed, or does it come to an abrupt end midstream, like the "pont d'Avignon"? Two such economists offer up useful evidence about the possibilities and limitations of such "bridge" construction

In *Economic Laws and Economic History* (1989) Charles Kindleberger makes the case for using history to validate economic laws, applying a broad brush that sets in relief general tendencies and trends, but with less attention and concern for detailed depiction: "I am interested in using history to test the validity and generality of economic laws and models" (Kindleberger 1989: ix). Thus, Kindleberger identified patterns in history whose general form can be abstracted into what he sees as "economic laws." The four laws he took up have a lengthy history of their own and include: Engel's law, Iron law of wages, Gresham's law, and the law of one price.

For Kindleberger economics is built upon historical experience, but takes shape as a field of inquiry only as classes of those experiences are categorized, though with a flexibility that transforms "laws" into "tools" for explanation. In his own overview of his craft he stated:

> The economic historian or the economist seeking to test his analysis against historical data should be prepared to put down one economic law or model, and pick up another, when the condition to be explained calls for it, and not to insist on using always the same tool.
>
> (Kindleberger 1989: x)

In Kindleberger's schema there is clearly a belief in a strong role for history in "proving" economics and a loose separation of history and economics into the largely neo-Kantian categories of the ideographical and the nomothetic, but with a recognition that history provides a picture of patterns. How much does the existence of historical patterns belie the notion that history is a particularist field of inquiry? Somewhat, since patterns can be found only if a larger and more general framework, which might take the form of a historical thesis, hypothesis, or narrative is established, usually beforehand. In the process this makes economic laws less universal statements and more ad hoc constructions, for which there could be a test of competing narratives, perhaps more correctly understood as models:

At a certain rhetorical level, however, laws and models are synonymous. Say's "law" that supply creates its own demand is in reality only a model that can be either confronted with other models, such as Keynes' model that demand creates its own supply, or refuted with historical counterexamples.

(Kindleberger 1989: x–xi)

The tension between the nomothetic and the idiographical does not altogether vanish. Kindleberger himself faced these contradictory pulls when he described the Industrial Revolution depicted by historians as both "unique" and "an event." How can a century-long development be seen as an event? Perhaps one might make an analogy with political or military history, so that "World War II," "Thirty Years War," and "Hundred Years War" all become unique events containing many sub-events. Even so, how does one deal with the effort by historians to weigh the possibility of other "industrial revolutions," as Lynn White did for the European Middle Ages (White 1962)? It is clear that historians deal in generalities, even if at its most primitive one takes history to be chronology, with little if any shaping except for the date line or timeline to provide the requisite structure.

At the same time, Kindleberger showed an appreciation of Fernand Braudel's work that was nonetheless tempered somewhat by his greater willingness to entertain models. Writing in *World Economic Primacy: 1500 to 1990*, Kindleberger stated:

The distinguished historian, Fernand Braudel, asserts that there surely is no such thing as a model of decadence. He objects especially to economists with simple theories of the collapse of vital functions such as public finance, investment, industry and shipping. "A new model has to be built from the structure of every case" (Braudel 1966 [1975: 1240]). I am not so certain, and readers are invited to judge for themselves. I do agree about the simplicity. The model cannot be exclusively economic.

(Kindleberger 1996: 4)

One might contrast John Hicks' view of the Industrial Revolution with that of Kindleberger. In tackling the relation between economics and economic history is his *A Theory of Economic History*, Hicks found the designation of the Industrial Revolution as an "event" as too limited. "Though there is a sense in which the Industrial Revolution is an event," Hicks noted, "it is itself a statistical phenomenon; it is a general tendency to which theory is unmistakably relevant" (Hicks 1969: 5). Hicks then saw the possibility of theorizing about the history of the Industrial Revolution because it is a "general phenomenon" (Hicks 1969: 5), although his willingness to comprehend it in statistical terms appears to place it within the orbit of economics. As Hicks noted, "Economics is rather specially concerned with such 'statistical' behavior" (Hicks 1969: 4).

The approach taken by Hicks, the economist, bears a certain resemblance to that of Carlo Cipolla, the economic historian, in that they both situate economic history at an intersection or crossroads between the two fields of inquiry. Nonetheless, as there is a sense in Hicks' case that generality resides in statistics, in Hicks' schema history appears to remain the more particularist, economics the more general. Hence, his identification of the generalizing mode in economics in the uniformity of patterns embodied in statistics bears potentially some kinship with Kuznets' approach to finding and exploring "invariant relations" built upon or out of statistical data. Yet in constructing a "theory of history" Hicks is explicitly "concerned with ... general phenomena" (Hicks 1969: 5).

What distinguishes Hicks' version of a generalist inquiry from that of many economists – and also Cipolla – is that while he identified the generalizing mode in economics in the uniformity of patterns embodied in statistics, he sees that as a means of "classify[ing] ... economic states of society," producing a "sequence" that he recognized has some similarities with those advanced by Marx or the German Historical School (Hicks 1969: 6). Hicks, though, is careful to characterize his own "presuppositions" as "less deterministic, less evolutionary than theirs" (Hicks 1969: 6).

As to the distinction between a reliance upon statistics or model building: Only if model building is based solely on statistical techniques and outcomes would the two approaches converge, and this is not the norm. Economic theorizing may make use of econometric models, but even when they are employed as central elements or configurations of propositions, they tend to be derivative, drawn from other, more primitive assumptions whose arrangement or configuration does indeed describe and contain the economic theory actually being put forward.

If history's ability to be general is derived from its capacity, under some circumstances, to be statistical, then, according to Hicks, the alternative is a history with "an interest in particular stories" (Hicks 1969: 4). By contrast, Kindleberger, the more literary or discursive economist, found the generalizing mode of economics through story or narrative, presenting in essence the "tales" of four laws.

As to Kindleberger, one may ask whether, as a historical economist, he bridged the gap between history and economics any more than Carlo Cipolla did as an economic historian? Does Kindleberger find himself between "two cultures," or is his situation, as he sees it, altogether different? For one, the case he presented was less a treatise on methodology than Cipolla's was. Nonetheless, it is unquestionably the case that for Kindleberger the second field, history, serves as handmaiden for the first, economics, while for Cipolla the relation is problematic and fraught with conflict rather than ancillary. This may be so because Kindleberger is exploring matters of proof and allows for the "third" criterion of historical proof, beyond logical and empirical testing, while Cipolla focused on the different ways that historians and economists go about their tasks, that is, how they proceed in their profession (rather than how much need they have of each other). Yet Kindleberger's approach is, in its own way, a study in method, if by example, as much as Cipolla's. As a consequence, there may be no fundamental inconsistency between the two, but they cannot be viewed as bridge-builders approaching from opposite ends.

And yet, for all the tensions noted above, one might also make a plausible case for a substantial overlap between the practitioners of economics and economic history, to the extent that it may be difficult to distinguish one from the other. Consider the case of and claims for two classic academic achievements: Alfred Marshall's *Industry and Trade* and H. J. Habbakuk's *American and British Technology in the Nineteenth Century*. While written decades apart, in ostensibly quite different eras of academic inquiry in both economics and economic history, Marshall in 1919, Habbakuk in 1962, both works discuss in great detail the nature and evolution of manufacturing in industrialized states over the course of the nineteenth century, and contain a mix of history and economics, in essence narratives replete with economic categories and interpretation, with Habbakuk's addressing more directly than Marshall's an economic thesis, albeit with a quest for establishing pertinent causes for the changes that occurred. Habbakuk examined the thesis that the relative scarcity and high cost of labor in the United States made for a greater willingness and interest in introducing labor-saving technology in manufacturing.

Nonetheless, both writers were at pains to disclaim any special knowledge, understanding, or insight outside their own discipline. Marshall was the economist, Habbakuk the economic historian. But if these works had been subject to a blind test, could any such distinction have been made?

In fact, Marshall's *Industry and Trade* figures prominently in John Clapham's criticism of the "empty boxes" of economics, specifically on the grounds that it demonstrates what ought to be conveyed, in essence economic history, without any reference to abstracted economic terminology or categories:

> He takes down, in memory and when he gets home from his shelves, *Industry and Trade: A Study of Industrial Technique and Business Organization*, with its nearly nine hundred pages packed full of things of life. Two references to Constant Returns – one in a footnote – and a handful of references to Diminishing and Increasing Returns in Allgemeinen, not so far as he can find in close relation to the facts of those British, French, German and American Industries of which the great book has taught him so much: these seem to be all.
>
> (Clapham 1922: 305)

Clapham did not make mention of the fact that he had assisted his old teacher and mentor in preparing this work.

## Braudel's critique in detail

Then there is the view from the perspective of the historians. As it turns out, Fernand Braudel's alignment with Karl Polanyi, noted above, went only so far. While both may have seen the market as a historical phenomenon, Braudel was quick to point out the wide gap between historians and economists, among whom he counted Polanyi, for he felt that the latter failed "to tackle the concrete and diverse reality of history and use that as a starting-point" (Braudel [1981] 1992: 227).

Braudel's critique begins with a challenge to economists of varying stripes and ideological perspectives:

> The self-regulating market – all-conquering and rationalizing the entire economy – is in this view essentially what is meant by the history of growth. Carl Brinkmann once wrote that economic history was the study of the origins, the development and the latter-day decomposition of the market economy. Such a simplification accords with the teachings of generations of economists. But it cannot satisfy the historian, who does not view the market as a simply endogenous phenomena. Nor is it merely the sum of various economic activities, not even a precise stage in their development.
>
> (Braudel [1981] 1992: 225)

A historical approach would entail something rather different:

> Since exchange is as old as human history, a historical study of the market should extend to cover all the known ages through which man has lived, and should seek assistance from the other social sciences: it should consider the possible explanations they offer, without which it would be impossible to grasp long-term developments and structures, and the combinations that created new life.
>
> (Braudel [1981] 1992: 225)

Since Brinkmann served as one of the leading representatives of the German Historical School in the 1930s, Braudel's criticism must be taken as a broadside against the German Historical School as well (Korner 1997: 159–65).

As for Polanyi and his followers:

> They have gone through [this mass of different evidence] as best they could, seeking to suggest an explanation, almost a theory: the economy is only a "sub-division" of social life, one which is enveloped in the networks and constraints of social reality and has only disentangled itself recently (sometimes not even then) from these multiple threads.
>
> (Braudel [1981] 1992: 225)

Braudel then goes on to state:

> The trouble with this theory is that it is entirely based on a distinction based (if it can be said to be based at all) on a number of heterogeneous

samples ... The question of the market in the "mercantilist" period is dismissed in twenty lines. Sociologists and economists in the past and anthropologists today have unfortunately accustomed us to their almost total indifference to history. It does of course simplify their task.

(Braudel [1981] 1992: 227)

The recurring theme here can be found in the limitations to economic explanation and the lack of any systematic basis for establishing a form of historical proof in economics. But Braudel also took aim at the notion that history, by dint of its concern with the "concrete" and the "diverse" was somehow particularist, in contrast to the general sweep of economic theorizing. In the "Foreword" to *The Wheels of Commerce* Braudel laid out the case for a general form of economic history, while remaining cognizant of its limitations. It runs as follows:

> In this second volume, I have tried to analyse the machinery of exchange *as a whole*, from primitive barter up to and including the most sophisticated capitalism. Starting from as careful and neutral a description as possible, I have tried to grasp regularities and mechanisms, to write a sort of *general economic history* (as we have "general principles of geography"; or, to use a different set of terms, to construct a *typology*, a *model*, or perhaps a *grammar* which will help us at least pin down the meaning of certain key words, or of certain evident realities, without however assuming that the general history can be totally rigorous, the typology definitive or at all complete, the model in any sense mathematically verifiable, or that the grammar can give us the key to an economic language or form of discourse – even supposing that one exists or is sufficiently consistent through time and space.
>
> (Braudel [1981] 1992: 21)

Braudel made clear that the task he sought to embrace was that of "grasp[ing] regularities and mechanisms" in an effort to produce a "general economic history," akin to the "general principles of geography." In effect, Braudel described his work in terms that economists had routinely used to establish the nomothetic characteristic separating economics from history. In acknowledging that such a history cannot be "totally rigorous," Braudel may be seen as situating economic history in that "middle ground" or "no-man's-land" to which Cipolla assigned economic history, that is, falling "between two cultures." Yet one cannot escape sensing that Braudel intended to effect something more: a construction of generalities as "typology," "model," or "grammar" from a wealth of detail, where the importance of historical specificity was fully recognized, and with an awareness of all that may be set in motion over the course of real or historical time. This cannot be viewed other than as a rebuke to the social sciences, but especially economics, for the limits to their capacity to explain.

Remarkably, Max Weber had produced a general economic history six decades earlier. His last lectures – he died in 1920 – were compiled into a volume entitled *Wirtschaftsgeschichte*, then translated into English by Frank Knight in 1927 as *General Economic History*. This work in crucial ways parallels Braudel's *Capitalism and Material Life, 1400–1800*.

There is a certain irony in this, as Braudel has been cited as blistering in his criticism of Weber's notion of an underlying "spirit of capitalism" to be found in Puritanism, seeing it as the kind of false and unsupported generalization in which economists and sociologists typically indulged, and which set them apart from historians (Swedberg 1998: 206). But, as Randall Collins pointed out, "[t]here is only one place in Weber's works where he brings together the full theory of capitalism as a historical dynamic. There is in the *General Economic History*" (Collins [1980] 1982: 86).

Yet one can see an intriguing bridge between Braudel and Weber, in that Braudel's effort to "grasp regularities and mechanisms" and Weber's effort to describe the "concrete reality" of what has taken place, leading both to a "general economic history," seem to land them in the middle ground between economics and history.

## "More history than economics"

Thomas Piketty has described himself as a successor to Kuznets, albeit a critical one, in virtue of his own exhaustive study of economic statistics drawn from historical records. In an interview published in the *Boston Globe* (April 24, 2014), Piketty, author of *Capital in the 21st Century*, characterized the statistics he had established from various governmental records as "historical facts," and hence not subject to dispute, whatever policy prescriptions may be drawn from them. One might well contend that, at least from the perspective of historiography, Piketty has taken a rather nineteenth-century positivist view, in which the facts are clearly "the facts." To be fair, Piketty's contention does comport with the methodology of economic historians like Carlo Cipolla, in that he engaged in a rigorous "mining" of available documents to uncover them, and this does further align Piketty with historians in the task that he sets for himself.

One might well ask, then, if Piketty has revived, for the moment at least, the tradition of historical economics as it might have been practiced by the German Historian School or the American Institutionalists. There are clearly differences or distinctions that are noteworthy. For one, Piketty's research and overall vision are not tied, in large measure, to broad cultural currents, but rather, to political debate and economic policy prescriptions. Moreover, Piketty's data gathering is less of a moment – one that may nonetheless be sustained over a period of time – and more an intensive inquiry into quantifiable measures over the course of two centuries, and one that was meant to buttress an overarching theme concerning the interplay between secular trends in the return on capital (or financial assets) and the rate of growth of industrializing – or industrialized – economies. It is to this latter point that one might consider Max Weber's critique of the methodology of the German Historical School, namely whether the amassing of fact, however voluminous, can possibly lead to broader, theoretical generalizations. Piketty seems to be saying that not only are such generalizations possible, but also that the "facts" lead inextricably to such a broader result. At the same time, the deepening concern with historical construction or imaginative reconstruction among historians, including the broad development of the subfield of the philosophy of history in recent decades, may not have figured significantly in Piketty's assessment of the relation between fact and theory.

Speaking at a Harvard Book Store Forum on April 18, 2014, Piketty described *Capital in the 21st Century*, concerned largely, but certainly not entirely, with "past trends" and "history," and "filled with historical data," as "more history than economics."

Piketty's thesis has been seen as a rejoinder to the thesis about the general development of economies posed by perhaps the most consummate gatherer of "historical data" among economists in the twentieth century, Simon Kuznets. In broad perspective, Piketty's work, which builds upon his earlier, exhaustive work examining the shifts in the distribution of income and wealth in France since the French Revolution, has also been cast somewhat paradoxically, in light of the above, as a return to the concerns of the classical tradition in economics, recalling themes and frames of reference common to both Smith and Marx.

These shadings of Piketty's work are worthy of further exploration, as they shed light on the central matter of the place of history in economics and offer insight into the striking, if not unique understanding of that relation among French economists. As an additional matter of more than passing nuance, there is the question besetting the history of economic thought as to whether a more fluid treatment of the relation between history and economics is one of the defining characteristics of political economy from Smith to Marx, a necessary adjunct of the "big picture/big question" outlook of the classical school along with greater attention to historical detail, even if ostensibly subordinated to grander laws.

It is the case that Piketty's effort to probe the impact of the interplay of differing rates of return on financial assets, that is, the return on capital, and that of economic growth, does take up both the Smithian concern about in what inheres the "wealth of nations" and its bearing upon the states of different national economies, as well as the Marxian concern about the centrality of capital in modern economic life and its implications for the future course of economic development, including notably a tendency toward growing inequality. But what stands out at least as decisively is Piketty's attempt to address "big questions" by advancing "big ideas." As Robert Heilbroner deftly noted in his widely read classic, *The Worldly Philosophers* (Heilbroner 1953), this was the hallmark of the first century of economic thought after the Physiocrats: the classical era in economics. Here one might note a continuing interest in "big ideas" in a not insignificant vein of more contemporary French economic thought. One suspects that this may be due in part to the generally broader public space accorded intellectual discourse in France, with the attendant popular render-ings of what would otherwise be regarded as abstruse subjects, a longstanding tradition that encompasses such figures as Voltaire, Laplace, and Poincaré.

But it is to Piketty's emphasis upon and use of historical data that the relation between history and economics may be best elucidated. Piketty's thesis is built upon an empirical foundation. In fact, it is thoroughly dependent upon historical records whose availability owes much, as Piketty acknowledges, to the centralizing and revolutionary aims associated with the French Revolution, transforming property rights – and holdings – and initiating new forms of taxation. Hence, on the surface it would appear that Piketty has much in common with Kuznets, who, Robert Fogel has suggested, made it possible for economics to become as "empirical science." At the same time, Piketty's work has a real resonance with what Cipolla described as the historian's task, "the mining of facts." The not altogether serendipitous existence and availability of French statistics, data compiled by the state or its agents, over a span of two centuries opened the door to Piketty's subsequent analysis and thesis construction. Yet while one may be guided by the data, its shaping involves the imposition of at least tentative theoretical constructs. This may appear to raise the tension between deduction and induction underlying the *Methodenstreit* – and rightly so – but it does not in any fundamental way distinguish the work of the economist from that of the historian. Exhaustive study of baptismal or probate records by historians entails a similar mix of theoretical construction and the tweaking of available data. All of this seems to comport with Piketty's own characterization of his work as "more history than economics." Is that in fact the case?

One place to begin is with a comparison of the assumptions made about the scope of economics by Kuznets and Piketty. Did Kuznets cobble together his quantitative measures from "historical data" or "economic facts"? His 1941 article in the *Journal of Economic History* leaves the matter ambiguous, though his notion that economics must rely upon the quantitative and the general in ways that history does not may be crucial, suggesting a divide that may be unbridgeable, notwithstanding Kuznets' own deep concerns about the historical development of economies.

If "historical facts," mined in the way that Cipolla suggested, can be used directly as, or be suitably transformed into, quantified data, do they become the "economic statistics" that underlie Kuznets' "empirical science" of economics? But, otherwise not; that is, they remain in the province of history. Here one must take into account Fernand Braudel's notion of the need for the historian to examine and "tackle the concrete and diverse reality of history" (Braudel [1981] 1992: 227) or Weber's allusion to the goal of presenting a "concrete reality" in the social or cultural sciences. Is it the mode of presentation that matters? Braudel, the French historian who left a profound mark on histor-iography through his work in the *Annales* school, offers up a mass of detail, sometimes as anecdote, sometimes as the extension of narrative (as an extended portrayal), but also on many occasions as economic data. How might one distinguish Braudel's use of detail from that of Kuznets? Presumably, both had an interest in assaying and discerning trends, even if Braudel clearly placed some emphasis upon the anecdotal as illustrative. Might one infer from this latter point that economic analysis precludes any reliance upon example, the episode or event singled out to demonstrate the virtue and efficacy of a general theme or principle? Not likely to be so. Kuznets himself pointed to the danger of economists making selective and even self-serving use of "historical facts" to buttress a general case already reached, acknowledging thereby the ready indulgence of economists to showcase "historical facts" when the occasion seemed propitious.

For his part, Braudel warned of the dangers of easy generalizing, especially by economists and sociologists (Braudel [1981] 1992: 227). Would this establish as an essential criterion of distinction between history and economics the degree or level of the "recalcitrant nature" of reality to generalization? But Braudel also spoke of creating a typology or grammar that underlay a "general economic history" which, even if incomplete, as Braudel suggested it would be, necessarily operated on an abstracted plane; accordingly, the resort to abstraction cannot, in and of itself, be deemed decisive, nor would it be inconsistent to see "imaginative construction" or reconstruction as attributes of both history and economics. Piketty confounds the dilemma posed further by relying upon novels, ostensibly works of fiction, to draw out, via the extremes endemic to or characteristic of its portrayals, "essential" elements of the broad thesis of his text (Piketty 2014: 113ff.)

I would contend that this approach or technique has real resonance with the origins of political economy in the eighteenth century (see Chapter 6), and reinforces the notion that economics, in crucial ways, works from fiction and fictive recreation as much as "historical facts" or "economic statistics." This in turn may place in jeopardy Wesley Mitchell's goal of replacing the "plausible" by the "proven," and, as Mitchell served as mentor to Kuznets, may also raise skepticism about what it meant for Kuznets to provide the essential breakthrough for economics to become an "empirical science." Moreover, it is clear that such reliance upon novels (or other works of fiction) would fall outside the bounds laid down by Kuznets in his *Journal of Economic History* article, since it would necessarily be regarded as qualitative and impressionistic rather than quantitative. Nonetheless, if one were to find or derive general statements or characteristic features from novels, as Piketty has done, would these not be taken to be abstractions, even the basis for models of other "mental constructs"? The broader question thus becomes: is economics as much guided and informed by narrative – and narratives – as history?

## On the role of the formative in economic history

There is also an understanding of "explanation" among historians that appears to fall outside the bounds of economic analysis in its emphasis upon the "formative." The past may well produce a powerful hold on the present, if such experiences are "formative." Barry Eichengreen noted its importance as he concluded his 1986 essay "Macroeconomics and History," suggesting that the differences between the British and the French in maintaining or abandoning the gold standard in the 1930s may best be understood by looking back to differences in their "historical experiences" in the 1920s, when inflation dogged France in a way that it did not Britain (Eichengreen 1986: 76).

Does this represent the purview of the historians to seize upon that which, among all pertinent historical experiences, rises to the "formative"? That is, are there no forms of model construction in economics that would afford a similar approach, nor, it would seem, from the econometric constructs upon which Eichengreen draws most of his theoretical insights?

Of course, there are such forms, most commonly constructed on the basis of path dependence, but these are typically limited to translating the "formative" into an historical accident establishing the initial conditions to which an economic model or set of rules is applied.

One might capture the distinctive nature of the formative in economic history in establishing a mold that transcends the application of economics rules to an initial set of conditions through the example of the rise to prominence of New York City as both the financial and commercial capital of the United States and then, at least with respect to finance, of the world. This provides an excursion into matters pertinent to the grand narrative occupying the attention of economic historians, and many economists as well: the story of the rise and disposition of capitalism.

The salient formative feature of New York's rise to prominence is not to be found in swells of geographical determinism, despite the advantages accorded to New York harbor in making New York City an inviting entrepot. In the eighteenth century Boston loomed larger as a North American commercial port, while Philadelphia was a more populous city, second in size only to London in what constituted the British Empire on the eve of the American Revolution.

Instead, in what might readily be cast in a Weberian perspective, New York's special advantage in becoming the cynosure of finance and commerce is commonly, but not universally, attributed to its founding as a city by the Dutch rather than the British in the 1620s, alone among its rivals like Boston, Philadelphia, Baltimore, or Charleston along the Eastern Seaboard. From the Dutch, then at their zenith as a European commercial power with colonial aspirations, New York City acquired a greater openness to making money and a greater tolerance toward diversity in religious outlook and in those engaging in exchange. Kenneth Jackson, a historian of New York City, spotlighted the Dutch legacy in its "tolerance, aspirational spirit, geography and diversity" (*New York Times*, 8/26/2014). Edwin Burrows and Mike Wallace take a similar tack in their exhaustive history of the city: "As the twenty-four-dollar saga suggests, New York would become a city of dealmakers, a city of commerce, a City of Capital" (Burrows and Wallace 1999: xvi). But they also note their role in writing history as an imaginative reconstruction:

> We are going to present New York's story as a narrative … Yet, like all histories, *Gotham* is not the simple reflection of an underlying reality, but a construction. The narrative embodies our selections, our silences. It is organized around patterns we discern amid the swirl of events.
>
> (Burrows and Wallace 1999: xvi)

Dutch rule came to an end in 1664, as New Amsterdam was renamed New York. Consequently, the direct presence of the Netherlands in what would become New York lasted only several decades, and it was well more than a century before New York would assume its dominant role in finance and commerce or its status, since 1800, as the most populous city in the United States. Nonetheless, New York's distinctive Dutch heritage, seen as highly conducive to a certain "spirit of capitalism," continues to be regarded as a decisive element underlying New York's subsequent history, now spanning three-and-one-half centuries. To the extent that one accepts this notion, one is adhering to the idea that a mold formed early on informs all succeeding developments; hence the mold serves to define terms of operation and behavior that go well beyond an initial set of conditions or circumstances.

The creation of this formative mold was followed by a number of actions or decisions that were crucial to the development and expansion of New York's preeminent role in finance and commerce that emerged in the first decades of the founding of the new American republic; hence these actions and decisions can rightly be ascribed to an active element of historical agency:

1   The decision by the first Secretary of the Treasury, Alexander Hamilton, for the federal government to assume the outstanding debts of individual states that had been incurred in the course of the Revolutionary War; the financing required to take on such debts created the need for new or enlarged banking institutions situated in close proximity; as New York was then the nation's capital, these banking and related financing institutions were located in Lower Manhattan, along Wall Street.

2   The "grand bargain" struck early on in the 1790s to initiate the establishment of a central bank, the Bank of the United States, modeled on the Bank of England, by allowing for the US Constitution to be interpreted on the basis of "implied powers." In exchange for moving the nation's capital to a district of swampland abutting the Potomac River dividing Maryland from Virginia; in the process reinforcing the federal government's role in finance and separating the political capital of the United States from its financial capital, an action consistent with the formative focus on commerce and money-making as the central economic activities underway in New York.

3   The highly ambitious "grid plan" laid out for Manhattan in 1811, envisioning the growth of the city so as to encompass, by century's end, the entirety of Manhattan. The actual transformation proved to be even more rapid and dramatic.

4   The highly ambitious "public works" plan put forward, fought for, and overseen by New York State governor, DeWitt Clinton, to build a canal linking Lake Erie to the Hudson River and ultimately New York City. Built between 1817 and 1825, the Erie Canal, when completed, linked the Great Lakes and the hinterlands of what is now called the Upper Midwest to New York City, so that goods – initially agricultural goods – could be shipped from the Midwest through the port of New York and on to Europe, broadening the potential national market in the United States and enhancing rather dramatically the role of New York City as a commercial entrepot from the 1830s on.

## Bridging theory and fact

If this construction of an historical narrative represents the problem posed by colligation, as Jonathan Hughes saw it (Hughes 1966: 79–83; 1970: 29–40, especially 30), then the divide between economics and history can never be fully bridged, and economic history, if indeed it falls between the two disciplines, will always remain in a somewhat fractured state. Under the circumstances, the primacy of one discipline or the other will be determining as to its presentation and, perhaps more crucially, the nature of the explanation it provides.

Yet one must consider the possibility of an alternative in which this fracturing is not the case. Max Weber's *General Economic History*, for all intents and purposes overlooked over the course of the last century, appears to blend three fields into one, where the economic, the historical, and the sociological all come together in some fashion.

How well has this bridge been constructed, or its limitations exposed, in more recent work by economic historians? Joel Mokyr's lengthy overview of the terms by which the – British – Industrial Revolution should be understood raises many of the same concerns as Eichengreen's inquiry into "Macroeconomics and History," especially with regard to differentiating "cause" and "explanation" from "analysis," even though Mokyr is clearly less wedded to the notion that economic history is "explained" by theoretical economic suppositions and propositions. To begin with, Mokyr, casting about in the middle ground between economics and history, entertains the question as to what is meant by an industrial revolution. Put in other terms, this translates into, variously, whether the Industrial Revolution took place at all, or how one might know that an Industrial Revolution had occurred? Framed as a matter of whether something did, or did not happen; or, in the alternative, whether one knew or could know if something happened, this form of inquiry seems decidedly historical in nature, and consequently would not come under the purview of economists.

Instead, the line of demarcation that emerges is based upon the state and scope of measurability, thus bringing into high relief the tension between the quantitative and the qualitative affecting the perspective and the modus operandi of the two disciplines. The problem confronting economic historians in this instance is that estimates of the growth of gross domestic product or national income in Great Britain from 1760 to 1830, identified by historians as the key period of economic transformation, do not support the claims of its being transformative, either in relation to the previous or the succeeding period. In macroeconomic, quantitative terms, was the British Industrial Revolution an illusion, a matter of perception rather than reality? (See also McCloskey 1985) As a side note, of course, one must ask how reliable the reconstruction of such macroeconomic measures might be, in light of both the sources available for producing these measures, as well as the time lag in their reconstruction. But one also faces what Kuznets referred to as the "recalcitrant nature" of reality, suggesting that the qualitative aspects of experience do not lend themselves to a ready translation into the quantitative.

But Mokyr does weigh the virtues and disadvantages of various economic notions in "explaining" how the Industrial Revolution did indeed take place. In the process he examined six categories of causes, both economic and non-economic: (1) geography; (2) technological creativity; (3) social and institutional factors; (4) government and politics; (5) demand vs. supply; and (6) foreign trade. Mokyr's analysis is built around a succession of economic concepts, as distinct from economic theories, however much they may be implicit in them. In the case of "technological creativity" these include: "gains from trade," "specialization," "gains from technological progress," and "economic development" (Mokyr 1993: 27–83).

Nor is Mokyr averse to employing quantitative measures in assaying those different "causes," but those are more likely statistical, as one might measure, say, the growth of foreign trade. However, those statistics are not made to conform typically to an economic, that is, econometric model, so that the resort to quantifiable measures is intended to provide a case, or to illustrate by persuasive example, so as to demonstrate the explanatory power of one economic concept or another.

Take Mokyr's treatment of the impact of technological change. He begins by asserting the need to quantify: "Yet economic historians have felt intuitively that if technological change is to be analyzed, it has to be quantified in some way" (Mokyr 1993: 23).

He then elaborates as follows:

> There are two alternative ways of measuring the level of technological change. One is the counting of patents or related statistics, which is a microeconomic approach. The other is estimating total factor productivity, which is mostly a macroeconomic approach.
>
> (Mokyr 1993: 23)

He then appears to reverse course, engaging in a disquisition on the validity of the concept of total factor productivity derived from the Solow growth model and the limitations in its use:

"Identifying the residual with technological change is, however, far from warranted. The residual is a measure of our ignorance rather than our knowledge" (Mokyr 1993: 25). This in turn leads to a broader critique, in which "historical reality," clearly not strictly quantitative, becomes the ultimate measure and arbiter:

> Thus gains from trade and specialization interacted with gains from technological progress, and such interactions led to a long and sustained path of economic development. Monocausal, linear models based on concepts of equilibrium or steady states will have difficulty doing justice to the historical reality.
>
> (Mokyr 1993: 27)

Hence, there is a substantive break between the approach taken by Mokyr and by Eichengreen, as the formulation of a model for the latter holds the key to the capacity to explain; causality itself is embedded within the model, even if "historical evidence" is required for corroboration and standard notions about the virtues of equilibrium are challenged.

Did prices in Spain rise because of the force and efficacy of the quantity theory of money, in operation once gold and silver flowed into the country after 1519? If this were so, and Eichengreen raises questions as to whether it would be the case, then it would comport with Pigou's dictum that economics provides "knowledge by implication." General laws, rules, and statements become causes of action, but only in the presence of certain "economic facts."

By contrast, one might see Mokyr's use of statistics for defined economic categories as consistent with the work and ways of economic historians, but there is also a certain resonance with the approach taken by economists of the classical school, as exemplified by Adam Smith, if with greater comfort in the use of numbers and "political arithmetic," as well as with the scope of economic inquiry laid out by Max Weber in his 1904 essay in the *Archiv fur Sozialwissenschaften und Sozialpolitik*.

The disjuncture between "explanation" and "analysis, though, remains unresolved. Is Mokyr's enumeration of the factors leading the Industrial Revolution a list of "causes" that explain, or a multifaceted "analysis" of what took place? One thinks of causes as answers to the question "why," as Hobsbawm suggested was the interest and role of the historian. If Great Britain, for example, experienced a major expansion in foreign trade that affected both the level and composition of overall economic activity, what brought about that surge in foreign trade? The causes must come from elsewhere. The measured increase in trade shows what happened, but not why.

There is also something of a "back-to-the-future" aspect to Mokyr's lengthy and exhaustive treatment of what constitutes the British Industrial Revolution, driven by the evident lack of measurability in terms of economic growth during its crucial decades, a problem that McCloskey saw as besetting efforts to comprehend the event or, as Mokyr put it, the "process" that constituted the Industrial Revolution (McCloskey 1985: 53–4; Mokyr 1985: 3).

Decades before, M. M. Postan, the economic historian, had written amidst challenges to the then fashionable theory of an economic "take-off" proposed by Walt Rostow:

> Even if some economic historians continue to believe that the movement of industrialization proceeded at about the same pace throughout its history, they would still be unable to deny that the cumulative effects of the transformation were more profound and more irrevocable than any other economic transformation since the end of the Roman Empire.
>
> (Postan [1962] 1971: 41)

Eric Hobsbawm put forward a similar claim:

> some time in the 1780s, and for the first time in human history, the shackles were taken off the productive power of human societies, which henceforth became capable of the constant, rapid, and up to the present limitless multiplication of men, goods, and services.
>
> (Hobsbawm 1964: 45)

Thus, the efficacy, even relevance of measurement is central to many of the leading concerns about the appropriate relation between macroeconomics and history. For one, what measures matter, or matter most, in gauging significant economic changes? Moreover, are such changes, for all that they might be comprehended as qualitative, necessarily rooted in quantitative and hence palpable measures?

The debate that has surrounded the advent and transformative nature of the Industrial Revolution offers up perhaps one of the most dramatic cases on point. Joel Mokyr surveyed a half-dozen such possible measures in assaying the timing of the British Industrial Revolution, as well as its impact. Barry Eichengreen would contend that efforts of this sort require a theoretical correlative, fleshed out in a well-delineated (or carefully specified) model. In the process, of course, this transforms what had appeared to be a quantitative undertaking into, essentially, a matter of selecting the "right" theory or model. M. M. Postan would have been dismissive of those endeavors, whether directly "quantitative" or somehow aligned with theory, as missing the fundamentally qualitative nature of such changes, which may not be at all amenable to quantification; instead, characterizing the overall result as "cumulative" in effect, a term that would have been invoked by the earlier American Institutionalists, who emphasized the importance of "cumulative causation." Nor is it likely that Postan would have accepted Kuznets' relegation of historical events and developments not producing regularities or general patterns suitable for quantification as forms of "white noise."

## The new Institutionalism and the new historical economics

One might imagine this as a conversation between Douglass North and Paul David. As to the former, North stands out as perhaps the leading representative of the new Institutionalism, in which the role of extra- or non-economic factors, a category of causal or inciting elements, determining or initiating, cited variously by Weber, Knight, and Braudel, is taken to be crucial in establishing the fate, or at least the status, of nation-states or communities. Among the new Institutionalists the legal disposition of property, most especially the guarantees associated with well-defined and safeguarded rights to private property, appears decisive. Economic success, in their view, is highly dependent upon the functioning aspects of the legal system. Critics of the new Institutionalism, among them Paul David, would argue that this approach was less genuinely historical and more confirmatory, both in the sense that it tended to justify the existing state of affairs, adducing a history that validated the current advantages held by certain states and in the way that this confirmatory outlook conformed to the stated principles of neoclassical economic theory.

Consequently, the question posed by Eichengreen as to the nature of the match-up between economic facts, drawn from history or "historical experience," and economic theory or models, holds for the new Institutionalists as well: are the facts matched to the theory, or is the theory matched to the facts? Can the new Institutionalists be rightly challenged on the basis that their constructions of economic history spring from the conclusions they expect to reach – or already have reached? From a Weberian perspective might one posit that the new Institutionalists replaced the emanationist notion of national culture or national spirit embraced by the fact-gathering German Historical School with a set of theoretical suppositions similarly embodied in the economic facts gathered? The "spirit of the nation" has been replaced by the "spirit of capitalist principles," perhaps just as it was the case that G. F. W. Hegel, who was associated with the idea of such "emanationism," was criticized for being as apologist for the state as it was currently constituted, a different but nonetheless existing state of affairs.

One might also see this following from a Weberian form of argument or disputation, namely the one he employed in seeking to eviscerate the "ethical standard" put forward by Gustav Schmoller as a way of gauging the value of economic activity, a matter central to Weber's effort to make value judgments in science explicit and to separate "science" from them in the process.

As to the latter, David tried to create a new bridge between economics and history through the notion of "path dependence," which drew upon a possible analogy between the physics of statistical mechanics and thermodynamics, on the one hand, and economic changes over time, on the other. To the extent that economic experience resembled the world of statistical mechanics, there was a tendency for economic situations to be resolved at equilibrium and for a freedom of movement that translated into the lack of any necessary connection between past and present, effectively rendering the economic experience outside of history. However, to the extent that economic experience more closely resembled the world of thermodynamics, there was a direction to economic experience that bound the present to the past. More particularly, from David's vantage point, "history matter[ed]," because such path dependence established a "formative" or "initiating" element to past experience that, at least on some level, might be viewed as the "colligation" philosophers of history described as an essential and defining characteristic of history and hence historical explanation. As a corollary disequilibrium, capturing the tentativeness of historical experience and perhaps as well an underlying mechanism for change, tended to prevail, rather than equilibrium.

The limitation presented by David's alignment of historical relevance and significance with "path dependence" rests with the emphasis it places on and the meaning it ascribes to the "formative" rather than the "contextual." There is no doubt that the inclusion of the "formative" in economic matters represents a huge advance in the integration of history into economics, but it may also, with reason, be comprehended as producing a relationship between history and economics whereby the former is often seen as a matter of "accident" or "coincidence," while the latter is formed and forged as a matter of "logical necessity," a position that to a substantial degree was put forward by Brian Arthur and Paul Krugman, though David advances the notion further by positing a succeeding "sequence of trades."

Curiously, in a way that seems to reflect affinities over the century that are not always recognized, the identification of economic rules, laws, or mechanism as conforming to a kind of "logical necessity" harkens back to Pigou's defense of economic abstraction as providing "knowledge by implication" and therefore is aligned with logic. In this, then, one might see the effort to create a new historical economics as grounded at least in part with Pigovian assumptions, but obviously with crucial differences. For one, both David and Arthur looked to physics to provide an analogy – a carefully delineated one, to be sure – to the functioning of the mechanisms of economics, rather than perceiving physics to have some special affinity with history. Second, the new historical economists all sought to find ways to better integrate history into economics, both as an affirmative act in and of itself, and as a clear recognition of the importance to be attached to history. Third, this in turn was linked to the importance they attached to disequilibrium as the "mover" of economic changes through real time.

Yet the question remains: does the reliance of the new historical economists upon Pigou's central contention about the nature of economics, even if there is no recognition of this possible link or linkage, weaken or strengthen the case that they are making? Despite the blurred lines about the role of physics between Pigou and the new historical economists, the mechanism Pigou described could be accommodated to a physical process, since it does appear that a major goal of the new historical economists was to produce a new kind of mechanism in economic experience that took place in time but was somehow – or nevertheless – not contingent, like historical experience itself.

For both the new Institutionalists and the new historical economists, then, attributes of what might be termed in more contemporary fashion as their "research programs" can be traced to an earlier period in which the problematic aspects of constructing a historical economics were directly addressed, as in Max Weber's critiques of Roscher and Knies, and the boundary conditions between economics and economic history were drawn with a new clarity, evidenced by the Clapham–Pigou controversy. Once again it is striking how much of that earlier history and controversy seems to have been lost, akin to the lost thread of historical economics itself.

## References

Braudel, Fernand ([1981] 1992) *The Wheels of Commerce*, trans. Sian Reynolds (1992), Berkeley: University of California Press.

Burrows, Edwin and Wallace, Mike (1999) *Gotham: A History of New York City to 1898*. New York: Oxford University Press.

Cipolla, Carlo ([1988] 1991) *Tra due culture*, trans. Christopher Woodall (1991). New York: W.W. Norton.

Clapham, John (1922) "Empty Economic Boxes." *Economic Journal*,38(127): 305–314.

Collins, Randall ([1980] 1992) "Weber's Last Theory of Capitalism." In Mark Granovetter and Richard Swedberg (eds), *The Sociology of economic life*,Boulder: Westview Press.

Eichengreen, Barry (1986) "Macroeconomics and History." In Alexander J. Field (ed.), *The Future of Economic History*. Boston: Kluwer-Nijhoff.

Fogel, Robert William et al. (2013) *Political Arithmetic*. Chicago: University of Chicago Press.

Fogel, Robert William and Engerman, Stanley L. (1974) *Time on the Cross*. London: Wildwood House.

Frisch, Ragner (1936) "On the Notion of Equilibrium and Disequilibrium." *Review of Economic Studies*, III (February): 100–105.

Gerschenkron, Alexander (1967) "The Discipline and I." *Journal of Economic History*, 27(4): 443–459.

Habakkuk, H. J. (1962) *American and British Technology in the Nineteenth Century: The Search for Labour-Saving Inventions*. Cambridge: Cambridge University Press.

Heilbroner, Robert (1953) *The Worldly Philosophers*. New York: Simon & Schuster.

Hempel, Carl (1952) *Fundamentals of Concept Formation in Empirical Science*. Chicago: University of Chicago Press.

Hicks, John (1969) *A Theory of Economic History*. Oxford: Oxford University Press.

Hobsbawm, Eric (1964) *The Age of Revolutions: 1789–1848*. New York: Mentor Books.

Hobsbawm, Eric ([1980] 1997) *On History*. London: Weidenfeld & Nicolson.

Hodgson, Geoffrey (2001) *How Economics Forgot History: The Problem of Historical Specificity in Social Science*. London: Routledge.

Hughes, Jonathan (1966) "Fact and Theory in Economic History." *Explorations in Economic History*, 2nd ser. 3: 75–100.

Hughes, Jonathan (1970) *Industrialization and Economic History: Theses and Conjectures*. New York: McGraw-Hill.

Keynes, John Maynard [1936] (1964) *The General Theory of Employment, Interest, and Money*. San Diego: First Harvest/Harcourt.

Kindleberger, Charles (1989) *Economic Laws and Economic History.* Cambridge: Cambridge University Press.

Kindleberger, Charles (1996) *World Economic Primacy: 1500 to 1990.* New York: Oxford University Press.

Korner, Heiko. (1997) "Carl Brinkmann: Eine wissenschaftsbiographische Skizze." In Reinhard Blomert,Hans Ulrich Esslinger, and Norbert Giovannini (eds), *Heidelberger Sozial- und Staatswissenschaften.* Marburg: Metroplis-Verlag, pp. 159–165.

Kuznets, Simon (1941a) "Statistics and Economic History." *Journal of Economic History,* 1: 26–41.

Kuznets, Simon (1941b) *National Income and Its Composition, 1919–1938,* vol. 1. New York: NBER.

Kuznets, Simon (1945) *National Product in Wartime.* New York: NBER.

McCloskey, Deirdre (1985) "The Industrial Revolution 1780–1869: A Survey." In Joel Mokyr (ed.), *The Economics of the Industrial Revolution: An Economic Perspective.* Boulder: Westview Press, pp. 53–74.

Maddison, Angus (1991) *Dynamic Forces in Capitalist Development: A Long-Run Comparative View.* Oxford: Oxford University Press.

Maddison, Angus (2001) *The World Economy: A Millennial Perspective.* Paris: Development Centre of the Organization for Economic Cooperation and Development.

Marshall, Alfred (1919) *Industry and Trade.* London: Macmillan.

Marshall, Alfred (1920) *Principles of Economics,* 8th edn. London: Macmillan.

Mokyr, Joel (ed.) (1985) *The Economics of the Industrial Revolution.* London: Allen & Unwin.

Mokyr, Joel (ed.) (1993) *The British Industrial Revolution: An Economic Perspective.* Boulder: Westview Press.

Morgenstern, Oskar (1937) *The Limits of Economics,* trans. Vera Smith. London: W. Hodge.

Neurath, Otto [1913] (1983) "The Lost Wanderers of Descartes and the Auxiliary Motive." In *Philosophical Papers 1913–1946,* ed. and trans. Robert S. Cohen and Marie Neurath.Dordrecht: Reidel, pp. 1–12.

Poincaré, Henri (1905) *Science and Hypothesis,* with special preface by Poincaré and introduced by Josiah Royce, authorized translated by George Bruce Halsted. New York: Science Press.

Postan, M. M. [1962] (1971) "Function and Dialectic in Economic History," *Fact and Relevance: Essays on Historical Method.* Cambridge: Cambridge University Press, pp. 35–47.

Rosenthal, Stuart and Strange, William (2004) "Evidence on the Nature and Sources of Agglomeration Economies." In Vernon Henderson and Jacques Thisse (eds), *Hand-book of Urban and Regional Economics,* vol. 4. Amsterdam: Elsevier, pp. 2119–2172.

Slicher van Bath, B. H. (1963) *The Agrarian History of Western Europe, A.D. 1500 1850,* trans. Olive Ordish. London: E. Arnold.

Solow, Robert M. and Temin, Peter (1985) "The Inputs for Growth." In Joel Mokyr (ed.), *The Economics of the Industrial Revolution.* London: George Allen & Unwin, pp. 75–96.

Swedberg, Richard (1998) *Max Weber and the Idea of Economic Sociology.* Princeton: Princeton University Press.

White, Lynn (1962) *Medieval Technology and Social Change.* London: Oxford University Press.

Wrigley, E. A. et al. (1997) *English population history from family reconstitution, 1580–1837.* Cambridge: Cambridge University Press.

## Newspaper articles and other sources

"French economist warns in new book of US' expanding wealth gap," *Boston Globe*, April 24, 2014.

Article by Kenneth Jackson on the origins of New York City, *New York Times*, August 26, 2014.

The author attended Thomas Piketty's talk at the Harvard Bookstore Forum, Cambridge, MA, April 18, 2014.

# 10 Toward a positive construction of historical economics

There are several foundational approaches from which a positive construction of historical economics might be launched. The first of these involves ascertaining the possibilities proffered by those schools of economic thought that have given great weight to seeking out and establishing an essential connection between history and economics, namely Marxian political economy, the German Historical School, and Institutionalism.

A second is more philosophical, and arises out of a recurrence, if not often noted, of a striking pattern in the plumbing of the foundations of economics over the course of a century: the concerns about the relation between theory and fact addressed by turn-of-the-century conventionalists and neo-Kantians, reappearing, if seemingly transmuted and somewhat transformed, in heightened interest in the structure of model building and the role of language and literary forms in an economics narratology raised by the late twentieth-century postmodernists.

The third looks to the matter of whether a bridge or a breach exists between the two fields of inquiry. In this regard one might consider the problems associated with the construction of economic history as well as the work and perspective of recent figures who skirt the boundaries between economics and history, like Charles Kindleberger or Thomas Piketty. However, it is also the case that the challenge taken on by Max Weber about the relation between subjective and objective experience, as well as the place of the particular and the general across intellectual disciplines, all framed as methodological questions starting with the "logical problems" facing "historical economics," may prove quite fruitful.

## The Marxian perspective

Among the Marxists – and here one must take into account both economists and historians – there are a variety of emphases in the linkage between economics and history. The notion that the state of national economies ought to be set in some historical framework, setting, or context, had roots in the formative period in which classical economics emerged. It was Anne-Robert-Jacques Turgot, a Physiocrat, who first gave full weight to the notion of economic transformation through set stages of history in *Réflexions sur la formation et la distribution des Richesses* (Turgot 1770), and it was Adam Smith who, beyond displaying a keen interest in historical details in *The Wealth of Nations*, advanced a framework for considering the question of comparative economic development, necessarily calling forth an infusion of history into economics.

However, it was Marx and his successors who put forth a system intended to encompass world history built around different sets of fundamental economic relations, making historical changes the product of economic circumstances, conditions, and arrangements, ones that conformed to a series of distinct determinants. In Marx's pithy aphorism from *The Poverty of Philosophy* (1847), the mill was emblematic of a feudal economy, the factory of an industrial economy: "The hand-mill gives you society with the feudal lord; the steam-mill society with the industrial capitalist." A variant upon this was the notion that these economic arrangements and series of stages were subject to laws that were analogous to physical laws, most directly Newton's laws; hence, the changes that occurred assumed an inevitability or inexorability that followed from the "law of motion of capital."

Maurice Dobb, a leading twentieth-century Marxist political economist in Great Britain, while characterizing the work of classical economics as analysis, gave it a decidedly historical and evolutionary cast, which also held for Marxian analysis. Citing Friedrich Engels, Dobb noted:

> In demonstrating the laws of laissez-faire [the classical economists] had provided a critique of previous orders of society, but they had not provided an historical critique of capitalism itself.
>
> (Dobb 1937: 55)

This task would fall to Marxian analysis, "in order to give capitalism its proper place in historical evolution and to provide a key to the forecast of its future" (Dobb 1937: 55).

Elsewhere Dobb stated that these laws were built upon empirical evidence, an approach he saw as informing in general the workings of political economy in the classical era and contrasting with a reliance upon logical relations from given assumptions in the succeeding era of neo-classical economics. If that is the case, then history is inexorably intertwined with economic analysis, as the resultant laws may be regarded as generalities that are capable of making the past intelligible and ordered, and, at the same time, capable as well of predicting the future in broad outline, though this latter capacity is in reality a projection of the course of future development.

Quoting Engels from his *Anti-Duhring*: "[What was necessary was] a socialist critique of the capitalist mode of production; that is, with the statement of its laws in their negative aspects, with the demonstration that this mode of production, through its own development, drives toward the point at which it makes itself impossible" (Dobb 1937: 56).

These laws, then, would "explain" the past, bridging the gap Hobsbawm found between historical explanation and economic analysis that typified mainstream economic thought. The Marxian framework those laws provided would be a system constructed as a series of stages in history, while the ability to extract generalities from particulars, the empirical evidence noted by Dobb, might be regarded as Hegelian, and was less a form of induction and more a fully realized set of conditions or states of affairs drawn from the gathering of inchoate signs from the particulars; in short, a kind of "emanation."

Yet a different variant of Marxian analysis gave great weight to the vagaries and outcome of the class struggle, where the categories of resources often demarcated in classical economics, that is, as factors of production or the payments made thereto (hence, wages and profits) were recast as more fundamentally socio-economic groups or classes. Significantly, differing historical outcomes could then be attributed to the power those different classes were able to exert, in the process introducing potentially a rather large role for historical agency, and challenging the inexorability of the "law of motion of capital," if not necessarily over a long trajectory.

This last point requires further elaboration, as many Marxists would contend that there is no inconsistency between the law of motion of capital and the class struggle, so that some sort of bridge between the apparent fluidity – even potentially indeterminate quality – of historical agency and the seeming inflexibility and determined state of laws underlying historical change might be achieved. Note Paul Sweezy's response in marking the centenary of *The Communist Manifesto*: "'The history of all hitherto existing society is the history of class struggles.' This is in no sense a contradiction of the theory of historical materialism but rather an essential part of it" (Sweezy 1953a: 8).

But does such a blending or synthesis exist? How might one go about proving or disproving such a possibility? Moreover, what would it mean in relation to the question at hand, namely the appropriate link between economics and history?

It is fair to say that one could construct a historical economics emphasizing historical agency, with the caveat that if only particulars matter, in a world in which the "accidents of history" and the decisions taken or abjured "drive" the actual course of events, then this would produce an economics for which generalizations and conceivably abstractions would play only a limited role.

Also, one might find it useful to delineate the dimensions of historical agency that comport with a Marxian understanding of economics and history. While it is undoubtedly the case that from a Marxian perspective classes and, more importantly, the state of the "class struggle" would be comprehended as the prime vehicle for historical agency, would it also be possible to treat power relations as expressed and asserted by what might be termed "interests," as in "business interests," as historical agents within a Marxian frame of reference? Or, might the more general or diffuse notion of "interests" fit more closely with the terms of Institutionalism, with its emphasis upon enlarging the "frontiers of economics so as to include … Economic Sociology," to use

Schumpeter's characterization (Schumpeter [1951] 1965: 246), and could just as easily be construed, as John Commons might have, as "producers" and "consumers," for example, as "capital" and "labor." From this vantage point those various "interests" would be set into a broader social configuration through which economic relations and meanings could be derived.

In this respect the array of interests, and their relations with one another, constitute a prevailing set of institutions, or institutional structures. If, following John Stuart Mill, one takes matters of distribution as the product of society and hence, to some significant degree, societal institutions that are created or maintained, as Mill put it, "[t]hat is a matter of human institution solely" (Mill 1857: 244), then there may be a wide berth for historical agency in economics, including versions of it that are strongly informed by Institutionalism, where the role of institutions in framing and making economic choices is decisive.

## The Institutionalist inversion

For their part, the German Historical School and the Institutionalists, both old and new, appear to have embraced history far more fully as essential to any comprehension of economic life than the mainstream of economic thought current during their periods of efflorescence. For the German Historical School the emphasis upon the differences played by national culture and the need to gather extensive, even exhaustive data before making any hasty economic generalizations appeared instead to prevent any meaningful economic analysis.

In his own – admittedly Institutionalist – take on the matter, Wesley Mitchell, lecturing at Columbia University in the 1930s, sought to contrast the work of Gustav Schmoller, the leading representative of the later generation of the German Historical School, with that of Thorstein Veblen. In Mitchell's view Veblen did not lose sight of the need to draw all the factual threads together in a systematic way, infusing theory thereby into his economics to the extent of avoiding a full presentation of factual details, so that there was a definite shape to his program of "economics as an evolutionary science." On the other hand, Mitchell found no such coherence in Schmoller's extensive fact-gathering (Mitchell 1949: 218–23).

Yet Institutionalism might also face contradictory pulls in that regard, as the notion of "economics as an empirical science," most closely associated with the work of Simon Kuznets, whom Mitchell mentored and encouraged, must be held in tension with Veblen's quest to make economics an "evolutionary science."

At the same time, a closer look at the later version of the German Historical School, though, especially through the work and ideas of Max Weber, whose economic thought bears a significant, if complex, relation to that school, would be instructive here. Weber sought to redefine the boundaries of all scientific disciplines, casting doubt upon the division between particularity and generalization that had been conventionally used to separate and segregate history from any scientific economics. Instead, he weighted more strongly the varying role of interpretation across all disciplines and the differences associated with their purpose or goal. Yet in the end Weber's engagement with a historical economics resulted in his "retreat" into sociology, and his preeminent role as a sociologist contrasts sharply with his diminished, even obscured place as an economist.

In the first instantiation of Institutionalism, the turn-of-the-twentieth century school of American economists, notably identified with Thorstein Veblen, Wesley Mitchell, and John Commons, among others, one might reasonably recognize the influences of both the German Historical School and Marxism, but that nonetheless produced an approach to and an understanding of economics sui generis. Economic life was treated broadly, flowing from the society in which it took place and clearly encompassing cultural phenomena. Data from and descriptions of this society were therefore deemed essential. All of this recalls at least elements of the historical and empirical approach associated with the German Historical School. The Institutionalists also gave great weight to the role of institutions and legal structures, effectively inverting the Marxian framework of substructure and superstructure, so that varying legal systems and laws themselves would play a significant role in shaping national economic activities. This was often accompanied by a critical outlook upon the state and mores of contemporary society, leading Paul Samuelson to cast Veblen as "the American Karl Marx" (Samuelson 1966: 1736), though Veblen, while a caustic critic, was clearly not a Marxist.[1] Instead, as his interest in "evolutionary science" suggests, Veblen was much more a Darwinian, perhaps more so than any other major Institutionalist.

This structural inversion can be captured through the juxtaposition of the works of two major heterodox economists from the United States: John Commons and Paul Sweezy. Commons, the early twentieth-century Institutionalist from Wisconsin, had served as the lead editor of a ten-volume, exhaustive study of the state of US industries under the auspices of the American Bureau of Industrial Research near the turn of the twentieth century (Commons 1910–11) that rivalled the vast, multi-volume series about the nature and composition of industry across the German Empire produced by the Verein zur Sozialpolitik, a leading academic society in Wilhelmian Germany long dominated by Schmoller.

But Commons also put forth a significant study of the evolving interpretation and reach of legal language and constitutional principles by the US Supreme Court affecting the powers of corporations and underpinning their centrality to US economic life in the second half of the nineteenth century. Entitled *Legal Foundations of Capitalism*, Commons' work sets legal structures as the base upon which economic structures are shaped, and reads more like a history, in this case of court decisions, than an economics text per se, with a pivotal role given to the elevation of corporations to the status of fictive persons protected by the due process provisions of the Fourteenth Amendment to the

US Constitution, largely thwarting the efforts of individual states to regulate their activities (Commons 1924).

In fact, Commons laid out the case for the centrality of law and history in economics early on in his career, in his own treatment of the subject of the "distribution of wealth" in 1893:

> The place of law in Political Economy is a subject which has received from English economists no attention at all commensurate with its far-reaching importance. The reason for this is mainly a lack of historical investigation.
>
> (Commons 1893: 59)

He goes on to state:

> The English economists have taken the laws of private property for granted, assuming that they are fixed and immutable in the nature of things, and therefore needed no investigation. But such laws are changeable – they differ for different peoples and places, and they have profound influence upon the production and distribution of wealth.
>
> (Commons 1893: 59)

Paul Sweezy, often regarded as the leading Marxist economist in the United States in the twentieth century, if at times regarded as an "unorthodox" one (King 1995: 50), wrote *The Theory of Capitalist Development* at least in part as a response to the early work of his mentor, Joseph Schumpeter, who had written *Theory of Economic Development* in central Europe prior to the outbreak of World War I (Schumpeter 1912). As the titles suggest, both of these latter works were far more abstract than Commons' text; moreover, there was little, if any, attention to historical detail. Instead, both attended to the general terms of how economies develop, but with one important exception: Schumpeter purported to lay down principles and mechanisms that had universal application, while Sweezy sought to show that the principles and mechanisms so engaged characterized a specific economic system, capitalism, and, accordingly, were subject to temporal and thereby historical limitations. Sweezy's focus, though, was more abstracted and theoretical; he elaborated, for example, upon a general theory of underconsumption to explain the onset of economic crises, building upon the work of the Austrian socialist Otto Bauer (Sweezy 1942: 179–89, especially 186–9). Hence, this was not a "history" amassed from details or "historical facts"; rather, its historical dimensions were derived, somewhat abstractly, from the underlying economic substratum.

The Institutionalist inversion noted above, though, could also lead to far less radical views. In fact, a second wave of Institutionalist thought emerged in the second half of the twentieth century with a decidedly more conservative cast in the hands of economic thinkers like Douglass North, as different legal structures, now focused strongly on such matters as property rights, were seen as the bases for the different experiences and outcomes found in different national economic experiences (North 1990). This later version of Institutionalism seemed less concerned with critiques of existing societies and possible alternatives to them, and more with explaining – critics like Paul David would say "justifying" – the existing state of such societies (David 1994: 206).

There is another inversion that occurs in the work of the early Institutionalists, most evident in the writings of Wesley Mitchell that is also pertinent to sorting out the nature of economics as a discipline.

Mitchell links causality in economics to the formation of hypotheses, which would then require confirmation through empirical evidence. As such, these hypotheses would serve a heuristic value, but in that state would function as a kind of scaffolding in the creation of economics as a rigorous discipline.

As Mitchell comprehended the role of theory, in particular with regard to business cycles, the centerpiece of his economic inquiries: "A theory of business cycles must therefore be a descriptive analysis of the cumulative changes by which one set of business conditions transforms itself into another set" (Mitchell 1941: ix). In the search for regularities among "the maze of sequences among business phenomena" only "substantially uniform" sequences are likely to be found, so that "[t]he purposes scientific theory serves are met by explanations that stop far short of radical thoroughness" (Mitchell 1941: x).

On its face Mitchell's notion of causality appears to invert the more commonly accepted view of factual description as more surface and theory the deeper level of inquiry, but it is consistent with Mitchell's highly critical stance toward contemporaneous economic theorizing as "more plausible than proven." One might reasonably see in that expression one element of a continuum in economic thought connecting Mitchell to Kuznets and ultimately to Fogel. If economics were to be a science, it would be an "empirical" one. Where does an "empirical science" fit into the grand division of sciences into the natural or physical and the human or social, if it does at all? What might one extract from the ability to create an "empirical science" in sorting through the tension between the nomothetic and the idiographical?

It would appear from Mitchell's perspective that in an empirical science the virtue of the general was to serve as a stepping stone to the particular: a factual demonstration. The alignment of economics with logic, the Pigovian paradigm, would give way to an economics that was "scientific" because it comported with the facts. As such, it would have more in common with Pigou's paradigm for history, as "knowledge in fact." And yet Mitchell was compelled to seek out "regularities" from the "tangled mass of facts" in order to find ways, using "imagination," in order to establish "causal connections," all of which muddies the relation between theory and fact (Mitchell 1941: x–xi).

The greater emphasis upon "knowledge in fact" in the claims put forward for economics as an empirical science would be all the more the case if the empirical evidence had to be found in historical data. Under these circumstances, it would suggest that Thomas Piketty may also have a place in this continuum as the – critical – successor to Kuznets, especially when he characterizes his own work as "more historical than economic."

Piketty described his sources as follows:

> To begin with income: in large part, my work has simply broadened the spatial and temporal limits of Kuznets's innovative and pioneering work on the evolution of income inequality in the United States between 1913 and 1948.
>
> (Piketty 2014: 16)

He goes on to state:

> Oddly, no one has every systematically pursued Kuznets's work, no doubt in part because the historical and statistical study of tax records falls into a sort of academic no-man's-land, too historical for economists and too economistic for historians. That is a pity, because the dynamics of income inequality can only be studied in a long-run perspective, which is possible only if one makes use of tax records.
>
> (Piketty 2014: 17)

Nonetheless, questions remain, casting doubt as to whether Piketty ought to be considered an Institutionalist, especially as his research centers around a theory of capital, as well as two related "laws of capitalism," one of which stands outside of the historical moment. On the other hand, he also devotes considerable attention to – historical – changes in the sources and nature of capital, and, in the end, sees a factual description as the culmination of economic explanation. One might see such use of descriptive laws as "Keplerian" rather than "Newtonian."

Moreover, it should be noted that Piketty's initial query about a longstanding "debate without data" (Piketty 2014: 2–3) fits neatly within Mitchell's construction of the problem besetting economics. In fact, one cannot help be struck by the seeming lack of progress in advancing the claims and aspirations of "economics as an empirical science" between Mitchell's caustic criticism in the 1920s, in which he bemoaned the lack of progress over the previous century, from the time of Malthus and Sismondi, and Piketty's introductory remarks, asserting much the same in the 2010s over the course of the twentieth century, making it two centuries of a seemingly stagnant economic science.

## The story of capitalism

To what extent has the broad trajectory of one question, the bases upon which capitalism came to arise first and, for long, overwhelmingly in the West and not elsewhere, figured in and across many seemingly distinct, even disparate efforts at comprehending the proper and pertinent relation between economics and history? Among Marxist political economists it has fueled a half-century debate initiated between Dobb and Sweezy in the 1950s.

Meanwhile, Fernand Braudel has spoken disparagingly of the treatment of the rise of capitalism as the central focus of an economic historiography from figures as distinguishable as Carl Brinkmann, from the late German Historical School, and Karl Polanyi (Braudel [1981] 1992: 226–8).

At the same time, it is also striking how similar Hobsbawm's and Weber's statements about the importance of this question were, especially in light of the differences in framework, perspective, and outlook which they brought to it. Hobsbawm, arguably the leading Marxist historian of the twentieth century, raised the question so as to distinguish the historian's role and interest in explanation from the economist's concern with analysis, here manifested in the possibility of gauging the import of counterfactuals, a variation, one might reasonably contend, on the Pigovian notion of the logic of economics as "knowledge by implication."

By contrast, Weber, with whom Hobsbawm did identify to a certain extent (see above), specifically in relation to the need to bridge economics and history in some fashion (and thus offering a link of sorts between Marxian historians and the German Historical School), was a non-Marxist whose relationship to Marxian ideas has spawned quite varied interpretations.

Weber raised the question about the rise of capitalism in corresponding with his former student Robert Liefmann, and broached it in the context of elevating the role of theory, presumably in economics, as against either economic history or sociology. In it he characterized the question as a "special relation" worthy of inquiry (Weber [1920] 2012: 410).

For his part, Hobsbawm tended to see the question of the rise of capitalism as a factual one rather than a counterfactual conjecture, emphasizing the importance of ascertaining why capitalism emerged as it did in the West (Hobsbawm 1997: 111). Moreover, in distancing the work of the historian from the relativism of postmodern narrative construction, Hobsbawm spoke of the need to maintain "the universality of the universe of discourse that is the essence of all history as a scholarly and intellectual discipline," which was grounded in "the belief that historians' investigations, by means of generally accepted rules of logic and evidence, distinguish between fact and fiction, between what can be established and what cannot, what is the case and what we would like to be so" (Hobsbawm 2002: 296).

The central concern, here as elsewhere, remains the same: what is the appropriate balance and relation between theory and fact in economics? Once again, the tension between the nomothetic and the idiographical, as well as the concomitant potential for a bridge or breach between the two disciplines, encountered directly in the conundrum of economic history, occupies center stage in this inquiry.

## Historical agency revisited

This survey of historically conscious perspectives in economics raises further questions about the role of historical agency. To what extent does the degree of contingency of historical agency correspond with the degree to which economics falls away from, or stands apart from, its status as nomothetic or nomological? Or, does the introduction of historical agency of any sort render nugatory any reliance upon or resort to the distinction between the nomothetic and the idiographical? In other words, has that distinction simply been superseded by other criteria, even other methods, of comprehending the nature and place of economics as an intellectual discipline?

One could imagine a form of historical agency in which laws play a central role, as in the Marxian assertion of governing, if ultimately subverting, laws of history. This might be cast as a Newtonian approach to economics, with the law of motion of capital at work. On the other hand, that which is contingent might suggest the approach taken by Arthur or Krugman in establishing a notion of inciting events as the "accidents of history," upon which economic rules, perhaps in line with Pigou's economics of logical relations, would then act.

As to the latter, I think it safe to say that historical agency, while it may well include inciting events, is clearly meant and able to affect the unfolding pathway followed at many other, succeeding turns. Why might it not be possible for such a pathway to be punctuated at numerous turns by historical events or, better, historical decisions or choices, holding the key to the overall path pursued?

Along those lines Paul David put forward the case for events to be interlocked, so that economic developments advanced through a "sequence of trades" (David 1997). In this version the nomothetic/idiographical divide does not altogether vanish; rather, it is the balance between the two that fundamentally shifts. The logical relations of economics continue to matter, only their importance in determining the actual outcome has been substantially diminished. Even this approach, though, does not fully capture the idea of context, which is less a sequencing of events and more a framework within which events unfold. In that sense historical agency is insufficient, in and of itself, in bringing the full weight of history to bear in economics.

Might a turn to "structure" be necessary to provide the full weight required? Paul Bairoch would contend that is the case, employing language that recalls and evokes that which was put forward by J. R. Firth and, ultimately, Bronislaw Malinowski, to capture the "situational" nature of "contextual meaning" in economic history: "So, other times, other situations" (Bairoch 1993: xv). He fleshed out a fuller version of this notion in what he referred to as "the paradox of economic history":

> If I had to summarize the essence of what economic history can bring to economic science it would be that there is no "law" or rule in economics that is valid for every period of history or for every economic structure.
>
> (Bairoch 1993: 164)

For Bairoch those varying economic structures are situational, arising at different moments, so that, "once again, different structures mean different evolutions and different laws. History does not necessarily repeat itself, and never exactly" (Bairoch 1993: 174).

Pursuing this understanding further calls for a deeper examination of the bases for and method of historical periodization. The historian Jacques Le Goff has tackled this question directly:

> The breaking down of time into periods is necessary in history, when one considers it in the general sense as the study of the evolution of societies or as a particular type of knowledge and instruction, or again as the simple unfolding of time. But this "decoupage" is not a simple matter of chronology; it also expresses the idea of passage, of a turning, that is to be seen as a disavowal vis-à-vis of the society and the values of the preceding period. The periods consequently have a particular "signification"; in their very succession, in the temporary continuity or, on the contrary, in the ruptures which this succession evokes, they constitute an object of reflection essential for the historian.
>
> (Le Goff 2014: 12–13)

From this perspective, in order to account for meaningful distinctions about both periodization and structure, the task facing the historian would then also fall to the economist. To do so means that, once again, matters of interpretation, requiring the intermingling of fact and theory, assume primacy, a subject at the center of Weber's methodological inquiries.

## The Weberian perspective and the recurrence

The most forthright statement of what might be termed "the Weberian perspective" can be found in the introductory essay Weber wrote, in concert with Werner Sombart and Edgar Jaffe, upon their assumption of the editorship of the *Archiv fur Sozialwissenschaften und Sozialpolitik* in 1904.

Economics, understood broadly, consisted not only of matters directly regarding economic activity, but also those activities and relations that are economic arising from non-economic sources, and those activities and relations that are non-economic arising from economic sources. Critically, Weber saw this as a reflection of changes wrought in economics after Roscher and Marx, suggesting an attunement to at least part of what both Marxist approaches and those from the German Historical School might offer to a rethinking of the scope of economics, with a greater historical consciousness no doubt a part. In fact, in this same essay Weber explicitly sought to preserve a version of "historical materialism" somehow divorced from the Marxian "world-view" (Weber [1904] 2012: 131–3).

How well is this schematic realized in practice, by Weber or others? The Weberian perspective both looks back, to the efforts of Marxists and earlier generations of the German Historical School, and forward, to the post-modernism within an emergent field of economic methodology, with its renewed emphasis upon narrative, "contextual meaning," and modeling. This is all the more striking because of a recurrence of concerns raised by the turn-of-the-century conventionalists and neo-Kantians, which might well be regarded as presaging much of what would later inform the subject of economic methodology and, to some extent, the late twentieth century "linguistic turn" in economics. Making sense of the role of narrative, in particular the extent to which such narratives were necessarily historical, or might also correspond to literary forms, would be crucial to establishing more clearly the historical component of economics, whether it be found in concepts, theoretical assumptions, and constructed models, or fitted to a set of events or policies.

Are narratives necessarily historical? Certainly one might point to Weber's adaptation of Johannes von Kries' notion of "objective possibility" and his adoption of a two-step process of causal imputation to suggest that a serious effort to address that question took place a century ago, in this instance more from the vantage point of the neo-Kantians, but likely as well on the part of at least some of the conventionalists. "Narrative" would not have been invoked explicitly by Weber, but he did evince an awareness of what might be termed the "primacy of text" by acknowledging that all writings constitute texts of one sort or another (and it is the sorting that distinguishes the routine or mundane from the significant) (Weber [1906] 2012: 175). In this turn-of-the-century context one narrative, or, perhaps better, one interpretation, would be deemed better suited to the facts, though the "pluralism" advanced by the conventionalists, discussed further below, would serve as a counterpoint to this notion or belief.

The degree of contingency of "historical agency" may complicate matters here. If the actions of historical agents are fully contingent, then it may fall to a discerning of the facts to establish a reasonable interpretation of outcomes. If, on the other hand, as is more likely the case, historical agents themselves are subjects of interpretation or theoretical suppositions, then "fact-checking" or "fact confirmation" will prove to be insufficient, as "fact selection" would follow from the interpretation or theory pursued. In short, the choice of narrative may trump any positivist notion of an assemblage of non-controversial and uncontroverted facts.

Moreover, as narratives are explicitly understood to be "texts," the emphasis upon narrative, or, rather, its reentry into discussions about the nature – and form – of economics, necessarily introduces a literary component into the analysis and philosophy of economics. Hence the notions of rhetoric and allegory, if "modernized" or "postmodernized," would reappear into matters of subtext. But this also should propel further consideration of forms associated with and meanings attached to narratives as literary texts. Might the choice of such forms indicate elements of historical context, if not be seen as shaping context overall? Might such choices not also address matters of meaning and significance, pointing to ways that the economic subject ought to be understood, that is, as an aspect of the plumbing of its foundation or philosophy; as in: "here is the proper atmosphere; there are the pertinent levels of meaning."

In advancing to the late twentieth century one finds that the great missing piece in the philosophical or methodology inquiry flowing from the "recurrence" has in fact been the lack of conscious or systematic criteria for selecting one narrative or another. This has been accompanied by, and indeed is linked to, another weakness: the incomplete treatment of historical context, reducing it to, for example, "path dependence" and "lock-in," both significant advances in the attempt to re-frame the relation between economics and history, but something less than what context must fully convey, though a useful entry point for taking up the matter of the "formative" in economics.

## Path dependence and formative construction

Brian Arthur's related notions of "lock-in" and "path dependence," which first appeared in a paper published in the late 1980s, along with the earlier notion of "cumulative causation" advanced by the American Institutionalists, may come as close as any put forward in exploring the construction of economics to capture the essence of the notion of "the formative" in establishing historical context, as it fixes earlier or prior developments as shaping the future course of development by limiting possible pathways. What "path dependence" misses is the related idea, from the standpoint of historical construction, of "setting the stage," built, metaphorically, on an analogy with the world of theater and the "putting on" of plays. That is so because, in a further borrowing from the literary lexicon ultimately drawn from epic poetry, but with both theatrical and cinematic attributes of presentation, the production necessarily begins in medias res. In historical presentation there is always a beginning before the beginning; if fully pursued this would produce its own infinite regress. Accordingly, when one translates the matter of "setting the stage" to economics, the conditions and circumstances that gave rise to the initial state must be ascertained, if not explored in some depth as well. In short, the "inciting event" itself must be viewed as formed within a "stage set," intelligible only if understood as the product of what preceded it, and whose appearance on the scene must be made comprehensible through a context that traces back to earlier events and circumstances. Moreover, it may only be historical periodization that makes it possible to avoid regarding and treating the chosen "stage set" as simply arbitrary. But this then requires a further exploration of the bases for such periodization, yet another question of interpretation.

The Institutionalist notion of "cumulative causation" does offer up real possibilities for capturing the in medias res quality of "setting the stage," but without illuminating the elements that go into its formation. Thus, Mitchell states: "Every business cycle, strictly speaking, is a unique series of events and has a unique explanation, because it is the outgrowth of a preceding series of events, likewise unique" (Mitchell 1941: x).

Yet these "unique" series must display "uniformities" sufficient to allow for generalization, at least as a description.

In addition, the notion of "lock-in" is built upon a concept drawn from mathematical physics, in which a "tipping point" is found leading to two rather different outcomes. In physical terms this is a measure of energy; in economic terms this translates into "the minimum cost to effect changeover to an alternative equilibrium" (Arthur 1994: 115). As Arthur elaborated upon what is entailed in this process:

> Self-reinforcement, almost by definition, means that a particular outcome or equilibrium possesses or has accumulated an economic advantage. This advantage forms a potential barrier. We can say that the particular equilibrium is locked in to a degree measurable by the minimum cost to effect changeover to an alternative equilibrium.
>
> (Arthur 1994: 115)

Under certain conditions "lock-in" could pose a barrier to other, potentially more productive pathways. It is in this way that Alexander Gerschenkron's thesis about the "economic advantages of relative backwardness" might be made manifest. For example, as portrayed by David Landes in *The Unbound Prometheus*, the widespread adoption of the Leblanc process in England for producing industrial soda and potash meant that the advances associated with the later Solvay process made little headway in Great Britain, in contrast to its rapid embrace in the industrializing states of continental Europe (Landes 1969: 270–3). But how far might one extend this notion of the possible gains from a certain marginality? If treated quite broadly, would it assume the form of a "law," as has been done rather loosely with Schumpeter's notion of "creative destruction"? Perhaps these might be thought of as "ideas as imperatives," which of course makes them more "plausible" than anything more exact or necessarily so.

In any event, this is hardly what is meant by "formative," as in the formation of a mold whose terms and conditions may not be subject, fully or perhaps even partially, to a quantitative measure; hence, one must return to the distinction between the quantitative core of economics and the qualitative essence of history that Kuznets laid out as defining.

This, of course, raises doubts about the ability to mathematize the phenomena of "formative construction," although one must also retain the possibility of introducing a more qualitative mathematics, as conventionalists like Poincaré championed. Moreover, beyond the potential for quantification as a matter of abstraction, one needs as well to contend with the requirements for translating this proposition into an economic calculus of cost and advantage. It was Paul David's insight that "lock-in," à la "QWERTY," might encumber costs that a more efficient and hence economically advantageous approach might not face (David 1985). David still tried to find a mechanism, via "path dependence" and non-Markov processes, to preserve an analogue with mathematical physics while giving central place to history.

## Historical circumstance and contextual meaning

From Marx's *The Eighteenth of Brumaire* one has the ringing phrase:

> Men make their own history, but they do not make it just as they please ... but under circumstances directly found, given and transmitted from the past.
>
> (Marx [1852] 2002: 19)

From Clifford Geertz, the anthropologist, one has humans "suspended in webs of significance" of their own making. If one assumes – rightly – that the "making" to which Geertz refers must have taken place over time, that is, in the past, as human history, then might it be possible to see these two statements, as they stand alone, as bearing a certain kinship, for all that Marx emphasized the economic ramifications of the past on the present and the prospects for revolutionary transformation in the future? "Circumstances" have been translated into "meanings," a transformation of events, institutions, and social relations into signs and language by which they are perceived and understood.

In fact, one might associate the new-found interest in language and signs in order to analyze different cultures, then extended to a wide array of intellectual disciplines, as rooted in the work of anthropologists. It was Bronislaw Malinowski's focus upon the logic of situation and the barriers attendant upon the translation of language and other signs from one culture to another that strongly influenced J. R. Firth, a professor of linguistics, to put forward the notions of "contextual meaning" and "colligation" in the middle of the twentieth century (Firth 1968: 137–46). While initially applied to matters of linguistics, these notions were soon absorbed into the discourse of the philosophy of history, and the latter of the two was seen by the economic historian Jonathan Hughes, by the mid-1960s, as one of the critical differences between history and economics (Hughes 1966: 79–83).

Perhaps of even greater significance and import was the work of Geertz, who ushered in a new era of "interpretive anthropology" in the 1970s, and caught the wave of symbolic interpretation and cultural analysis that appeared to underlie the "linguistic turns" found in various fields of inquiry and in the advent of the relativism and cultural pluralism of late twentieth-century postmodernism. The impact of Geertz's work and the shift toward comprehending human activity in terms of different cultures was noted by Hobsbawm as marking the decline of a more economics-based history with its greater emphasis upon "structure" that had taken its "inspiration" from Braudel (Hobsbawm 2002: 294). Curiously, what it did not appear to do was reawaken interest in an economics in which such cultural concerns either played a leading role or even set the main framework for constructing an economics. In essence, this would have entailed a revival of the emphasis upon culture and social organization found in the German Historical School, but effectively stripped of its nationalist mythos.

   This is all the more noteworthy in that Geertz himself acknowledged the influence of Max Weber as the critical forerunner of his intellectual mission, alluding to him in what has become the most well-known statement of Geertz's assertion of the primacy of interpretation in the human (or cultural) sciences:

> Believing with Max Weber that man is an animal suspended in webs of significance he himself has spun, I take culture to be those webs and the analysis of it to be therefore not an experimental science in search of law but an interpretive one in search of meaning.
>
> (Geertz 1973: 5)

> It is explication I am after, construing social expression on their surface enigmatical.
>
> (Geertz 1973: 5).

   The reference to Weber does shed light on the recurrence of related concerns across a century-long arc. Geertz points to the centrality of matters of meaning in any discipline in which culture matters, then eschews the task of law-making. In this latter tack Geertz appears to open up the possibility that disciplines which are "cultural" may not be nomothetic, but clearly are subject to a kind of "analysis" that may take the form of "explication." And, of course, as "explication," one can see the embarkation upon a new course, where the place of signs and language is elevated.
   Differences with Weber's approach do emerge as well. Geertz's focus upon explication of this sort is combined with, or complemented by, a diminution of interest in the kind of fictive construction associated with Weber's "ideal types," although construction of that sort remains central to questions of model-building. At the same time, Geertz's reference to probing beneath or through "surface[s] enigmatical" evokes the allegorical layering that can be linked to the interpretation of models.

## Economics, narrative, and history

Economic models, even thought-experiments, constitute the standard mode for inquiry in economics, consequently relying greatly upon their underlying assumptions and rendering both central and problematic the relation between such theoretical construction and historical or empirical evidence. For one, is it typically the case that "theory is matched to facts," or are "facts matched to theory"? Moreover, how pervasive is the place of narrative whenever and whichever way the match-up is constructed? Theory matched to facts might be understood as an empirically based construction, where the amassing of facts leads inexorably to the resultant theory, forging an economics as "empirical science." Is such a process or procedure possible, that is, without the introduction of at least a working hypothesis? Mitchell's efforts in laying out an "empirically based" construction make plain the need for working hypotheses, even if only as an intermediate or heuristic step. At this juncture, then, the matter of narrative selection and the narratology of economics arises, for even the "match-up" noted just above is based upon a narrative chosen.

In fact, whether as model or thought-experiment, whether discursively or mathematically constructed, economic ideas are conveyed by, or tell stories. Hence, if economics is to proceed systematically rather than on an ad hoc basis, it must be subject to a thorough assessment of the array of narratives available. While it is a truism that every theory and every hypothesis (working or otherwise) tells a story (see McCloskey 1983 and Morgan 2012), unless one accepts a postmodernist "soup" of completely relativist outcomes and possibilities, then there must be a way to make the case for better or worse storylines, and preferably on a systematic foundation and platform. Moreover, as these narratives must bear some connection to an economic and social world, they must derive their force from the historical context in which they are found.

Toward that end, one may ask if economics has foundered on the question posed by the choice of narrative, implied by the problem of plausibility raised by both Mitchell and Solow? Can it be redeemed, in part or full, by a linkage reestablished between economics and history, so that history might be seen as informing the choice of narrative that comported with more systematically based criteria? Such criteria might themselves be subject to variation and no lack of controversy: (1) a separation of fact from fiction, applying a juridical standard; (2) a separation of fact from fiction, applying a statistical or probabilistic standard; (3) the application of operable laws of history, effectively placing interpretation and theory in primary position; or (4) the embedding within a larger cultural or societal net that has been shaped by historical circumstances and conditions.

## Toward a narratology

For all the light shed upon the role of narrative in economics in recent decades, perhaps most notably by Deirdre McCloskey (McCloskey 1983) and Mary S. Morgan (Morgan 2012), one can find a clear expression of this notion of the centrality of narratives in Otto Neurath's *Foundations of the Social Sciences*, which was published in 1944. Neurath is best known for his role in spearheading the Vienna Circle of philosophers and for his advocacy of economic planning and in-kind calculation. This treatise, written late in his career, was, to a significant degree, a critique of the language of economics, and in it he introduces the idea of multiple hypotheses underlying narratives as especially evident in the social sciences, drawing upon turn-of-the-twentieth-century conventionalists:

> That leads us to a kind of "pluralism," which appears even within physics, as Duhem and others have pointed out. In the social sciences this

pluralism is more conspicuous because relatively simple stories are full of hypotheses. But we should not overlook that even the simplest report is based on hypotheses, and, therefore, pluralist.

(Neurath 1944: 14)

Compare this notion of pluralism with that introduced by Hayden White in the 1970s in his influential work entitled *Metahistory*:

It is different with history. There are different possible ways of comprehending historical phenomena because there are different, and equally plausible ways of organizing the social world which we create and which provides one of the bases of our experience of history itself.

(White 1973: 283–4)

Neurath had long since seen the need for establishing a metatheory to arrange and order hypotheses about the physical and social world. For his part, Max Weber, like Neurath associated with or influenced by the German Historical School in his early career, noted that facts were "molded" by theory (Colliot-Thélène 2006: 21), recalling Goethe's aphorism that "fact" was inseparable from "theory" in his 1906 methodological essay critiquing the German economic historian Eduard Meyer (Weber [1906] 2012: 175). On a separate note, Goethe's aphorism also found its way as a guiding idea in the work of the British linguist J. R. Firth, who advanced the notion of "contextual meaning" (Firth 1968: 146, 168).

And that may stand as a critique of the postmodern focus upon the role of narrative. The recognition of the ubiquity or universality of narratives to effect interpretation and the construction of models makes it incumbent to establish the criteria by which narratives are selected, and through which historical elements will come to the fore, making "historical experience" itself comprehensible. Hence, the examination of narratives in economics must extend beyond the criteria noted above linking economics and history to an inquiry into the different modes of interpretation of narrative itself.

One such mode would be through the assortment of plotlines or genres of dramatic presentation, along the lines first marked out by Hayden White in the 1970s for historical interpretation in his *Metahistory*.

A second would be through the notion of the layering of narrative as one might treat texts as allegories. Adam Smith, trained and practiced in rhetoric, himself alluded to the uses of allegory. While one might treat "subtext" as a modern-day version of allegory, contrasting surface content with the actual meaning inscribed in subterranean fashion within the text, it is also possible to translate, update, and secularize the more complex layering of medieval allegory, perhaps most famously laid out by Dante Alighieri in his letter to Can Grande della Scala as fourfold allegory (see Auerbach [1959] 1973: 64–76), Hollander 1969), to the narratology of economics. In brief, one such transmuted accounting of fourfold allegory set on a temporal basis, and, implicitly, a historical one, might hew to the following outline: (1) the literal or historical: a recounting of past events; (2) the moral or tropological: the meaning to be found in present events, or the "ought" contained in the literal or historical, in essence, what is often thought of as the "message"; (3) the topological: the connection of past with present, conceived of as a correspondence or resonance between past and present events, but with an emphasis upon prefiguration; and (4) the anagogical: the end result in the future, or the culmination of economic activity.

A third would be based upon the appearance and use of tropes and figures, offering up representations of "something other" through turns of phrase or speech most notably through metaphor, metonymy, and synecdoche. Smith had characterized metaphor as "contracted allegory" (Smith 1983: 30), highlighting thereby its ability to convey a message, but in representing "something other" in the broadest of terms these figures of speech open a window upon the use of narratives in economics that are derived from other disciplines, whether they be mechanics, biology, or thermodynamics.

Finally, a fourth would be built upon the literary elements in the origins and development of economics, drawing upon both the renewed interest in the fable as a literary form in the late seventeenth century (with greater attention to La Fontaine than to de Mandeville, as has generally been the case). Nancy Cartwright has contended that fables, offering up morals that need to be fitted to a given set of conditions, rather than concealing deeper messages, as allegories might, provide the royal way to framing models, including economic ones (Cartwright 2010: 27). I would contend that even more important was the rise to prominence of the novel in the eighteenth century, with its heightening of fiction all the better to convey fact and reality, and shaping the longstanding and often dominant role of conjecture in economics.

Hence, there are at least four elements of the textual inquiry into narrative that are pertinent. In turn, they all must be set in some relation to a context made explicit. That is because even if a story provides a message, its interpretation may depend upon the context in which it is set. A fable may be taken, at least in certain instances, as the subtext for an economics narrative, as, for example, in the narratology of the recent financial crisis, where one views greed or excess as the character flaw that leads to the downfall – and downturn. John Kenneth Galbraith's *The Great Crash, 1929* (Galbraith 1955) presents a model for an historical account of a financial crisis with an allegorical subtext fixed upon the wages of excess – and the perils of historical amnesia.

But if the fable is not simply viewed as a universal statement about human nature, then it must be situated somehow. Such an effort is necessarily historical in nature, as it draws from a selected set of facts pertaining to events and developments that have already occurred. In fact, one might contend that economics narratives are fundamentally historical, set in shape by the period or moment in time. There is a bit of a reflexive loop here: interpretation requires that a context be found or established, but that context as well requires an act of interpretation, namely the selection of certain facts to form it. Have we once again entered the world of the infinite regress? One might well see in all this Neurath's notion embodied in an epigraph made famous by Willard van Orman Quine about the necessity in philosophical terms of engaging in "drydock" reconstruction while at sea (Quine 1960: vii).

## Plotlines and "atmosphere" in economics

To pursue the matter of plotlines, or genres of presentation, further, it is necessary to elaborate upon or disentangle the theatrical categories laid out by Hayden White, like comedy or satire, and the literary or cinematic forms, like the fable or "film noir," that provide crucial frames of reference through their form of presentation.

White's actual focus was on the imaginative constructions of nineteenth-century historiography. Within that context White accorded the most significant role to four writers of history, each of whom, while attempting to capture and portray an understanding of historical realism, was linked to a different genre of literary or dramatic presentation. Thus, Michelet's work offered up a romance, Ranke's a comedy, de Tocqueville's a tragedy, and Burckhardt's a satire (White 1973: 235–4).[2] Can these rightly be thought of as subtexts or plotlines? In some sense, neither; in another sense, both. On the one hand, none of these provides the kind of message associated with allegory, as no details about the nature of any of these forms of presentation are disclosed. One is left to ask: a comedy or satire about what? That is, these forms are just that, devoid – seemingly – of content. Yet on the other hand they all convey a sense about the nature of things, or, in this setting, the course of history, hence an atmosphere or context, even in the absence of specific content.

How might this translate into a narratology of economics? First of all, for all that White's work helped catapult to prominence the notion of a "linguistic turn" first in history, then extended to other fields, there are distinct differences between reading history as a text, with underlying subject, and divining narratives in history that comport with these various genres of "artistic" (literary or dramatic) presentation – as well as, of course, the possibility of a certain murkiness in-between.

Consider the interpretive strands of the following example, drawn from the Solow growth model: (1) a subtext trumpeting the virtues of efficiency through the introduction and development of labor-augmenting technology, taken as the key to long-term, sustained growth; (2) a fairy tale, à la Fontaine, but ultimately from Aesop, in which a subtext is clearly in evidence, say in the tale of the "squirrel and the grasshopper," or the triumph of prudent saving, as the model places a premium on saving, contrasting the nation that saves with the one that does not, with a far higher steady-state level of capital; (3) a comedy, as its genre of presentation, for its fundamentally optimistic conclusion about the possibilities for long-term growth and the convergence of the economies of developed, highly industrialized economies; all in contrast to the tragedy posed by the "razor's edge" of Harrod-Domar; and (4) a historical narrative constructed from the "facts" of renewed prosperity and economic expansion entered into following the end of World War II.

Second, might a reliance upon identifying and classifying forms of presentation, as noted above, open the door to capturing the more elusive matters of context in a historical economics? Neither the notion of pathway, mathematized as non-Markov processes, nor the idea of a rough fit between narrative and model, advanced by Morgan, provides one of the crucial components of context, namely atmosphere, but might it be the case that White-like plotlines, or, better, genres of presentation, would serve that purpose? This, it should be noted, would also convey context in a way that Weber's ideal-types do not.

One might object, and rightfully so, that genres of presentation can provide only a generic type of atmosphere. In "Of Puzzles and Problems" I suggested that the "prisoner's dilemma" be cast through the filter of the highly atmospheric "film noir." In the main, as evidenced in Morgan's survey, among others, the "context" for the prisoner's dilemma has been taken to be the Cold War (Morgan 2012: 306–7, 345–48). These are not mutually exclusive, as film noir was, on more than one occasion, appropriated for use in representing the atmospherics or narrative themes associated with the Cold War. This comes, though, with complications, for the atmospherics and sensibility of film noir convey a grayness, weariness, and even a subverting irony that stand in contrast to the black-and-white global division also called up by the Cold War. (In reality, perhaps both were in play simultaneously.)

As to the unfolding methodological questions: one source of the applicable context is literary or cinematic, an extension, one might argue, of the dramatic or theatrical forms of presentation pertinent to the representation of history in the nineteenth century, while the other is plainly historical. Does this make a case for the relevance of both in fleshing out a suitable context for economics? With matters of history one tends to think in terms of periodization, as indeed one might regard the reference to the Cold War. Should the literary, the dramatic, or the cinematic be regarded as a separate entry into matters of context, like distinct "strata" of context, or are they effectively melded into the pertinent history?

All of this goes to the independence of White's plotlines in framing economics. It seems to me that the literary aspects of economics are so strong and salient that the genres of presentation do maintain a certain autonomy, as one might even translate White's four categories to the "explanations" evoked about the most recent financial crisis, or financial crises in general: do we see the unfolding of a romance, comedy, tragedy, or satire?

So far these criteria have been drawn from history or literature. I suspect a third might involve the specific use or role of language, and that this criterion in turn is linked to the infusion of anthropological considerations. This last element reflects the large impact anthropological insights have had on other disciplines that have directly or indirectly affected economic thought (see above for more details). Is it possible to apply the criteria drawn from these anthropological insights about the nature of language to the Solow growth model as well? For example, are the terms in which it is couched culturally bound in some way? From the vantage point of Institutionalism, does it assume or presume certain social or legal structures or relations?

## A special case: the role of the novel in undergirding Piketty's *Capital*

On the surface there appears to be a specter haunting Piketty's work that takes the form of Balzac's pen, perhaps Jane Austen's as well. Consequently, what is the role of literature in Piketty's economic thought? One way to address this is to scrutinize a short but incisive subsection of Piketty's work within the part devoted to "The Metamorphoses of Capital," entitled, "The Nature of Wealth: From Literature to Reality," as a literary text.

At the outset Piketty describes this engagement with literature as a "detour" (Piketty 2014: 113), but is that actually the case? He begins with a general assertion:

> In the classic novels of the nineteenth century, wealth is everywhere, and no matter how large or small the capital, or who owns it, it generally takes one of two forms: land or government bonds.
>
> (Piketty 2014: 113)

Then, after distancing the nineteenth-century world from the "modern era," Piketty makes a turnabout of sorts, stating: "It would be quite wrong, in fact, to assume that the study of nineteenth-century capital has nothing to teach us today" (Piketty 2014: 114).

Piketty goes on to note a conflation of "two types of capital asset – land and government bonds" by novelists of the period "for narrative convenience" that ought to be attended to separately. To establish the larger case of greater contemporary relevance, Piketty notes:

> There is also another, even more important complication: many other forms of capital, some of them quite "dynamic," played an essential role not only in classic novels but in the society of the time," embarking then on a detailed description of the careers of two Balzac "characters" and one Jane Austen "hero."
>
> (Piketty 2014: 114–15)

The gravamen of his case now seems to rest on the following:

> So which was it: quiet capital or risky investments? … . What actual changes have occurred in the structure of capital since the eighteenth century? Père Goriot's pasta may have become Steve Jobs' tablet, and investments in the West Indies in 1800 may have become investments in China or South Africa in 2010, but has the deep structure of capital really changed?
>
> (Piketty 2014: 115)

Curiously, and perhaps significantly, Piketty has made a seamless transition from the world of fiction, representing the nineteenth century, to the world of fact (that is, historical fact) in the twenty-first. The elevation of this earlier, fictional world is complete as this subsection comes to an end:

> What, then, gives us the vague sense that social inequality today is very different from social inequality in the age of Balzac and Austen?
>
> (Piketty 2014: 116)

I think it is fair to say that this literary excursion is much more than a "detour," as the two authors noted come to define the essence of an historical period through its economic relations, but also comprehended in terms of its social fabric or make-up. One may regard these literary works as critical interpretive elements, which surely is the case, but that may understate both their role and importance: they in fact form the narrative framework about which an economic model may be configured. Here the source of the pertinent narrative is narrative itself, but only of a special sort: the novel. As such, it would enhance the affinity between literature and economics in a bold way. In place of Weber's "fictive assumptions" one resorts instead to fiction outright. The novel, a work of fiction, provides a heightened sense of reality, perhaps better, a capacity to encapsulate reality, as factual accounts and accounting somehow fail to do. Piketty refers to this as a kind of "intensification," which bears a striking resemblance to Weber's notion that his "ideal-types" offered up an "accentuation" of certain aspects of reality, while shunting aside others.

Piketty's reference to "the age of Balzac and Austen" is itself a form of metonymy, as the "age" represented is captured in the writings of Balzac and Austen, and is constituted by the economic and social world portrayed in them. All of this goes to the unearthing of the figurative element in economics, harkening back to Smith's engagement with rhetoric and allegory, or to the seemingly unlikely resonances of postmodernism (and the heightened concern with language of more contemporary writers and critics) with economic thinkers from earlier periods, including Marx, who created a theatrical stage to capture the historical moment and setting for the accession of Louis Napoleon in *The Eighteenth of Brumaire*. First he characterized the recurrence of the signal event of a Napoleonic coup d'etat as "the first time as high tragedy, the second time as low farce," then saw the 1851 coup as the "second imprint," invoking literature itself as a metaphor for historical events and personages (Marx [1852] 2002: 19).

## Historical context: four critical elements

Is the infusion of historical data, understood as such or translated into economic statistics, into economic analysis sufficient to make economics suitably historical? This, one might contend, is the position taken by both Kuznets and

Piketty, demonstrably the case in their compilation and use of data, and, if deemed sufficient this approach informs what Fogel called "economics as an empirical science." But to engage that which is historical at the theoretical, even interpretive level requires something more, for it is a truism that historical facts, along the lines of Goethe's oft-cited aphorism, cannot exist in isolation, so organizing principles of some sort, drawing upon theory and necessitating interpretation, must be introduced and examined.

Can these matters of theory and interpretation be subsumed under the overarching notion of "historical context"? While Weber spoke of the use of historical research to bring the "fictive" aspects of ideal-type construction more in line with the world of fact, what I have proposed instead entails the construction of historical context as the crucial step in grounding economics in history.

In summary form I've identified four critical elements involved in the fleshing out of historical context in economics, which in turn draw consistently from the arts and linguistics. The first of these calls for the "setting of the stage," that is, establishing the formative "mold" within which subsequent events and developments occur or take shape; the first acknowledgment as well of the hold of the past on the present. The "hold" then extends to the second element, noted, with a borrowing from linguistics, as "colligation," but advanced into the discourse of economic history by Jonathan Hughes (Hughes 1966: 79–83; 1970: 30), whereby meaning is taken to be situational or "contextual"; but in this instance applied to the linkage between past and present, and open to the possibility of a temporal inversion in which the present remakes the past.

This last, seemingly paradoxical mechanism brings to the fore the way that contemporary perspectives often vary the weight of past historical facts, rendering the past as currently understood the product of a changing selection of facts and the significance attributed to them.

One might read such efforts as a contemporary version of prefiguration, whereby the meaning of the past is highlighted through its connection, typically on the basis of a set interpretation, to the present.

Third, there is the historian's penchant for periodization, distinct divisions in time taken to be meaningful in interpreting historical events and developments. Colligation may call for a rethinking of the pertinent divisions to be made. Finally, there is the appearance of and role to be assigned to "genres of presentation," hence a more literary, dramatic, or cinematic element, that offer little in the way of specifics, but crucially provide the atmosphere, thereby linking contextual impressions with a kind of metonymy expressed through such art forms.

'Narrative" and "context" are clearly meant to offer an alternative in historical reconstruction to pathway, often broached by those, like David and Arthur, who have sought to show why "history matters" in economics. Yet colligation, as a notion of some force in historiography and the philosophy of history, presents a serious challenge to the translation of historical influences in economics into a pathway. For one, colligation may be viewed as conveying the sense of the "formative" in history, whereby the initial set of conditions may coalesce into a mold, within which all subsequent events are shaped as well.

Economists may well contend that this is simply a reformulation, in other terms, of the decisive advantage gained by initial steps undertaken, like the case of "human capital" informing a "positive externality" often cited by Paul Krugman, the centering of the carpet-making industry in Dalton, Georgia (Krugman 1991: 35).

What does this example fail to take into consideration? There may be other ways in which such molds form and operate. Political acts, and their consequences, may prove decisive, or, as set forth by Institutionalists of various stripes, changes in legal structures or cultural norms may set crucial changes in motion. The appropriation of Church lands and properties in the course of the French Revolution was of major economic consequence, yet it would be a mistake to treat it as an initiating event upon which economic rules were then applied, both because of the transformation of possibilities, economic and otherwise, like new forms of economic development and enrichment, afforded by it and because of the changed economic relations recasting the prevailing economic rules themselves. This may also entail the introduction of human agency into the relation between past and present.

Moreover, a second major consideration has to do with the temporal inversion of past and present in historical reconstruction, namely that the present has the capacity, indeed the likelihood, of remaking the past, contrary to the notion of economists like Joan Robinson (Robinson 1979) and John Hicks (Hicks 1976) that the future differs from the past in that the former is unknown or perhaps incomplete, while the latter is "spoken for" or "set in stone." This is because of the requisite selectivity involved in appropriating the "facts" of the past, hence the necessary role of establishing and applying criteria out of which a narrative will emerge.

## The nomothetic paradox resolved

The question as to whether the gap or division between economics and history constitutes a divide that might be bridged or a breach that cannot be repaired may be regarded as a restatement of the challenge posed by the nomothetic paradox in economics: the not altogether clearly delineated – perhaps even discerned – mixture of the general and the particular. One view of a substantially reinvigorated historical economics would be to see this paradox (or tension) "successfully" resolved, though "success" and resolution might well need to be carefully qualified. "Knowledge by implication," to cast the matter in Pigovian terms, makes economics a set of rules or, conceivably, mechanisms, allowing for "conditional prediction" or, perhaps better, conjecture.[3] In this way Pigou's alignment of economics with logic makes sense, but only to a certain degree.

Here one of the classic problems bedeviling economics emerges: are there links that provide overall coherence to the sets of economic rules found or constructed, on the model of a system of logic, or does the grounding of economics in the social world result in the ad hoc creation of such rules, with a concomitant lack of what one might term "organic" interrelation or coherence? Paul Bairoch cast the matter as situational, with different laws or rules operative at different times and within different structures. As a parallel, but only in part, the Marxian perspective outlined by Dobb identified different rules governing different stages of historical development, subsumed, though, by more sweeping laws of history. In less flattering terms the ad hoc selection of rules might be described as "willy-nilly" rule creation.

On the other hand, could history contribute in some way to the overall coherence of these rules? In a Marxian construct the rules follow from "laws of history," but could such laws transcend the limitations of the Newtonian model and by what means would they be ascertained? In a Weberian construct historical research smoothes out the "fictive" framework of economic models "extruded" from economic rules posited, that is, theory, though the overall coherence of these rules is not addressed. Keener attention to the elements of historical context, extending even to atmosphere, would provide a means toward at least contemplating what coherence would entail, so that whether cast as law, rule, model, or concept, economic construction would be comprehended as "contextual" or "situational," and economics itself, in philosophical terms, would be set within a "social epistemology."

It is also the case that the seeming congruence of Weber's and Braudel's notion of producing a "general economic history" may capture what might be a bridge between the general and the particular. In particular, Braudel spoke of a grammar and a typology amidst a wealth of detail that might nonetheless fall short of full rigor and precision. From a seemingly quite distant and different vantage point, Mitchell saw economic theorizing facing much the same limitation. An imperfection of this sort might prove less a difficulty, from a philosophical or methodological perspective, than a potentially "incoherent" logic of economics.

## Notes

1 See Veblen (1906); Mitchell (1936: xlvii–xlviii).
2 While there is no reason to see Max Weber's historical inquiries as somehow ultimately satirical, it is noteworthy that in attempting to explain what a historical economics might achieve he alluded to the possibility of producing a work akin to that of Burckhardt. See his letter to Heinrich Rickert, dated April 28, 1905 (Weber [1905] 2012: 381).
3 As to the gap between "historical prediction" and "conditional prediction": Paul Sweezy tried to narrow this gap by countering Karl Popper's charge that "historical prediction" was vacuous through the "following theorem: a conditional prediction can become a historical prediction if the conditions which it specifies are sufficiently accurately reproduced in an actual historical situation" (Sweezy 1953b: 332). Sweezy's theorem, though, comports quite well with the distinction Pigou drew between economics and history in his response to Clapham.

## References

Arthur, W.Brian (1994) *Increasing Returns and Path Dependency in the Economy.* Ann Arbor: University of Michigan Press.

Auerbach, Erich [1959] (1973) *Scenes from the Drama of European Literature.* Gloucester, MA: Peter Smith.

Bairoch, Paul (1993) *Economics and World History: Myths and Paradoxes.* Chicago: University of Chicago Press.

Braudel, Fernand (1981) *The Wheels of Commerce*, trans. Sian Reynolds (1992). Berkeley: University of California Press.

Cartwright, Nancy (2010) "Models: Parables v Fables." In Roman Frigg and Matthew C. Hunter (eds), *Beyond Mimesis and Convention.* Dordrecht: Springer, pp. 19–31.

Colliot-Thélène, Catherine (2006) *La sociologie de Max Weber.* Paris: La Découverte.

Commons, John R. (1893) *The Distribution of Wealth.* New York: Macmillan and Co.

Commons, John R. et al. (eds) (1910–1911) *A Documentary History of American Industrial Society*, prepared by the American Bureau of Industrial Research, 10 vols. Cleveland: A.H. Clark.

Commons, John R. (1924) *Legal Foundations of Capitalism.* New York: Macmillan.

Dantzig, Tobias (1930) *Number: The Language of Science.* New York: Macmillan.

David, Paul (1985) "Clio and the Economics of QWERTY." *American Economic Review*, 75(2): 332–337.

David, Paul (1994) "Why Are Institutions the 'Carriers of History'?" *Structural Change and Economic Dynamics*, 5(2): 205–220.

David, Paul (1997) "Path Dependence and the Quest for Historical Economics." *Discussion Papers in Economic and Social History*, no. 20. University of Oxford.

Dobb, Maurice (1937) *Political Economy and Capitalism.* New York: International Publishers.

Firth, J. R. (1968) *Selected Papers of J. R. Firth 1952–59*, ed. F. R. Palmer. London: Longmans, Green and Co.

Galbraith, John Kenneth (1955) *The Great Crash, 1929.* Boston: Houghton Mifflin.

Geertz, Clifford (1973) *The Interpretation of Cultures: Selected Essays.* New York: Basic Books.

Gerschenkron, Alexander (1962) *Economic Backwardness in Historical Perspective.* Cambridge, MA: Belknap Press of Harvard University Press.

Hicks, Sir John R. (1976) "Some Questions of Time in Economics." In A. M. Tang, F. M.Westfield, and J. S. Worley (eds), *Evolution, Welfare, and Time in Economics.* Lexington, MA: Lexington Books, pp. 135–151.

Hobsbawn, Eric (1997) *On History.* London: Weidenfeld & Nicolson.

Hobsbawn, Eric (2002) *Interesting Times: A Twentieth-Century Life.* New York: Pantheon Books.

Hollander, Robert (1969) *Allegory in Dante's Commedia.* Princeton: Princeton University Press.

Hughes, Jonathan (1966) "Fact and Theory in Economic History." *Explorations in Entrepreneurial History*, 3(20), ser. 2: 75–100.

Hughes, Jonathan (1970) *Industrialization and Economic History: Theses and Conjectures.* New York: McGraw-Hill.

King, J. E. (1995) *A History of Post Keynesian Economics Since 1936.*Cheltenham, UK: Edward Elgar.

Krugman, Paul (1991) *Geography and Trade.* Cambridge, MA: The MIT Press.

Landes, David (1969) *The Unbound Prometheus*. London: Cambridge University Press.

Le Goff, Jacques (2014) *Faut-il vraiment découper l'histoire en tranches?* Paris: Editions du Seuil.

McCloskey, Deirdre (1983) "The Rhetoric of Economics." *Journal of Economic Literature*, 21: 481–517.

Marx, Karl (1852) "The Eighteenth of Brumaire of Louis Bonaparte." In Mark Cowling and James Martin (eds) *Marx's Eighteenth Brumaire: (Post)modern Interpretations*, trans. Terrell Carver (2002). London: Pluto Press, pp. 19–109.

Mill, John Stuart (1857) *Principles of Political Economy with Some of Their Applications*, vol. 1, 4th edn. London: John W. Parker & Son.

Mitchell, Wesley (1936) *What Veblen Taught*. New York: Viking Press.

Mitchell, Wesley (1941) *Business Cycles and Their Causes*. New edition of Mitchell's Business Cycles: Part III. Berkeley and Los Angeles: University of California Press.

Mitchell, Wesley (1949) *Lecture Notes on Types of Economic Theory*, vol. I. New York: Augustus M. Kelley. [notes at Columbia University, 1934–5]

Morgan, Mary S. (2012) *The World in the Model: How Economists Work and Think*. Cambridge: Cambridge University Press.

Neurath, Otto (1944) *Foundations of the Social Sciences*. Chicago: University of Chicago Press.

North, Douglass (1990) *Institutions, Institutional Change, and Economic Performance*, Cambridge: Cambridge University Press.

Piketty, Thomas (2014) *Capital in the Twenty-First Century*. Cambridge: Harvard University Press.

Quine, Willard van Orman (1960) *Word and Object*. Cambridge, MA: MIT Press.

Robinson, Joan (1979) "History versus Equilibrium," in *Collected Economic Papers*, vol. 5. Oxford: Basil Blackwell, pp. 48–58.

Samuelson, Paul (1966) "Economic Thought and the New Industrialism," in Joseph E. Stiglitz (ed.), *The Collected Scientific Papers of Paul A. Samuelson*, vol. II. Cambridge, MA: MIT Press, pp. 1729–1747.

Schumpeter, Joseph (1912) *Theorie der wirtschaftlichen Entwicklung*. Leipzig: Duncker & Humblot.

Schumpeter, Joseph ([1951] 1965) *Ten Great Economists: From Marx to Keynes*. New York: Oxford University Press.

Schumpeter, Joseph (1954) *History of Economic Analysis*, ed. Elizabeth Boody Schumpeter.New York: Oxford University Press.

Smith, Adam (1983) *Lectures on Rhetoric and Belles Lettres*, ed. J. C. Bryce. Oxford: Clarendon.

Sweezy, Paul (1942) *The Theory of Capitalist Development: Principles of Marxian Political Economy*. New York: Oxford University Press.

Sweezy, Paul (1953a) "The Communist Manifesto after 100 Years," *The Present as History*. New York: Monthly Review Press: 3–29.

Sweezy, Paul (1953b) "Science, Marxism, and Democracy," in *The Present as History*. New York: Monthly Review Press, pp. 330–337.

Turgot, Anne-Robert-Jacques ([1770] 1788) *Réflexions sur la formation et la distribution des richesses*. [n.p.].

Veblen, Thorstein (1906–7) "The Socialist Economics of Karl Marx and His Followers." *Quarterly Journal of Economics*, August 1906 and February 1907.

Weber, Max [1904] "The 'Objectivity' of Knowledge in Social Science and Social Policy." In Hans Henrik Bruun and Thomas Shimpler (eds), *Max Weber: Collected Methodological Writings*, trans. Hans Henrik Bruun (2012). London: Routledge, pp. 100–138.

Weber, Max [1905] "Letter to Heinrich Rickert," in *Max Weber: Collected Methodological Writings* (2012). London: Routledge, p. 381.

Weber, Max [1906] "Objective Possibility and Adequate Causation in the Historical Causal Approach," in *Collected Methodological Writing* (2012). London: Routledge, pp. 169–184.

Weber, Max ([1920] 2012) "Letter to Robert Liefmann," in *Collected Methodological Writing*. London: Routledge, p. 410.

White, Hayden (1973) *Metahistory*. Baltimore: Johns Hopkins Press.

# Index

For Product Safety Concerns and Information please contact our EU
representative  GPSR@taylorandfrancis.com
Taylor & Francis Verlag GmbH, Kaufingerstraße 24, 80331 München, Germany